FamilyCircle

ANNUAL RECIPES 2014

SHRIMP
MARINARA,
PAGE 88

Meredith® Consumer Marketing
Des Moines, Iowa

BERRY CHEESECAKE POPS,
PAGE 128

DIFFERENT TASTES, SHARED GOALS

When it comes to one of the most important aspects of our lives—what we eat—our families all have different tastes, preferences and needs. Even within families, members can vary greatly in what makes each person happy at mealtime. But ultimately, we all have the same goal: to feed the people we love most in the world well. That's where *Family Circle®* comes in. It's our job as editors to help equip you with the tools for a good life—in the kitchen and out of it.

In *Family Circle Annual Recipes 2014*, you will find a wealth of fresh ideas and recipes—all of which appeared on the pages of *Family Circle* magazine throughout 2014. The variety of recipes is both broad and deep, so you are sure to find the perfect recipe for any occasion. Whether it's a fast, family-friendly and healthy meal or a celebratory sit-down dinner; something light and low-calorie or deliciously indulgent comfort food—you will find it in this one volume.

Indulge in chocolate treats for Valentine's Day, such as Red Velvet Trifle (page 53), Flourless Brownie Sundaes (page 55) and marshmallow-topped S'Mores Cake (page 60). Celebrate peak-season produce with a feast that includes Summer Minestrone (page 223), Organic Baby Lettuces and Quinoa Salad (page 224), Rustic Grilled Vegetable Tart (page 227) and Blueberry-Thyme pie (page 227). Or tuck into seriously good comfort food with updated casseroles such as Indian Madras Pie (page 275) and Greek Baked Eggs and Wheat Berries (page 276).

It's no secret that weeknights present cooking challenges, so in every issue—in regular features such as Healthy Family Dinners and Slow Cooker Suppers—we focus on fast, simple and budget-minded ways to help you get delicious, nutritious food on your table any night of the week.

Cooking for family and friends isn't just about fueling up—it's also about spending time together around the table. See you there!

Linda

Linda Fears, Editor in Chief
Family Circle® Magazine

Family Circle® Annual Recipes 2014

Meredith® Consumer Marketing
Vice President, Consumer Marketing: Janet Donnelly
Consumer Marketing Product Director: Heather Sorensen
Consumer Marketing Billing/Renewal Manager: Tami Beachem
Business Director: Ron Clingman
Consumer Marketing Product Manager: Wendy Merical
Senior Production Manager: Al Rodruck

Waterbury Publications, Inc.
Editorial Director: Lisa Kingsley
Associate Editor: Tricia Bergman
Creative Director: Ken Carlson
Associate Design Director: Doug Samuelson
Associate Design Director: Cathy Brett
Graphic Designer: Mindy Samuelson
Contributing Copy Editors: Susan Kling, Carrie Schmitz
Contributing Indexer: Elizabeth T. Parson

Family Circle® Magazine
Editor in Chief: Linda Fears
Creative Director: Karmen Lizzul
Food Director: Regina Ragone, M.S., R.D.
Executive Food Editor: Julie Miltenberger
Associate Food Editor: Michael Tyrrell
Associate Food Editor: Melissa Knific
Editorial Assistant: Megan Bingham

Meredith National Media Group
President: Tom Harty

Meredith Corporation
Chairman and Chief Executive Officer: Stephen M. Lacy

In Memoriam: E.T. Meredith III (1933–2003)

DIG IN! Gathering around the family table at the end of a long day to enjoy a fresh, flavorful home-cooked meal soothes away the day's stresses and satisfies on so many levels. This collection of recipes from the 2014 issues of *Family Circle*® magazine makes it easier than ever to serve tasty food you cook yourself—whether it's a fast weeknight dinner or a special evening with friends. Recipes are organized by month to take advantage of peak-season produce and to make it easy to find just the perfect recipe for any occasion.

Chicken and Grilled Pineapple Salsa (page 168) is part of the "Grill Happy" story that appeared in the July issue. Other flame-kissed dishes from that issue include Coffee-Rubbed Steak with Charred Zucchini (page 167), BBQ Burgers (page 168), Pork and Plum Skewers (page 171), Grilled Ratatouille (page 171), and Chili-Lime Swordfish and Grilled Corn (page 173).

STRAWBERRY
SHORTCAKES,
PAGE 229

BLUEBERRY-PEACH PARFAITS,
PAGE 229

PEANUT BUTTER S'MORES,
PAGE 229

CONTENTS

THAI FISH SOUP,
PAGE 35

JANUARY

33

16

25

QUICK COMFORT

Make a bubbling casserole in minutes with jarred marinara and refrigerated ravioli.

BAKED RAVIOLI

When you're craving lasagna but don't have time to make the filling and layer the noodles, this Italian-style dish hits the spot. A generous dose of fresh basil and parsley give purchased marinara a flavor boost.

Baked Ravioli

MAKES 8 servings **PREP** 5 minutes **COOK** 5 minutes **BAKE** at 350° for 20 minutes **BROIL** 2 minutes

1	**pound lean ground beef**
1	**jar (24 ounces) marinara sauce**
¼	**cup fresh basil leaves, chopped, plus more for garnish (optional)**
¼	**cup fresh parsley, chopped**
1	**package (20 ounces) refrigerated cheese ravioli**
1	**package (9 ounces) refrigerated cheese ravioli**
1	**bag (8 ounces) shredded mozzarella cheese**
2	**tablespoons grated Parmesan cheese**

• Heat oven to 350°. Coat a 2-quart oval baking dish with nonstick cooking spray. Bring a large pot of lightly salted water to a boil.

• Crumble ground beef into a large nonstick skillet. Cook for 5 minutes over medium-high heat, until browned. Remove from heat and stir in 1 cup of the marinara sauce, half the basil and half the parsley.

• Meanwhile, cook ravioli for 5 minutes in boiling water. Drain and return to pot. Stir in remaining sauce, basil and parsley.

• Pour half the ravioli into prepared dish, spreading level. Top with meat sauce and ¾ cup of the shredded mozzarella. Add remaining ravioli to dish and top with remaining 1¼ cups shredded mozzarella and the Parmesan.

• Bake at 350° for 20 minutes. Increase oven temperature to broil; broil ravioli for 2 minutes. Garnish with additional chopped basil, if desired.

PER SERVING 542 **CAL**; 22 g **FAT** (12 g **SAT**); 34 g **PRO**; 50 g **CARB**; 5 g **FIBER**; 1,135 mg **SODIUM**; 115 mg **CHOL**

COUNT YOUR CHICKENS

10 ways with the country's most beloved and versatile bird.

GRILLED CHICKEN CUTLET
WITH BASIL-TARRAGON AIOLI,
PAGE 15

CHICKEN TAGINE
WITH OLIVES AND FIGS,
PAGE 19

POPCORN CHICKEN

GRILLED CHICKEN CUTLET WITH
BASIL-TARRAGON AIOLI

Crunchy-fried and served with hot peppers and dipping sauce or grilled and served on a salad, chicken suits every mood, occasion, and palate.

Popcorn Chicken

MAKES 6 servings **PREP** 20 minutes
COOK 9 minutes

1½	**pounds boneless, skinless chicken breasts, cut into 1-inch pieces**
1	**tablespoon salt-free Cajun seasoning**
1	**teaspoon salt**
1	**cup all-purpose flour**
¾	**cup beer**
8	**pepperoncini peppers**
1	**quart vegetable oil**
	Cocktail sauce and ranch dressing for dipping (optional)
	Lemon wedges for squeezing (optional)

• Toss chicken with 1½ teaspoons of the Cajun seasoning and ½ teaspoon of the salt. In a large bowl, whisk flour, beer and remaining 1½ teaspoons Cajun seasoning and ½ teaspoon salt. Toss chicken and peppers in batter and coat completely.

• In a Dutch oven, heat oil to 375°. Working in 3 batches, drop chicken pieces and peppers into oil, one piece at a time. Fry for 3 minutes, gently stirring halfway through cooking time.

• With a slotted spoon, remove chicken and peppers from oil and place on a paper-towel-lined baking sheet. Serve immediately with, if desired, cocktail sauce, ranch dressing and lemon wedges.

PER SERVING 372 **CAL**; 22 g **FAT** (2 g **SAT**); 25 g **PRO**; 17 g **CARB**; 1 g **FIBER**; 842 mg **SODIUM**; 63 mg **CHOL**

Grilled Chicken Cutlet with Basil-Tarragon Aioli

MAKES 4 servings **PREP** 15 minutes **COOK** 5 minutes

AIOLI

½	**cup light mayonnaise**
2	**tablespoons chopped fresh basil**
1	**tablespoon chopped fresh tarragon**
1	**clove garlic, finely chopped**
2	**teaspoons lemon juice**

CHICKEN AND SALAD

2	**tablespoons extra-virgin olive oil**
2	**tablespoons lemon juice**
⅛	**teaspoon salt**
⅛	**teaspoon black pepper**
4	**chicken cutlets (about 4 ounces each)**
6	**cups mixed salad greens**
1	**cup grape tomatoes, halved**
½	**cucumber, peeled and sliced**

• **Aioli.** In a small bowl, whisk together mayonnaise, basil, tarragon, garlic and lemon juice. Cover and refrigerate until serving.

• **Chicken and Salad.** In a medium bowl combine olive oil, lemon juice, salt and pepper. Add chicken and toss to coat. Reserve marinade.

• Heat a stovetop grill pan over medium-high heat. Grill chicken for 2 minutes per side or until temperature reaches 165°. Remove to a plate. Place reserved marinade in a small saucepan and add 1 tablespoon water. Bring to a boil; boil for 1 minute.

• To serve, arrange greens, tomatoes and cucumber on a large serving platter; pour marinade over greens and top with chicken. Serve aioli on the side.

PER SERVING 313 **CAL**; 20 g **FAT** (4 g **SAT**); 25 g **PRO**; 10 g **CARB**; 3 g **FIBER**; 400 mg **SODIUM**; 73 mg **CHOL**

CHICKEN TIKKA MASALA

Chicken Tikka Masala

MAKES 4 servings   PREP 20 minutes   BROIL 12 minutes   COOK 24 minutes

2	tablespoons chopped fresh ginger
2½	teaspoons garam masala
3	cloves garlic, chopped
½	teaspoon salt
¼	teaspoon cayenne pepper
1	cup plain low-fat yogurt
8	small boneless, skinless chicken thighs (about 1¾ pounds)
1	tablespoon vegetable oil
1	large onion, thinly sliced
1	can (28 ounces) whole, peeled tomatoes
¼	cup heavy cream
¼	cup fresh cilantro leaves
1	cup basmati rice, cooked following package directions, substituting chicken broth for water
	Naan (optional)

● Heat broiler to high. Line broiler pan with nonstick foil.

● In a small bowl, combine ginger, garam masala, garlic, salt and cayenne.

In a large bowl, combine 1 tablespoon of the ginger mixture and ½ cup of the yogurt. Add chicken and toss to coat. Place on prepared broiler pan and broil 6 inches from heat source for 6 minutes per side.

● Meanwhile, heat oil in a large nonstick skillet over medium-high heat. Add onion and cook 5 minutes; stir in remaining ginger mixture and cook 1 minute. Stir in tomatoes, cream and remaining ½ cup yogurt. Simmer, covered, for 10 minutes, breaking up tomatoes with a wooden spoon. Add chicken to skillet; simmer, covered with lid slightly ajar, for 6 to 8 minutes or until internal temperature reaches 165°.

● Garnish with cilantro. Serve with rice and, if desired, naan.

PER SERVING 611 CAL; 22 g FAT (8 g SAT); 49 g PRO; 59 g CARB; 4 g FIBER; 995 mg SODIUM; 217 mg CHOL

Rigatoni with Gorgonzola Sauce and Chicken

MAKES 8 servings   PREP 10 minutes
COOK 6 minutes   LET STAND 5 minutes

2	tablespoons vegetable oil
1½	pounds boneless, skinless chicken breasts, cut into 1½-inch pieces
¼	teaspoon salt
⅛	teaspoon black pepper
2	cloves garlic, sliced
⅓	cup white wine
½	cup chicken broth
½	cup heavy cream
1½	cups crumbled Gorgonzola cheese
1	cup shredded Parmesan cheese
1	pound rigatoni, cooked following package directions
½	cup fresh basil leaves, sliced
½	cup toasted walnuts, coarsely chopped
	Freshly cracked black pepper (optional)

● Heat oil in a large skillet over medium-high heat. Season chicken with ⅛ teaspoon of the salt and the black pepper. Cook chicken 4 minutes, turning once. Remove to a plate.

● Add garlic and wine to skillet and cook 1 minute. Stir in broth and cream; add back chicken and simmer 1 minute. Take off heat and stir in Gorgonzola and ½ cup of the Parmesan. Add pasta and toss to coat with sauce. Allow to stand 5 minutes.

● To serve, spoon into a large bowl; stir in basil, walnuts, remaining ⅛ teaspoon salt and remaining ½ cup Parmesan cheese. Add freshly cracked black pepper, if desired.

PER SERVING 552 CAL; 26 g FAT (11 g SAT); 35 g PRO; 44 g CARB; 3 g FIBER; 636 mg SODIUM; 9 mg CHOL

RIGATONI WITH
GORGONZOLA SAUCE
AND CHICKEN

CHIPOTLE CHICKEN
MEATBALL HEROES

Chipotle Chicken Meatball Heroes

MAKES 6 servings **PREP** 20 minutes
BAKE at 400° for 25 minutes
COOK 10 minutes **BROIL** 1 minute

1	pound ground chicken
½	cup finely chopped onion
3	cloves garlic, chopped
⅓	cup unseasoned bread crumbs
1	egg, lightly beaten
1	chipotle pepper in adobo sauce, seeded and chopped, plus 1 tablespoon adobo sauce
¾	teaspoon salt
½	teaspoon dried oregano
1	can (14.5 ounces) diced tomatoes, fire-roasted or with chipotle
6	hero rolls (about 2 ounces each), split
¾	cup shredded Monterey Jack cheese or sharp white cheddar cheese

• Heat oven to 400°. Line a baking sheet with nonstick foil.

• In a large bowl, combine chicken, onion, garlic, bread crumbs, egg, chipotle, adobo, salt and oregano. Form into 18 meatballs and place on prepared pan. Bake at 400° for 15 minutes. Turn and bake an additional 10 minutes.

• In a large saucepan, combine diced tomatoes and 1 cup water; bring to a boil. Add meatballs and simmer on medium heat, covered, for 10 minutes.

• Spoon 3 meatballs and some sauce into each roll. Sprinkle 2 tablespoons cheese over each and broil about 1 minute, until lightly browned and cheese is melted. Serve immediately with any remaining sauce.

PER SERVING 415 **CAL**; 16 g **FAT** (6 g **SAT**); 24 g **PRO**; 44 g **CARB**; 3 g **FIBER**; 1,053 mg **SODIUM**; 139 mg **CHOL**

CHICKEN TAGINE WITH OLIVES AND FIGS

Chicken Tagine with Olives and Figs

MAKES 8 servings **PREP** 20 minutes **COOK** 40 minutes

3	tablespoons vegetable oil
1	large broiler-fryer chicken (about 4 pounds), cut into 8 pieces
1	teaspoon salt
½	teaspoon black pepper
1	large onion, chopped
3	cloves garlic, sliced
2	tablespoons fresh ginger, chopped
½	teaspoon ground cumin
½	teaspoon cinnamon
1	cup reduced-sodium chicken broth
½	cup chopped dried figs
½	cup pitted green cocktail olives
1	lemon, cut into wedges
2	cups Israeli couscous, cooked following package directions
2	tablespoons sliced almonds

• In a large Dutch oven, heat oil over medium-high heat. Season chicken with ¾ teaspoon of the salt and ¼ teaspoon of the pepper. Cook chicken about 5 minutes per side or until browned. Remove to a plate. Add onion, garlic, ginger, cumin, cinnamon and remaining ¼ teaspoon each salt and pepper; cook 5 minutes, stirring occasionally.

• Add back chicken, skin side up, and spoon some of the onion mixture on top. Add broth and simmer, covered, for 15 minutes over medium heat. Stir in figs, olives and half the lemon wedges; simmer, covered, for an additional 10 minutes or until temperature of chicken reaches 165°.

• To serve, spoon couscous onto a large serving platter and place chicken over top. Spoon liquid from pot over chicken and garnish with almonds and remaining lemon.

PER SERVING 513 **CAL**; 24 g **FAT** (5 g **SAT**); 33 g **PRO**; 39 g **CARB**; 3 g **FIBER**; 675 mg **SODIUM**; 89 mg **CHOL**

CHICKEN-FRIED
CHICKEN AND TOMATO
GRAVY AND DIRTY RICE

Chicken-Fried Chicken and Tomato Gravy

MAKES 4 servings **PREP** 15 minutes **COOK** 20 minutes

1½	**pounds plum tomatoes, seeded, cut into 1-inch pieces**
3	**tablespoons unsalted butter**
¼	**teaspoon salt**
⅛	**teaspoon plus ½ teaspoon black pepper**
4	**boneless, skinless chicken breasts (about 6 ounces each)**
1	**teaspoon seasoned salt**
¾	**cup all-purpose flour**
2	**tablespoons cornstarch**
½	**cup vegetable oil**

• In a medium saucepan, combine tomatoes, butter, salt and ⅛ teaspoon of the pepper. Cover and simmer 20 minutes, stirring occasionally.

• Meanwhile, season chicken with seasoned salt and remaining ½ teaspoon black pepper. Combine flour and cornstarch in a bowl; dredge chicken in mixture.

• In a large nonstick skillet, heat oil over medium-high heat. Add chicken and sauté for 4 minutes per side or until internal temperature reaches 165°.

• Serve chicken with tomato gravy and, if desired, Dirty Rice (recipe at right).

PER SERVING 446 **CAL**; 27g **FAT** (8 g **SAT**); 37 g **PRO**; 14 g **CARB**; 2 g **FIBER**; 587 mg **SODIUM**; 117 mg **CHOL**

Dirty Rice

• In a medium saucepan, heat 1 tablespoon vegetable oil over medium-high heat. Add 2 sweet Italian sausages, casings removed, and 2 ounces chicken livers; cook 2 minutes. Add 1 cup chopped onion, ½ chopped sweet red pepper, 1 rib chopped celery and 4 minced cloves garlic. Cook 6 minutes, stirring occasionally. Add 1½ cups RiceSelect Royal Blend, 2¼ cups water, ¼ cup salt and ⅛ teaspoon cayenne pepper. Bring to a boil; simmer, covered, on medium-low 20 to 24 minutes or until tender. Garnish with chopped scallions.

Roasted Chicken and Greek-Style Potatoes

MAKES 8 servings   **PREP** 15 minutes   **ROAST** at 425° for 70 minutes

6	tablespoons olive oil
3	tablespoons lemon juice
1	large shallot
2	cloves garlic
¼	cup fresh parsley leaves
2	tablespoons fresh oregano leaves
¾	teaspoon salt
½	teaspoon black pepper
1	whole chicken (about 4 pounds)
2½	pounds russet potatoes, cut into thin wedges

● Heat oven to 425°.

● Add olive oil, lemon juice, shallot, garlic, parsley, oregano, ½ teaspoon of the salt and ¼ teaspoon of the pepper to a blender; blend until combined. Liberally season chicken with half the mixture and place on a rack in a large roasting pan. Season with ⅛ teaspoon each of the salt and pepper. Roast at 425° for 60 to 70 minutes or until internal temperature reaches 165°.

● Meanwhile, toss potatoes with remaining olive oil mixture. Place on a baking sheet and roast with chicken for 40 to 45 minutes, until browned and fork-tender. Season with remaining ⅛ teaspoon each salt and pepper.

● Slice chicken and serve with potatoes.

PER SERVING 461 **CAL**; 26 g **FAT** (6 g **SAT**); 31 g **PRO**; 26 g **CARB**; 2 g **FIBER**; 305 mg **SODIUM**; 89 mg **CHOL**

EASIEST-EVER ONE-DISH
CHICKEN TAMALES

Easiest-Ever One-Dish Chicken Tamales

MAKES 8 servings **PREP** 15 minutes
BAKE at 400° for 40 minutes **COOL** 10 minutes

1	package (8.5 ounces) corn muffin mix
1	can (14.75 ounces) cream-style corn
2	eggs, lightly beaten
½	cup milk
1	teaspoon chili powder
½	teaspoon ground cumin
1	package (8 ounces) shredded taco cheese blend
1	can (10 ounces) hot enchilada sauce
3	cups shredded cooked chicken, from rotisserie chicken
1	cup sour cream (optional)
	Lime wedges (optional)

• Heat oven to 400°. Coat a 13 x 9 x 2-inch baking dish with nonstick cooking spray.

• In a large bowl, combine muffin mix, corn, eggs, milk, chili powder, cumin and 1 cup of the cheese. Spoon into prepared baking dish. Bake at 400° for 20 minutes.

• Pierce casserole with a small knife in about 12 places and spread enchilada sauce over top. Scatter chicken and remaining 1 cup cheese over casserole; bake for an additional 20 minutes.

• Allow to cool for 10 minutes and cut into 8 squares. If desired, serve with sour cream and lime wedges.

PER SERVING 415 **CAL**; 20 g **FAT** (9 g **SAT**); 27 g **PRO**; 36 g **CARB**; 1 g **FIBER**; 780 mg **SODIUM**; 128 mg **CHOL**

Sweet and Spicy Coleslaw

• In a large bowl, combine ½ cup light mayonnaise, ½ sliced red onion, 1 sliced seeded jalapeño, 4 sliced small sweet gherkins and a dash of hot sauce. Fold in 1 bag (12 ounces) broccoli slaw. Chill at least 1 hour before serving.

HONEY SESAME WINGS

SWEET AND SPICY COLESLAW

Honey Sesame Wings

MAKES 12 wings **PREP** 15 minutes **ROAST** at 375° for 60 minutes

¼	cup honey
2	tablespoons sesame oil
2	tablespoons reduced-sodium soy sauce
1	tablespoon chopped fresh ginger
2	cloves garlic, chopped
2½	pounds chicken wings (about 12)
1	tablespoon sesame seeds
3	scallions, chopped

• Heat oven to 375°. Line a large shallow baking pan with nonstick foil.

• In a small bowl, whisk together honey, sesame oil, soy sauce, ginger and garlic.

• Place wings on prepared baking pan and roast at 375° for 45 minutes. Brush with half the honey-sesame mixture and roast an additional 10 minutes. Brush with remaining sauce and sprinkle with sesame seeds; roast 5 minutes. If desired, broil 1 to 2 minutes to crisp skin.

• Garnish with chopped scallions. Serve with Sweet and Spicy Coleslaw (recipe at left), if desired.

PER WING 263 **CAL**; 18 g **FAT** (4 g **SAT**); 18 g **PRO**; 7 g **CARB**; 0 g **FIBER**; 173 mg **SODIUM**; 71 mg **CHOL**

GRAIN CHANGERS

Think beyond brown rice and barley—these ancient grains are the new ticket to delicious meals your family will love.

KAMUT WITH BRUSSELS
SPROUTS, CARROTS
AND CHERRIES

Whole grains offer fiber, flavor, and interesting textures that range from chewy to crunchy. Pair with meat or vegetables or both—or turn into a wholesome dessert.

CREAMY MILLET PORRIDGE AND RASPBERRY CHIA REFRIGERATOR JAM

Kamut with Brussels Sprouts, Carrots and Cherries

MAKES 9 cups **SOAK** overnight **PREP** 15 minutes **COOK** 40 minutes

- 1½ **cups kamut**
- 2 **cups Brussels sprouts (about ½ pound)**
- 2 **cups shredded carrots**
- 1 **cup dried cherries**
- 1 **cup walnuts, toasted and roughly chopped**
- ⅓ **cup fresh parsley, chopped**
- ¼ **cup olive oil**
- ¼ **cup lemon juice**
- 2 **tablespoons honey**
- 1¼ **teaspoons salt**
- ¼ **teaspoon black pepper**

• Soak kamut in cold water overnight. Drain. In a medium lidded pot, add kamut and 4½ cups water. Cover and bring to a boil. Reduce heat to low and simmer 30 to 40 minutes, until tender. Drain and cool.

• Shred Brussels sprouts with a food processor slicing blade or a coarse grater. Mix with kamut, carrots, cherries, walnuts and parsley.

• In a small bowl, whisk olive oil, lemon juice, honey, salt and pepper. Stir into salad. Serve at room temperature or chilled.

PER CUP 305 **CAL**; 14 g **FAT** (2 g **SAT**); 7 g **PRO**; 43 g **CARB**; 6 g **FIBER**; 347 mg **SODIUM**; 0 mg **CHOL**

Creamy Millet Porridge

MAKES 4 servings **PREP** 5 minutes **COOK** 20 minutes

- 1 **cup millet**
- 2 **cups milk**
- ⅓ **cup packed brown sugar**
- ¼ **teaspoon salt**

• Process millet in a food processor until about half of it has a flourlike texture, approximately 1 minute.

• In a medium lidded pot, combine millet, milk, 1 cup water, the brown sugar and salt. Cover and bring to a boil. Reduce heat to low, cover and simmer 15 to 20 minutes, until mixture reaches a porridge consistency. (If too much liquid has evaporated, stir in more water, if desired.)

• Serve immediately. If desired, serve with Raspberry Chia Refrigerator Jam (recipe at right), cream, additional brown sugar or butter.

PER SERVING 172 **CAL**; 2 g **FAT** (1 g **SAT**); 6 g **PRO**; 34 g **CARB**; 1 g **FIBER**; 207 mg **SODIUM**; 6 mg **CHOL**

Raspberry Chia Refrigerator Jam

MAKES 24 servings **PREP** 5 minutes **COOK** 20 minutes

- 3 **cups raspberries**
- ¼ **cup sugar**
- 1 **tablespoon lemon juice**
- ¼ **cup chia seeds**

• In a pot, combine raspberries, sugar and lemon juice over medium heat; cook 5 minutes. Reduce heat to medium-low. Stir in chia seeds and cook until thickened, about 15 minutes.

• Cool slightly and transfer to a canning jar (makes approximately 12 ounces). Refrigerate until using. Jam will keep for about a week.

PER SERVING 25 **CAL**; 1 g **FAT** (0 g **SAT**); 0 g **PRO**; 5 g **CARB**; 2 g **FIBER**; 1 mg **SODIUM**; 0 mg **CHOL**

WINTER VEGETABLE
AND SPELT SOUP

Spelt and farro are ancient cereal grains that are related to modern wheat. Both are native to southern Europe, and farro especially is used widely in Italian cooking.

Wild Mushroom Farro Risotto (Farrotto)

MAKES 4 servings SOAK 30 minutes
PREP 15 minutes COOK 56 minutes

1	cup farro
1	box (32 ounces) organic mushroom broth
2	tablespoons unsalted butter
1	tablespoon olive oil
1	pound wild mushrooms, sliced
3	shallots, diced (½ cup)
1	tablespoon chopped fresh thyme
⅓	cup dry white wine
¼	cup chopped fresh parsley, plus more for garnish
½	teaspoon salt
⅛	teaspoon black pepper
2	ounces soft goat cheese, crumbled (optional)

• Soak farro in cold water for 30 minutes. Drain. Set aside. In a lidded pot, heat broth and 2 cups water.

• In a large sauté pan, heat 1 tablespoon of the butter and the olive oil over medium-high heat. Add mushrooms. Cook 10 minutes, stirring a couple times. Mix in remaining 1 tablespoon butter, the shallots and thyme. Cook 3 minutes. Stir in drained farro and the wine. Cook 3 minutes.

• Reduce heat to medium. Pour in ½ cup of the heated broth; cook until mostly evaporated. Add remaining broth in ½-cup increments until farro is tender, 30 to 40 minutes. Stir in parsley, salt and pepper. Top with goat cheese, if desired.

PER SERVING 348 CAL; 11 g FAT (4 g SAT); 13 g PRO; 46 g CARB; 8 g FIBER; 763 mg SODIUM; 15 mg CHOL

Winter Vegetable and Spelt Soup

MAKES 6 servings SOAK overnight PREP 20 minutes COOK 45 minutes

1	cup spelt
1	tablespoon olive oil
3	links (3 ounces each) sweet Italian sausage, casings removed
2	cups peeled and cubed butternut squash (cut into 1-inch pieces)
1½	cups peeled and sliced carrots (cut into 1-inch pieces)
1½	cups peeled and sliced parsnips (cut into 1-inch pieces)
1	large onion, diced
3	cloves garlic, chopped
1	tablespoon chopped fresh thyme
4	cups low-sodium chicken broth
¾	teaspoon salt
¼	teaspoon black pepper

• Soak spelt in cold water overnight. Drain and set aside.

• In a large lidded pot, heat olive oil over medium heat. Add sausage, breaking up with a wooden spoon. Cook 8 to 10 minutes, until browned. Stir in butternut squash, carrots, parsnips, onion, garlic and thyme. Cook 5 minutes, stirring occasionally. Add chicken broth, 1 cup water and the spelt. Bring to a boil. Reduce heat to a simmer and cook, covered, for 30 minutes or until spelt is tender. Stir in salt and pepper.

PER SERVING 277 CAL; 9 g FAT (2 g SAT); 11 g PRO; 41 g CARB; 7 g FIBER; 623 mg SODIUM; 12 mg CHOL

WILD MUSHROOM FARRO
RISOTTO (FARROTTO)

MADE TO ORDER

Staffers' slow-cooker faves for chilly winter nights.

SLOW COOKER CHILI
WITH THREE BEANS

Slow Cooker Chili with Three Beans

MAKES 8 servings **PREP** 20 minutes
SLOW COOK on HIGH for 4 hours or LOW for 8 hours, plus 15 minutes on HIGH

1	**pound lean ground beef**
2	**cans (14.5 ounces each) diced fire-roasted tomatoes, undrained**
1	**can (15 ounces) each black beans, pinto beans and dark red kidney beans, drained and rinsed**
1	**can (14.5 ounces) beef broth**
3	**medium yellow onions, chopped (1½ cups)**
1	**can (8 ounces) tomato sauce**
1	**tablespoon chili powder**
1	**canned chipotle pepper in adobo sauce, finely chopped**
6	**cloves garlic, minced**
1	**teaspoon ground cumin**
½	**teaspoon ground cinnamon**
½	**teaspoon ground coriander**
2	**ounces bittersweet or semisweet chocolate, chopped**
1	**tablespoon honey**
	Sour cream (optional)
	Chopped green onions (optional)

• In a large skillet, cook ground beef over medium-high heat until browned, using a wooden spoon to break up meat as it cooks. Drain off fat.

• Transfer meat to a 4- to 5-quart slow cooker. Stir in tomatoes, black beans, pinto beans, kidney beans, broth, yellow onions, tomato sauce, chili powder, chipotle pepper, garlic, cumin, cinnamon and coriander.

• Cover and cook on LOW for 6 to 8 hours or HIGH for 3 to 4 hours. Stir in chocolate and honey. Cover and cook on HIGH about 15 minutes more, until heated through. If desired, serve with sour cream and green onions.

PER SERVING 298 **CAL**; 9 g **FAT** (4 g **SAT**); 22 g **PRO**; 37 g **CARB**; 8 g **FIBER**; 1,076 mg **SODIUM**; 36 mg **CHOL**

LENTIL SOUP WITH BEEF

Lentil Soup with Beef

MAKES 6 servings **PREP** 25 minutes **SLOW COOK** on HIGH for 4 hours or LOW for 8 hours

1	**pound boneless beef sirloin steak**
4	**cups reduced-sodium beef broth**
1	**cup lentils, rinsed and drained**
¾	**cup coarsely chopped red sweet pepper**
½	**cup chopped onion**
½	**cup sliced carrot**
½	**cup sliced celery**
2	**cloves garlic, minced**
1	**teaspoon ground cumin**
¼	**teaspoon cayenne pepper**
⅓	**cup snipped fresh parsley**

• Trim fat from meat. Cut into ¾-inch pieces. For a richer soup, cook beef in a nonstick skillet over medium-high heat until browned; otherwise, use uncooked meat. Place in a 3½- or 4-quart slow cooker. Stir in broth, lentils, 1 cup water, the sweet pepper, onion, carrot, celery, garlic, cumin and cayenne.

• Cover and cook on HIGH for 3½ to 4 hours or LOW for 7 to 8 hours. Stir in parsley. Ladle soup into bowls.

PER SERVING 265 **CAL**; 7 g **FAT** (2 g **SAT**); 26 g **PRO**; 24 g **CARB**; 11 g **FIBER**; 353 mg **SODIUM**; 50 mg **CHOL**

Steamed Kielbasa, Sauerkraut and Pierogies

MAKES 6 servings PREP 10 minutes
SLOW COOK on HIGH for 4 hours or LOW for 8 hours, plus 40 minutes on HIGH

2	tablespoons country-style Dijon mustard
1	tablespoon packed brown sugar
1	tablespoon apple cider vinegar
4	cooked chicken apple sausage links (3 ounces each), cut up
½	yellow onion, thinly sliced (½ cup)
2	cups sauerkraut (16 ounces), undrained
7	frozen mini potato and cheese pierogies (from a 12.84-ounce package of 14)

• In a large bowl, combine mustard, brown sugar and vinegar. Add sausage and onion and toss to coat.

• Place sauerkraut in a 4-quart slow cooker. Spoon sausage and onion mixture on top of sauerkraut.

• Cover and cook on HIGH for 3 to 4 hours or LOW for 6 to 8 hours.

• When ready to serve, add frozen pierogies on top. Cover and cook on HIGH about 40 minutes more, until pierogies are heated through.

• Stir gently to combine and serve.

PER SERVING 196 CAL; 7 g FAT (2 g SAT); 12 g PRO; 22 g CARB; 2 g FIBER; 733 mg SODIUM; 42 mg CHOL

Chipotle Baby Back Ribs

MAKES 8 servings PREP 15 minutes BROIL 10 minutes
SLOW COOK on HIGH for 3½ hours or LOW for 7 hours, plus 15 minutes on HIGH

3	pounds pork loin back ribs or meaty pork spareribs
¾	cup no-salt-added tomato sauce
½	cup bottled barbecue sauce
2	canned chipotle chiles in adobo sauce, finely chopped
2	tablespoons cornstarch
	Shredded coleslaw mix and/or thinly sliced jalapeños (optional)

• Heat broiler. Cut ribs into 2-rib portions. Place ribs on unheated rack of a broiler pan. Broil 6 inches from heat for about 10 minutes or until browned, turning once. Transfer ribs to a 4- to 5-quart slow cooker.

• In a medium bowl, combine tomato sauce, barbecue sauce and chipotle chiles. Pour over ribs in cooker.

• Cover and cook on HIGH for 3 to 3½ hours or LOW for 6 to 7 hours.

• Transfer ribs to a serving platter, reserving cooking liquid. Cover ribs to keep warm. Skim fat from cooking liquid.

• In a small bowl, combine cornstarch and 2 tablespoons cold water. Stir into liquid in slow cooker. Cover and cook on HIGH about 15 minutes more or until thickened. Top ribs with sauce. If desired, serve ribs over coleslaw mix and/or thinly sliced jalapeños.

PER SERVING 286 CAL; 8 g FAT (3 g SAT); 40 g PRO; 10 g CARB; 1 g FIBER; 526 mg SODIUM; 91 mg CHOL

STEAMED KIELBASA,
SAUERKRAUT AND
PIEROGIES

HEALTHY FAMILY DINNERS

Fresh ideas for busy weeknights.

CHILI-RUBBED ROAST PORK
WITH SPAGHETTI SQUASH

SUNDAY PREP

- ☐ **Cook quinoa.** (see recipe, below)
- ☐ **Make chicken marinade.** (see recipe, right)
- ☐ **Cook brown rice.** (see recipe, below right)
- ☐ **Make curry broth.** (see recipe, far right)
- ☐ **Roast pork and squash.** (see recipe, far right)

Quinoa (for Monday and Wednesday)

MAKES 5 cups PREP 5 minutes
COOK 20 minutes LET STAND 5 minutes
COOL 15 minutes

1½	cups dry quinoa
¼	teaspoon salt

• Rinse quinoa. Heat a dry saucepan over medium-high heat for 1 minute. Add quinoa and cook, stirring constantly, until fragrant, 2 minutes. Stir in 3 cups water and the salt. Bring mixture to a boil. Cover, reduce heat to low and simmer 15 to 20 minutes, until water is absorbed. Let stand, covered, 5 minutes. Fluff with a fork and cool 15 minutes.

• Divide quinoa evenly into 2 separate lidded containers (2½ cups each) and refrigerate.

Lemon-Herb Chicken Marinade (for Monday)

MAKES about ⅔ cup PREP 5 minutes

⅓	cup lemon juice
2	tablespoons Dijon mustard
2	tablespoons olive oil
3	cloves garlic, minced
1	tablespoon chopped fresh oregano
½	teaspoon salt
¼	teaspoon black pepper

• In a small bowl, whisk together all ingredients until smooth. Transfer dressing to a jar with a tight-fitting lid and refrigerate until ready to use.

Brown Rice (for Tuesday and Friday)

MAKES 3 cups PREP 5 minutes COOK 40 minutes
LET STAND 5 minutes COOL 25 minutes

1	cup brown rice
½	teaspoon salt

• In a medium saucepan, combine 2 cups water, the rice and salt. Bring to a boil and stir once. Cover, reduce heat to medium-low and simmer 40 minutes, until almost all water is absorbed. Let stand, covered, 5 minutes.

• Cool 25 minutes. Divide rice evenly into 2 separate containers (1½ cups each) lidded and refrigerate.

Curry Broth (for Friday)

MAKES about 5 cups PREP 10 minutes
COOK 14 minutes COOL 30 minutes

2	teaspoons canola oil
1	shallot, finely chopped
3	cloves garlic, minced
1	tablespoon curry powder
½	teaspoon sugar
1	box (32 ounces) reduced-sodium chicken broth
¾	cup light coconut milk
2	teaspoons grated fresh ginger
½	teaspoon salt

• Heat oil in a large saucepan over medium-high heat. Add shallot and sauté until softened, 3 minutes. Add garlic, curry and sugar. Cook, stirring constantly, until fragrant, 1 minute. Stir in chicken broth, coconut milk, ginger and salt. Heat to boiling, then reduce heat to medium-low and simmer 10 minutes. Cool 30 minutes. Transfer to a container with a tight-fitting lid and freeze.

SUNDAY

Chili-Rubbed Roast Pork with Spaghetti Squash

MAKES 4 servings, plus leftovers for Thursday
PREP 15 minutes COOK 4 minutes
ROAST at 350° for 1½ hours LET STAND 10 minutes

SQUASH

1	spaghetti squash (about 3¾ pounds)
1	tablespoon butter, melted
1½	teaspoons ground cumin
½	teaspoon smoked paprika
¼	teaspoon salt

2　tablespoons fresh cilantro leaves, chopped

ROAST PORK

1	tablespoon chili powder
2	teaspoons ground cumin
1	teaspoon smoked paprika
½	teaspoon salt
¼	teaspoon black pepper
1	center-cut boneless pork roast (2 pounds)
2	teaspoons canola oil
4	baking potatoes, scrubbed

• Heat oven to 350°. Cut squash in half lengthwise and scrape out seeds. In a small bowl, combine butter, cumin, paprika and salt. Brush butter mixture onto cut sides and into cavities of squash. Place squash cut side down on a rimmed baking sheet. Pour ¼ cup water into pan. Roast at 350° for 1½ hours or until squash is fork-tender.

• Meanwhile, make roast pork. In a small bowl, combine chili powder, cumin, paprika, salt and pepper. Place pork on a sheet of wax paper and apply dry rub to meat evenly, patting so rub adheres.

• Heat oil in a large nonstick skillet over medium-high heat. Add pork and cook, browning on all sides, about 4 minutes. Transfer meat to a roasting pan. Pierce potatoes with a fork. Place pork in oven with potatoes and squash and roast until internal temperature reaches 135°, about 40 to 45 minutes. Let pork rest on cutting board under tented foil for 10 minutes; let squash stand on baking pan for 10 minutes. Remove potatoes.

• With a fork, scrape flesh of one squash half into a serving bowl and sprinkle with cilantro. Wrap the other half tightly in plastic wrap and refrigerate for Pork and Veggie Burritos on Thursday (page 35).

• Cut roast in half. Slice and serve one half with spaghetti squash and baked potatoes. Wrap other half in plastic wrap and refrigerate for Thursday.

PER SERVING 380 CAL; 9 g FAT (3 g SAT); 30 g PRO; 44 g CARB; 7 g FIBER; 356 mg SODIUM; 75 mg CHOL

LEMON-HERB CHICKEN WITH QUINOA

MONDAY

Lemon-Herb Chicken with Quinoa

MAKES 4 servings, plus leftovers for Wednesday　PREP 10 minutes　MARINATE 30 minutes
ROAST at 400° for 15 minutes　COOK 20 minutes　MICROWAVE 3 minutes

	Lemon-Herb Chicken Marinade (page 32)
8	boneless, skinless chicken breasts (5 to 6 ounces each)
1	pint grape tomatoes
2	teaspoons olive oil
½	teaspoon salt
¼	teaspoon black pepper
2½	cups cooked quinoa (page 32)
2	cups firmly packed arugula leaves
	Lemon wedges

• Set aside ¼ cup of the marinade. Place remaining marinade and chicken breasts in a shallow dish, cover and refrigerate 30 minutes.

• Heat oven to 400°. On a baking sheet, toss tomatoes, olive oil, ¼ teaspoon of the salt and the pepper. Roast at 400° for 15 minutes, until tomatoes are softened and slightly charred.

• Coat pan with nonstick cooking spray. Heat a grill pan over medium heat. Remove chicken from fridge; discard marinade and season chicken with remaining salt. Cook breasts, 4 at a time, until cooked through, 5 minutes per side.

• Transfer 4 chicken breasts to a container with a tight-fitting lid. Refrigerate for Greek Chicken-Quinoa Salad on Wednesday (page 34).

• Spoon quinoa into a large glass bowl. Microwave until warm, 3 minutes. Stir in reserved marinade, roasted tomatoes and arugula. Serve with chicken breasts. Garnish with lemon wedges.

PER SERVING 395 CAL; 11 g FAT (2 g SAT); 45 g PRO; 28 g CARB; 3 g FIBER; 806 mg SODIUM; 99 mg CHOL

BAKED CILANTRO TILAPIA
WITH BROWN RICE AND SNOW PEAS

TUESDAY

Baked Cilantro Tilapia with Brown Rice and Snow Peas

MAKES 4 servings, plus leftovers for Friday PREP 10 minutes BAKE at 350° for 12 minutes
MICROWAVE 9 minutes STEAM 4 minutes

¼	cup chopped fresh cilantro leaves, plus more for garnish (optional)
3	tablespoons fresh lime juice
2	teaspoons olive oil
1	shallot, minced
1	clove garlic, minced
½	teaspoon salt
½	teaspoon black pepper
8	defrosted tilapia fillets (5 ounces each)
1	bag (12 ounces) frozen Steam Fresh vegetables (asparagus, gold and white corn, and baby carrots mix)
½	pound fresh snow peas, trimmed
1½	cups cooked brown rice (page 32)
	Lime wedges (optional)

• Heat oven to 350°. In a small bowl, whisk together cilantro, lime juice, olive oil, shallot, garlic, salt and pepper. Place fish in a shallow baking pan and pour on cilantro mixture. Bake at 350° for 12 minutes or until fish is opaque and cooked through. Transfer 4 of the fillets to a container with a tight-fitting lid. Freeze for Thai Fish Soup on Friday (page 35).

• Meanwhile, microwave frozen vegetables according to package directions, about 4 to 7 minutes. Divide vegetables in half. Place ¾ cup in a lidded container; refrigerate for Thai Fish Soup on Friday (page 35).

• Heat 2 inches water in a pot set over high heat until boiling. Top with a steamer basket; add snow peas, cover and steam until crisp-tender, 4 minutes. Transfer ¾ cup to a lidded container. Refrigerate for Friday.

• Microwave rice until warm, 2 minutes. Stir in remaining half of mixed vegetables. Serve with remaining snow peas and tilapia. Garnish with lime wedges and cilantro, if desired.

PER SERVING 330 CAL; 4 g FAT (1 g SAT); 34 g PRO; 35 g CARB; 5 g FIBER; 249 mg SODIUM; 71 mg CHOL

WEDNESDAY

Greek Chicken-Quinoa Salad

MAKES 4 servings PREP 10 minutes
LET STAND 10 minutes MICROWAVE 4 minutes

3	tablespoons white wine vinegar
1	tablespoon lemon juice
1	tablespoon olive oil
1	clove garlic, minced
¼	teaspoon salt
⅛	teaspoon black pepper
1	English cucumber (seedless), peeled, halved and sliced
1	pint grape tomatoes, halved
¼	large red onion, chopped
¼	cup chopped fresh dill
2½	cups cooked quinoa (page 32)
4	cooked chicken breasts (page 33), diced
¼	cup reduced-fat feta cheese

• In a large bowl, whisk together vinegar, lemon juice, oil, garlic, salt and pepper. Stir in cucumber, tomatoes, onion and dill; mix to combine. Let stand 10 minutes.

• Meanwhile, combine quinoa and chicken in a medium bowl and microwave until warm, 4 minutes. Stir quinoa-chicken mixture into bowl with vegetables. Divide among serving plates and top with feta.

PER SERVING 403 CAL; 11 g FAT (2 g SAT); 47 g PRO; 29 g CARB; 4 g FIBER; 608 mg SODIUM; 101 mg CHOL

GREEK CHICKEN-
QUINOA SALAD

PORK AND VEGGIE BURRITOS

THURSDAY

Pork and Veggie Burritos

MAKES 4 servings **PREP** 10 minutes
COOK 11 minutes **MICROWAVE** 4 minutes

2	teaspoons canola oil
1	large red sweet pepper, seeded and sliced
¾	red onion, sliced
¼	teaspoon salt
¼	teaspoon black pepper
½	pork roast, cut into ½-inch strips (page 32)
3	tablespoons chopped fresh cilantro
½	cooked spaghetti squash (page 32)
4	10-inch multigrain wraps
	Lime wedges (optional)
	Reduced-fat sour cream (optional)

• In a large nonstick skillet, heat oil over medium-high heat. Add red pepper, onion, salt and black pepper; cook, stirring frequently, until softened and lightly browned, about 8 minutes. Stir in pork and cilantro and warm through, about 3 minutes.

• Using a fork, scrape spaghetti squash into a medium bowl and microwave until warm, 3 minutes. Warm wraps in microwave for 30 to 45 seconds.

• Place one-fourth of squash down center of each wrap. Top each with one-fourth pork-vegetable mixture. Wrap and serve with lime wedges and sour cream, if desired.

PER SERVING 423 **CAL**; 15 g **FAT** (4 g **SAT**); 32 g **PRO**; 42 g **CARB**; 6 g **FIBER**; 763 mg **SODIUM**; 75 mg **CHOL**

THAI FISH SOUP

FRIDAY

Thai Fish Soup

MAKES 4 servings (about 7 cups) **COOK** 10 minutes **MICROWAVE** 3 minutes

5	cups defrosted curry broth (page 32)
4	defrosted cooked tilapia fillets (page 34)
¾	cup cooked mixed vegetables (page 34)
¾	cup cooked snow peas (page 34), halved
1½	cups cooked brown rice (page 32)
	Fresh cilantro leaves (optional)
	Lime wedges (optional)

• In a large saucepan, heat broth over medium heat until warm, about 4 minutes. Stir in tilapia (breaking apart with a spoon), vegetables and snow peas. Heat until warmed through, about 6 minutes.

• Microwave rice until warm, 3 minutes; serve on the side or spoon into bowls. Divide soup among bowls. Garnish with cilantro and lime wedges, if desired.

PER SERVING 390 **CAL**; 11 g **FAT** (4 g **SAT**); 38 g **PRO**; 34 g **CARB**; 3 g **FIBER**; 669 mg **SODIUM**; 524 mg **CHOL**

RED VELVET TRIFLE,
PAGE 53

FEBRUARY

40

46

62

HEALTHY FAMILY DINNERS

Transform heart-healthy ingredients into a week of great-tasting suppers.

LEMONY SHRIMP
LINGUINE, PAGE 45

PEAR-AND-PECAN-
STUFFED SQUASH,
PAGE 42

ROASTED CHICKEN WITH ITALIAN
WHEAT BERRY SALAD

SUNDAY

Roasted Chicken with Italian Wheat Berry Salad

MAKES 4 servings **PREP** 20 minutes **ROAST** at 425° for 30 minutes **LET REST** 5 minutes

1½	**cups wheat berries**
2½	**tablespoons olive oil**
¼	**cup white balsamic vinegar**
½	**teaspoon Dijon mustard**
1	**teaspoon chopped oregano**
¾	**plus ⅛ teaspoon salt**
¼	**plus ⅛ teaspoon black pepper**
3	**bone-in chicken breast halves (about 2¼ pounds)**
1	**pint cherry tomatoes, halved**
⅓	**cup chopped pitted Kalamata olives**
1	**cup packed fresh basil, roughly chopped**
½	**cup baby bocconcini (small mozzarella balls)**

• In a medium pot, cook wheat berries according to package directions. Drain and cool. Place 1 cup of cooked wheat berries in a resealable container for Tuesday.

• Heat oven to 425°. In a bowl, whisk together oil, vinegar, mustard, oregano and ⅛ teaspoon each of the salt and pepper. Pour ⅓ cup of the dressing into a large bowl. Toss with remaining cooked wheat berries (about 3 cups), tomatoes, olives, basil, bocconcini, ½ teaspoon of the salt and ⅛ teaspoon of the pepper. Set aside.

• Meanwhile, place chicken breast halves on a baking sheet and season under skin with remaining ¼ teaspoon salt and remaining ⅛ teaspoon pepper. Brush chicken with remaining dressing. Bake at 425° for 30 minutes, until internal temperature reaches 160°. Let rest 5 minutes. Slice 2 of the chicken breast halves. Refrigerate remaining chicken for Chicken, Apple and Spinach Empanadas on Wednesday (page 42). Divide chicken among 4 plates and serve with wheat berry salad.

PER SERVING (without skin) 482 **CAL**; 18 g **FAT** (3 g **SAT**); 37 g **PRO**; 41 g **CARB**; 7 g **FIBER**; 660 mg **SODIUM**; 77 mg **CHOL**

CAST-IRON STEAK WITH ROASTED CAULIFLOWER SOUP

MONDAY

Cast-Iron Steak with Roasted Cauliflower Soup

MAKES 4 servings **PREP** 10 minutes **COOK** 23 minutes **LET REST** 5 minutes

1	**tablespoon olive oil**
½	**medium onion, sliced**
3	**cloves garlic, sliced**
1	**head roasted cauliflower florets***
2	**cups reduced-sodium chicken broth**
1	**tablespoon lemon juice**
1	**tablespoon canola oil**
1¼	**pounds flatiron or flank steak, about 1 inch thick**
¼	**plus ⅛ teaspoon salt**
⅛	**teaspoon black pepper**
4	**cups arugula**
¼	**cup fresh parsley, chopped**

• Heat olive oil in a large pot over medium heat. Add onion; sauté 5 minutes, until softened. Stir in garlic and cook 2 minutes. Add cooked cauliflower, chicken broth and 1 cup water. Increase heat and bring to a boil. Cover, reduce heat to a low simmer and cook 10 minutes. Turn off heat. Carefully transfer to a blender and process until smooth. Return to pot and stir in 1 teaspoon of the lemon juice. Cover and set aside.

• Heat canola oil in a 10-inch cast-iron skillet over medium-high heat. Season steak with ¼ teaspoon of the salt and the pepper. Add steak and cook 3 minutes. Flip and cook 2 to 3 minutes, more until medium-rare. Let rest 5 minutes.

• Toss arugula with parsley, remaining 2 teaspoons lemon juice and remaining ⅛ teaspoon salt. Slice steak and serve over arugula. Serve with soup.

*Roast cauliflower: Heat oven to 400°. Cut 1 head cauliflower into florets. Toss with 1 tablespoon olive oil, ¼ teaspoon salt and ⅛ teaspoon black pepper. Place on a baking sheet. Roast at 400° for 25 minutes, turning once halfway through, until browned. Cool, place in a resealable container and refrigerate.

PER SERVING 359 **CAL**; 18 g **FAT** (4 g **SAT**); 36 g **PRO**; 13 g **CARB**; 4 g **FIBER**; 792 mg **SODIUM**; 49 mg **CHOL**

PEAR-AND-PECAN-STUFFED SQUASH

TUESDAY

Pear-and-Pecan-Stuffed Squash

MAKES 4 servings PREP 20 minutes ROAST at 400° for 30 minutes MICROWAVE 1 minute
BROIL 3 minutes COOK 5 minutes

4	delicata or acorn squash, halved lengthwise and seeded (about 4 pounds)
2	tablespoons plus 1 teaspoon olive oil
¾	teaspoon salt
1	cup cooked wheat berries (page 41)
1	pear, peeled, cored and diced into small cubes
½	cup shredded Parmesan cheese
⅓	cup roughly chopped pecans
2	teaspoons chopped fresh sage
¼	teaspoon black pepper
4	cloves garlic, chopped
1	bag (10 ounces) frozen kale
1	can (15.5 ounces) butter beans, drained and rinsed
1	teaspoon lemon juice

• Heat oven to 400°. Coat squash halves with 2 tablespoons of the olive oil. Sprinkle cavities with ¼ teaspoon of the salt. Place cut side down on 2 baking sheets. Roast at 400° for 30 minutes. Let cool slightly and scoop flesh out of 4 of the 8 halves and discard skins; place in a resealable container and refrigerate for Pork Scaloppine with Winter Squash on Thursday (page 45).

• Turn on broiler. In a microwave-safe bowl, combine cooked wheat berries, pear, ¼ cup of the Parmesan, the pecans, sage, ¼ teaspoon of the salt and ⅛ teaspoon of the pepper. Microwave for 1 minute. Carefully fill remaining 4 squash halves with mixture. Sprinkle with remaining ¼ cup Parmesan and broil for 2 to 3 minutes, until cheese is melted and lightly browned.

• Meanwhile, in a medium pot, heat remaining 1 teaspoon olive oil over medium heat. Stir in garlic; cook 1 minute. Mix in frozen kale and ½ cup water. Bring to a boil. Cover and cook 3 minutes. Stir in butter beans, lemon juice, remaining ¼ teaspoon salt and remaining ⅛ teaspoon pepper. Cook 2 minutes, until beans are heated. Serve with squash.

PER SERVING 516 CAL; 16 g FAT (3 g SAT); 21 g PRO; 83 g CARB; 16 g FIBER; 787 mg SODIUM; 9 mg CHOL

WEDNESDAY

Chicken, Apple and Spinach Empanadas

MAKES 5 servings PREP 15 minutes
BAKE at 400° for 20 minutes COOK 15 minutes

4	teaspoons olive oil
1	medium sweet onion, diced (1 cup)
1	Gala apple, peeled and diced
1	bag (9 ounces) fresh baby spinach
1	roasted bone-in chicken breast half (page 41)
¾	cup shredded sharp white cheddar cheese
½	teaspoon plus ⅛ teaspoon salt
¼	teaspoon black pepper
1	package (10 ounces) empanada dough wrappers, thawed
1	egg, beaten
1	bag (12 ounces) frozen corn
3	cloves garlic, minced
2	teaspoons fresh lemon juice

• Heat oven to 400°. In a large skillet, heat 2 teaspoons of the olive oil over medium heat. Stir in ½ cup of the onion and the apple; cook 5 minutes. Stir in half of the spinach. Cook 2 minutes, stirring, until wilted. Transfer mixture to a bowl; cool slightly. Shred chicken and stir into filling, along with cheddar, ¼ plus ⅛ teaspoon of the salt and ⅛ teaspoon of the pepper.

• Fill each wrapper with 2 tablespoons of the filling. Fold into half-moons and seal open ends with a fork. Place on a baking sheet and brush tops of empanadas with egg. Bake at 400° for 20 minutes, until golden brown.

• Meanwhile, in same skillet, add remaining 2 teaspoons oil over medium heat. Stir in remaining ½ cup onion and the frozen corn. Cook 5 minutes, until onion is soft and corn is heated through. Stir in garlic; cook 1 minute. Mix in remaining spinach until wilted, about 2 minutes. Stir in lemon juice, remaining ¼ teaspoon salt and remaining ⅛ teaspoon pepper. Serve empanadas with warm corn salad.

PER SERVING 521 CAL; 18 g FAT (7 g SAT); 24 g PRO; 72 g CARB; 5 g FIBER; 722 mg SODIUM; 66 mg CHOL

CHICKEN, APPLE
AND SPINACH
EMPANADAS

PORK SCALOPPINE WITH
WINTER SQUASH

THURSDAY

Pork Scaloppine with Winter Squash

MAKES 4 servings **PREP** 20 minutes
COOK 22 minutes

3	tablespoons canola oil
½	pound sliced cremini mushrooms
¼	cup sliced shallots
1	tablespoon chopped fresh sage
4	thick boneless center-cut pork chops (about 1¼ pounds)
½	cup all-purpose flour
1	teaspoon salt
½	teaspoon black pepper
1	cup low-sodium chicken broth
1	teaspoon Dijon mustard
	Cooked delicata squash (page 42)
½	cup milk

• Heat oven to 200°. In a large skillet, heat 1 tablespoon of the oil over medium-high heat. Add mushrooms and cook 8 minutes, stirring a couple of times, until lightly browned. Add sliced shallots; cook 2 minutes. Mix in sage; remove to a bowl. Turn off heat and reserve pan.

• Carefully split pork chops in half lengthwise (knife parallel to cutting board), making 8 thin chops. Pound each to ⅛-inch thickness in between 2 pieces of plastic wrap on a cutting board. On a plate, combine flour, ½ teaspoon of the salt and ¼ teaspoon of the pepper. Dredge chops in flour mixture, gently shaking to remove any excess; place on another plate.

• In same skillet, over medium-high heat, add 1 tablespoon of the oil. Sauté 4 of the chops for 2 minutes; flip and cook another 2 minutes. Remove to a baking sheet and place in warm oven. Add remaining 1 tablespoon oil to skillet and repeat with remaining 4 chops.

• Pour chicken broth into empty skillet. Whisk in mustard and release browned bits on bottom of pan. Bring to a simmer. Reduce heat to medium and simmer 3 to 4 minutes, until slightly thickened. Stir in mushroom mixture.

• Meanwhile, reheat squash in a lidded medium pot with milk, remaining ½ teaspoon salt and remaining ¼ teaspoon pepper. Serve pork over squash. Ladle mushroom sauce on top.

PER SERVING 429 **CAL**; 19 g **FAT** (3 g **SAT**); 36 g **PRO**; 30 g **CARB**; 6 g **FIBER**; 543 mg **SODIUM**; 91 mg **CHOL**

LEMONY SHRIMP LINGUINE

FRIDAY

Lemony Shrimp Linguine

MAKES 6 servings **PREP** 15 minutes **COOK** 13 minutes

1	box (12 ounces) whole wheat linguine
¼	cup olive oil
⅓	cup fresh lemon juice, plus 1 tablespoon lemon zest
½	teaspoon salt
¼	teaspoon black pepper
1½	pounds peeled and deveined shrimp
1	bulb fennel, cored, thinly sliced
½	sweet onion, thinly sliced
3	cloves garlic, sliced
½	cup chopped pitted Kalamata olives
½	cup fresh parsley, chopped

• Bring a pot of lightly salted water to a boil. Add linguine and cook 9 minutes or until al dente.

• Meanwhile, in a small bowl, whisk 2 tablespoons of the olive oil with the lemon juice, lemon zest, salt and pepper. Set aside.

• Heat 1 tablespoon of the olive oil in a large skillet over medium heat. Add shrimp. Sauté 1 minute; flip and sauté 1 to 2 minutes more, until just cooked. Remove to a plate. Add remaining 1 tablespoon olive oil to skillet; stir in fennel and onion. Cook 7 minutes, until softened. Stir in garlic; cook 1 minute. Stir in reserved olive oil-lemon mixture. Bring to a simmer and cook 1 minute.

• Remove cooked pasta from pot with tongs and add to skillet, along with 1 cup of the pasta water, the cooked shrimp and olives. Bring to a simmer and cook 1 minute. Stir in parsley. Serve immediately.

PER SERVING 402 **CAL**; 14 g **FAT** (2 g **SAT**); 27 g **PRO**; 49 g **CARB**; 9 g **FIBER**; 582 mg **SODIUM**; 168 mg **CHOL**

SUPER BOWLS!

Crowd-pleasers for the big day, straight from the slow cooker.

Red Wine Braised Chicken

MAKES 6 servings **PREP** 15 minutes **SLOW COOK** on HIGH for 6 hours or LOW for 8 hours

- ½ large onion, chopped
- 3 pounds bone-in skinless chicken thighs
- 1 packet (1.3 ounces) McCormick slow cookers red wine braised roast seasoning mix
- 1 cup small peeled baby carrots, halved
- 10 ounces white button mushrooms, quartered
- 1 bag (14.4 ounces) frozen pearl onions, thawed
- ½ cup dry red wine
- ½ cup fresh parsley, chopped
  Mashed potatoes and green peas (optional)

• Coat a 5- to 6-quart slow cooker with nonstick cooking spray.

• Place chopped onion in slow cooker; season chicken with seasoning mix and place on top of onion. Add carrots, mushrooms and pearl onions. Pour red wine and ½ cup water over top.

• Cover and cook on HIGH for 6 hours or LOW for 8 hours.

• Stir in parsley and serve with mashed potatoes and peas, if desired.

PER SERVING 343 CAL; 9 g FAT (2 g SAT); 47 g PRO; 12 g CARB; 3 g FIBER; 832 mg SODIUM; 188 mg CHOL

BUTTERNUT SQUASH
AND BLACK BEAN CHILI

Butternut Squash and Black Bean Chili

MAKES 8 servings **PREP** 20 minutes **SLOW COOK** on HIGH for 6 hours or LOW for 8 hours

2	large onions, chopped
4	cloves garlic, chopped
1	butternut squash (2 pounds) seeded, peeled and cut into 1½-inch pieces (5 cups)
1	large green bell pepper, seeded and chopped
1	large jalapeño pepper, seeded and chopped
2	cans (14.5 ounces each) stewed tomatoes
4	teaspoons ancho chili powder
2	teaspoons ground cumin
1	teaspoon salt
2	cans (15 ounces each) black beans, drained and rinsed
½	red sweet pepper, seeded and cut into 1-inch dice
½	yellow sweet pepper, seeded and cut into 1-inch dice
½	orange sweet pepper, seeded and cut into 1-inch dice

¼	cup fresh cilantro, chopped
1	cup shredded taco cheese
2	scallions, thinly sliced

• Coat a 4-quart slow cooker with nonstick cooking spray.

• Add onions, garlic, squash, green bell pepper and jalapeño. Combine tomatoes, chili powder, cumin and salt. Pour over squash and peppers.

• Cover and cook on HIGH for 6 hours or LOW for 8 hours. Add beans and red, yellow and orange sweet peppers during last 30 minutes.

• To serve, stir in cilantro. Top with cheese and scallions.

PER SERVING 209 **CAL**; 5 g **FAT** (3 g **SAT**); 10 g **PRO**; 38 g **CARB**; 11 g **FIBER**; 977 mg **SODIUM**; 13 mg **CHOL**

Atlanta Brisket

MAKES 8 servings **PREP** 10 minutes
SLOW COOK on LOW for 8 hours
COOL 10 minutes

2	sweet onions, sliced
1	beef brisket (about 3 pounds), trimmed
1	packet (1 ounce) dry onion soup mix
1½	cups ketchup
1	can (12 ounces) cola
	French fries and coleslaw (optional)

• Coat a 5- or 6-quart slow cooker with nonstick cooking spray.

• Place onions in bottom of slow cooker. Season brisket with soup mix and place on top of onions. Combine ketchup and cola; pour over brisket.

• Cover and cook on LOW for 8 hours.

• Remove brisket to a cutting board and allow to cool 10 minutes. Slice against the grain. Serve with french fries and coleslaw, if desired.

PER SERVING 329 **CAL**; 8 g **FAT** (3 g **SAT**); 38 g **PRO**; 26 g **CARB**; 1 g **FIBER**; 1,238 mg **SODIUM**; 73 mg **CHOL**

ATLANTA BRISKET

Cajun Chicken and Dumplings

MAKES 8 servings **PREP** 20 minutes
SLOW COOK on HIGH for 5 hours or LOW for 7 hours, plus 1 hour

1	large onion, thinly sliced
2½	pounds boneless, skinless chicken thighs, cut into 1½-inch pieces
2	tablespoons salt-free Cajun seasoning
4	cloves garlic, finely chopped
¼	teaspoon salt
7	ounces light kielbasa (from a 14-ounce package), sliced
1	can (14.5 ounces) fire-roasted diced tomatoes
1	cup reduced-sodium chicken broth
2	tablespoons all-purpose flour
1	green bell pepper, seeded and cut into ½-inch slices
2	ribs celery, cut into ½-inch slices
1	can (15 ounces) pinto beans, drained and rinsed
2	cups biscuit baking mix
⅔	cup milk
2	tablespoons chopped fresh cilantro

• Coat a 5- to 6-quart slow cooker with nonstick cooking spray.

• Place onion in bottom of slow cooker. Season chicken with Cajun seasoning, garlic and salt; distribute evenly over onion. Add kielbasa and tomatoes. Combine broth and flour; pour over tomatoes. Scatter bell pepper and celery over top.

• Cover and cook on HIGH for 5 hours or LOW for 7 hours.

• Add beans. Combine biscuit mix and milk; spoon heaping tablespoonfuls over top and cover again. Cook 1 hour more (on either HIGH or LOW).

• Spoon into individual bowls and sprinkle with cilantro.

PER SERVING 432 **CAL**; 17 g **FAT** (5 g **SAT**); 39 g **PRO**; 34 g **CARB**; 5 g **FIBER**; 956 mg **SODIUM**; 156 mg **CHOL**

SWEET AND SPICY BEEF STEW

Sweet and Spicy Beef Stew

MAKES 6 servings **PREP** 20 minutes
SLOW COOK on HIGH for 6 hours or LOW for 8 hours **COOK** 2 minutes

1	large onion, chopped
4	cloves garlic, chopped
1¾	pounds beef chuck, cut into 1½-inch pieces
1	teaspoon salt
¼	teaspoon ground cinnamon
⅛	teaspoon cayenne pepper
2	sweet potatoes (about 1¼ pounds), peeled and cut into 2-inch pieces
½	cup dried fruit bits
1	can (14.5 ounces) petite diced tomatoes
1¼	cups reduced-sodium beef broth
2	tablespoons cornstarch
3	cups cooked couscous
½	cup chopped peanuts

• Coat a 4- to 5-quart slow cooker with nonstick cooking spray.

• Place onion and garlic in bottom of slow cooker. Season beef with ½ teaspoon of the salt, the cinnamon and cayenne; place over onion. Scatter sweet potatoes and fruit bits over top; add tomatoes and 1 cup of the broth.

• Cover and cook on HIGH for 6 hours or LOW for 8 hours.

• Pour liquid from slow cooker into a small saucepan and bring to simmer. Dissolve cornstarch in remaining ¼ cup broth and stir into saucepan. Simmer for 2 minutes, until thickened. Add remaining ½ teaspoon salt and stir mixture back into slow cooker.

• Serve stew with cooked couscous and sprinkle each serving with peanuts.

PER SERVING 538 **CAL**; 12 g **FAT** (3 g **SAT**); 38 g **PRO**; 67 g **CARB**; 7 g **FIBER**; 719 mg **SODIUM**; 56 mg **CHOL**

SWEET TEMPTATIONS

Irresistibly good chocolate desserts.

SWEETHEART CAKE POPS,
PAGE 54

MINI CUPCAKES,
PAGE 62

RED VELVET TRIFLE

With a rosy red hue that's perfect for celebrating Valentine's Day, this rich and chocolaty Southern layer-cake classic has been turned into cupcakes, cake pops, brownies—and here, a trifle layered with cream cheese filling and topping. No matter what form it takes, red velvet always inspires love.

Red Velvet Trifle

MAKES 16 servings **PREP** 30 minutes **BAKE** at 350° for 40 minutes **COOL** 10 minutes **REFRIGERATE** overnight

CAKE

- 2½ cups all-purpose flour
- ¼ cup unsweetened cocoa powder
- 1 teaspoon baking soda
- ½ teaspoon salt
- 2 sticks (1 cup) unsalted butter, softened
- 1½ cups packed light brown sugar
- 3 large eggs
- 1 cup sour cream blended with ¼ cup milk and 1 bottle (1 ounce) red food coloring
- 2 teaspoons vanilla extract

FILLING AND TOPPING

- 1 package (8 ounces) Neufchâtel cheese, softened
- ½ stick (¼ cup) unsalted butter, softened
- 1½ cups heavy cream
- 2 cups plus 2 tablespoons confectioners' sugar
- ½ cup sour cream
- ½ cup milk
- ¾ teaspoon vanilla extract

• Heat oven to 350°. Coat a 13 x 9 x 2-inch pan with nonstick baking spray with flour.

• **Cake.** In a medium bowl, whisk together flour, cocoa, baking soda and salt. In a large bowl, beat butter until smooth. Beat in brown sugar until light colored and fluffy, 2 minutes. Beat in eggs, one at a time. On low, beat in half the flour mixture. Scrape down side of bowl and beat in sour cream mixture, followed by remaining half of the flour mixture. Stir in vanilla.

• Spread batter into prepared pan and bake at 350° for 35 to 40 minutes, until a toothpick inserted in center of cake comes out clean. Cool in pan on a wire rack for 10 minutes, then turn out onto rack and cool completely.

• **Filling and topping.** In a bowl, beat together Neufchâtel, butter and ¾ cup of the heavy cream until smooth. On low, beat in 2 cups of the confectioners' sugar, the sour cream, milk and ½ teaspoon of the vanilla extract.

• Trim edges from cake and cut cake into 1½-inch cubes (set aside 1 cube for topping). Place one-third of the cake cubes in a trifle dish or large bowl. Top with half the filling. Repeat layering with cake cubes and remaining filling, then top with remaining one-third of the cake. Beat remaining ¾ cup heavy cream with remaining 2 tablespoons confectioners' sugar and ¼ teaspoon vanilla. Spread over top of trifle. Crumble reserved cake cube over trifle. Cover with plastic and refrigerate overnight.

PER SERVING 522 **CAL**; 31 g **FAT** (19 g **SAT**); 7 g **PRO**; 54 g **CARB**; 1 g **FIBER**; 256 mg **SODIUM**; 134 mg **CHOL**

SWEETHEART
CAKE POPS

Sweetheart Cake Pops

MAKES 16 servings **PREP** 15 minutes **FREEZE** 1 hour **REFRIGERATE** 30 minutes
MICROWAVE 6 minutes **DECORATE** 1 hour

1	loaf (12 ounces) Entenmann's marble cake
¼	cup canned chocolate frosting
1	Wilton silicone Petite Hearts pan
3	packages (14 ounces each) white, red and pink candy melts
	Paper lollipop sticks
3	tablespoons vegetable oil
	Red, pink and white decorating sugar
	White and red nonpareils
2¼	cups confectioners' sugar
1	tablespoon cocoa powder
	Red gel food coloring

• Finely crumble cake into a large bowl. Stir in frosting, pressing crumbs together with a silicone spatula or the back of a spoon to make a dough.

• Press a heaping tablespoon of the dough into one of the cavities of the Petite Hearts pan. Repeat with remaining cavities. Pop out shaped cakes onto a wax-paper-lined sheet pan. Repeat with remaining dough. Freeze 1 hour.

• Place white candy melts in a glass bowl. Microwave at 50% for 1 minute. Stir and continue to melt at 50% in 30-second increments until a few lumps remain. Sir until smooth.

• Remove half the hearts from the freezer. Dip a lollipop stick about ¾ inch into white candy, then insert into cake. Repeat with all hearts. Refrigerate for 20 to 30 minutes.

• Reheat white candy melts until smooth. Stir in 1 tablespoon of the oil. Dip a pop into white candy and gently tap so excess coating drips back into bowl. Return to wax-paper-lined sheet. Repeat with a third of the cake pops (removing from refrigerator one at a time), adding decorating sugar or nonpareils to some of the pops and leaving others plain.

• Melt red and pink candy melts in same way as white ones, stirring 1 tablespoon of the oil into each. Dip pops into desired coating and add decorating sugar or nonpareils to some, leaving others plain.

• Make a quick icing: Beat confectioners' sugar and 7 teaspoons water in a bowl (this will be stiff). Divide into thirds. Add cocoa powder and a little more water to one bowl; add red gel food coloring to another bowl. Transfer to pastry bags fitted with small writing tips. Pipe messages onto white pops in red icing; use cocoa icing on pink pops and white icing on red pops. Let dry.

PER SERVING 348 CAL; 16 g FAT (10 g SAT); 2 g PRO; 48 g CARB; 1 g FIBER; 180 mg SODIUM; 7 mg CHOL

Cocoa Horchata Martini

MAKES 2 servings **PREP** 5 minutes

1	tablespoon confectioners' sugar
1	tablespoon cocoa powder
1½	cups ice
¾	cup (6 ounces) RumChata (horchata-and-rum liquor; see Note)
6	tablespoons (3 ounces) crème de cacao
¼	cup chocolate milk

• In a small bowl, combine confectioners' sugar and cocoa powder. Whisk to combine, then spread onto a shallow dish. Fill another shallow dish with ¼ inch of water.

• Fill a cocktail shaker with ice. Add RumChata, crème de cacao and chocolate milk. Cover and shake until chilled.

• Dip 2 martini glass rims in water and edge each glass in cocoa-sugar. Divide martini into prepared glasses.

Note: Horchata is a milky rice- or nut-base Latin beverage. RumChata is sold in grocery and liquor stores.

PER SERVING 479 CAL; 9 g FAT (6 g SAT); 3 g PRO; 63 g CARB; 0 g FIBER; 69 mg SODIUM; 24 mg CHOL

COCOA HORCHATA
MARTINI

Flourless Brownie Sundaes

MAKES 6 servings **PREP** 15 minutes **MICROWAVE** 45 seconds **BAKE** at 350° for 20 minutes

- ¼ **cup (½ stick) unsalted butter**
- 2 **ounces unsweetened chocolate, chopped**
- ⅔ **cup sugar**
- 1 **egg plus 1 egg yolk**
- 1½ **teaspoons vanilla extract**
- ¼ **cup unsweetened cocoa powder**
- ½ **cup mini semisweet chocolate chips**
- 6 **small scoops ice cream (any flavor)**
  Chocolate sauce, for drizzling

• Heat oven to 350°. Coat a jumbo muffin pan with nonstick cooking spray.

• Combine butter and chocolate in a medium glass bowl. Microwave for 45 seconds, then stir until smooth.

• Whisk in sugar, then egg and egg yolk. Whisk in vanilla extract and sift cocoa powder over mixture. Fold in cocoa with a rubber spatula; stir in mini chips. Divide among 6 prepared pan indents (¼ cup in each), spreading tops level. Bake at 350° for 15 to 20 minutes, until tops are shiny.

• Run a knife around edge of cakes; remove from pan. Cool a few minutes on a rack; transfer to plates. Top each with a scoop of ice cream; drizzle with chocolate sauce and serve.

PER SERVING 493 **CAL**; 26 g **FAT** (16 g **SAT**); 7 g **PRO**; 62 g **CARB**; 3 g **FIBER**; 52 mg **SODIUM**; 106 mg **CHOL**

MILK CHOCOLATE ICEBOX PIE

Milk Chocolate Icebox Pie

MAKES 8 servings **PREP** 30 minutes **COOK** 6 minutes **COOL** 15 minutes **REFRIGERATE** overnight

CRUST

1⅔	cups finely crushed Nabisco Famous wafer cookies (28 cookies)
6	tablespoons unsalted butter, softened
1	tablespoon sugar
	Pinch salt

FILLING

3	Hershey's milk chocolate bars (1.55 ounces each)
4	large eggs
⅔	cup sugar
2	tablespoons unsweetened cocoa powder
½	cup (1 stick) unsalted butter, softened
⅛	teaspoon salt
1	container (8 ounces) frozen whipped topping, thawed

• **Crust.** In a medium bowl stir together cookie crumbs, butter, sugar and salt. Press into bottom and up side of a 9-inch pie pan (not deep dish). Refrigerate while preparing filling.

• **Filling.** Chop 2½ of the chocolate bars; set aside Combine eggs and ⅓ cup of the sugar in a large metal bowl or double boiler. Bring 2 inches of water to a simmer in a large pot or Dutch oven. Place bowl or double boiler over pan without touching water. Cook, beating constantly with a hand mixer, until mixture is light colored and fluffy, and registers 160° on an instant-read thermometer, 5 to 6 minutes. Watch carefully; if eggs get too hot, they will scramble.

• Remove bowl from heat. Whisk in chopped chocolate and cocoa powder until smooth. Set aside to cool for 15 minutes, whisking occasionally.

• Once egg mixture is cooled, combine remaining ⅓ cup sugar with the butter and salt in a large bowl. Beat on high speed until very light colored, about 2 minutes. On medium, beat in egg mixture, scraping down side of bowl. Fold in half of the whipped topping and spread into prepared crust. Refrigerate overnight.

• Just before serving, spread center of pie with remaining whipped topping. Use a vegetable peeler to make large curls from reserved ½ chocolate bar, or cut into shards and sprinkle over pie.

PER SERVING 551 **CAL**; 35 g **FAT** (21 g **SAT**); 6 g **PRO**; 52 g **CARB**; 2 g **FIBER**; 284 mg **SODIUM**; 166 mg **CHOL**

CHOCOLATE
MOUSSE CONES

Chocolate Mousse Cones

MAKES 12 servings **PREP** 5 minutes
MICROWAVE 1½ minutes **COOK** 10 minutes
COOL 20 minutes **REFRIGERATE** 20 minutes

- **1** bag (12 ounces) semisweet chocolate chips
- **¼** cup solid vegetable shortening
- **12** small ice cream cones (from a 3-ounce package)
- **1** package (3.13 ounces) cook-and-serve chocolate pudding mix
- **1** envelope (0.25 ounce) unflavored gelatin
- **2** cups 1% milk
- **¼** teaspoon almond extract
- **4** ounces cream cheese, softened
- **1** cup heavy cream
- **2** tablespoons sugar
- **2** tablespoons chopped sliced almonds (optional)

• Combine chocolate chips and shortening in a glass bowl. Microwave for 1 minute, then stir until smooth. With a small brush, coat insides of cones with some of the melted chocolate. Turn cones upside down on a rack over a sheet of wax paper and let harden in refrigerator.

• Whisk together pudding mix and gelatin in a medium saucepan. Whisk in milk. Cook, stirring, over medium heat for 8 to 10 minutes, until pudding comes to a full boil. Remove from heat and stir in almond extract. Cool for 20 minutes, stirring occasionally.

• In a medium bowl, beat cream cheese with an electric mixer until very smooth. Add heavy cream and sugar and beat until medium peaks are formed. Fold one-third of the cream cheese mixture into cooled pudding mixture to lighten. Fold in remaining cream cheese mixture and transfer to a large piping bag or resealable plastic bag. Snip off a corner of the bag.

• Flip over cones and place them in a cupcake pan (to help balance them). Pipe mousse into cones, dividing equally. Refrigerate for 20 minutes.

• Reheat chocolate in microwave for 30 seconds. Stir until smooth. Dip cones into melted chocolate; sprinkle half with chopped almonds, if desired.

PER SERVING 278 **CAL**; 20 g **FAT** (10 g **SAT**); 4 g **PRO**; 25 g **CARB**; 1 g **FIBER**; 103 mg **SODIUM**; 40 mg **CHOL**

MINI PAIN AU CHOCOLAT

Mini Pain au Chocolat

MAKES 12 servings **PREP** 10 minutes **BAKE** at 400° for 18 minutes

- **1** package (17.3 ounces) frozen puff pastry, thawed
- **1** egg, beaten with 1 tablespoon water
- **¾** cup (4.5 ounces) Ghirardelli bittersweet chocolate morsels
- **2** tablespoons seedless raspberry jam or orange marmalade
- **1** tablespoon sugar

• Heat oven to 400°. Unfold pastry sheets on a cutting board and cut each into 6 equal pieces. Roll one piece out lengthwise to 7 inches. Brush edges with egg wash. Place a scant tablespoon chocolate in center of pastry. Top with ½ teaspoon raspberry jam. Starting on a short side, fold one end over chocolate, then fold over other end to resemble an envelope. Place on a baking sheet. Repeat with all pastry pieces, chocolate, and jam. Brush pastries with egg wash; top with sugar.

• Bake at 400° for 18 minutes or until puffed and golden brown. Cool slightly before serving.

PER SERVING 241 **CAL**; 16 g **FAT** (5 g **SAT**); 4 g **PRO**; 23 g **CARB**; 2 g **FIBER**; 205 mg **SODIUM**; 18 mg **CHOL**

S'mores Cake

MAKES 16 servings PREP 30 minutes BAKE at 350° for 35 minutes BROIL 30 seconds

CAKE

2⅓	cups all-purpose flour
½	cup unsweetened cocoa powder
1	teaspoon baking soda
½	teaspoon salt
1	cup (2 sticks) unsalted butter, softened
2	cups granulated sugar
4	large eggs
1	cup milk, mixed with 1 teaspoon white vinegar
1	tablespoon vanilla extract

FILLING AND TOPPING

1½	cups confectioners' sugar
1⅓	cups marshmallow creme
¼	cup (½ stick) unsalted butter, softened
2	jars (11.75 ounces each) hot fudge topping
2	graham cracker boards, crushed
1½	cups mini marshmallows

• Heat oven to 350°. Coat three 9-inch round cake pans with nonstick spray for baking.

• **Cake.** In a medium bowl, whisk together flour, cocoa, baking soda and salt. In a large bowl, with an electric mixer, beat butter until smooth. Add sugar and beat for 2 minutes, until light and fluffy. Beat in eggs, one at a time. On low speed, beat in half the flour mixture, then the milk mixture, followed by remaining flour mixture. Stir in vanilla and divide batter among prepared pans. Bake at 350° for 30 to 35 minutes, or until cake springs back when lightly pressed. Cool in pans on wire racks for 10 minutes. Run a thin knife around edge of pans; turn cakes out of pans and cool completely.

• **Filling.** While cake layers cool, combine confectioners' sugar, marshmallow creme, butter and ½ teaspoon water in a bowl. Beat on low speed until blended and a good spreading consistency.

• Once cakes have cooled, place one cake layer on a plate. Spread top with ⅔ cup of the fudge topping. Sprinkle with 1 tablespoon of the crushed graham crackers. Spread a second cake layer with half the marshmallow frosting, then invert onto cake layer on platter. Spread top with ⅔ cup of the fudge topping and carefully spread with remaining marshmallow filling (may look marbled). Sprinkle with 1 tablespoon crushed graham crackers. Spread remaining layer with remaining ⅔ cup fudge sauce (do not stack onto cake yet). Sprinkle with remaining crushed graham crackers and top with marshmallows.

• Arrange oven rack so cake layer can be about 3 to 4 inches from heat source (see Note). Heat broiler. Broil marshmallows for 30 seconds, until they just begin to brown. Carefully place layer on cake.

Note: You may use a crème brûlée torch (Bonjour, bedbathandbeyond.com, $30).

PER SERVING 570 **CAL**; 21 g **FAT** (11 g **SAT**); 7 g **PRO**; 90 g **CARB**; 2 g **FIBER**; 262 mg **SODIUM**; 92 mg **CHOL**

S'MORES CAKE

MINI CUPCAKES

Studies have shown that eating chocolate releases endorphins—chemicals made by the body that produce feelings of happiness and euphoria.

Mini Cupcakes

MAKES 48 servings **PREP** 15 minutes **MICROWAVE** 2½ minutes
BAKE at 350° for 15 minutes **REFRIGERATE** 15 minutes

CUPCAKES

2	ounces semisweet chocolate, chopped
1¼	cups all-purpose flour
¼	cup unsweetened cocoa powder
2	teaspoons baking powder
¼	teaspoon salt
¼	cup (½ stick) unsalted butter, softened
⅔	cup sugar
2	large eggs
½	cup sour cream blended with ½ cup water
½	teaspoon vanilla extract

FROSTING

1	cup heavy cream
8	ounces semisweet chocolate, chopped
	Chocolate sprinkles

• Heat oven to 350°. Line 48 indents of mini muffin pans with paper or foil liners. If you have only 1 or 2 pans, bake batter in batches.

• **Cupcakes.** Place chocolate in a small glass bowl. Microwave for 45 seconds, stir and microwave for 45 seconds more. Stir until smooth; set aside to cool slightly. In a medium bowl, whisk flour, cocoa, baking powder and salt.

• With a hand mixer, beat butter until smooth. Beat in sugar until fluffy, then beat in melted chocolate. Beat in eggs, one at a time, beating well after each. On low speed, beat in half the flour mixture, followed by sour cream mixture and remaining flour mixture. Add vanilla.

• Transfer batter to a large resealable plastic bag and snip off a corner. Pipe into cupcake liners. Bake at 350° for 14 to 15 minutes; cool completely.

• **Frosting.** While cupcakes are baking, microwave heavy cream for 1 minute, until steaming. Pour over chocolate in a bowl and whisk until smooth. Refrigerate for 15 minutes or until fairly cool. Beat on medium-high speed until thickened and good spreading consistency (about 5 minutes; frosting will be the color of milk chocolate). Transfer to a piping bag fitted with a small star tip and pipe frosting onto mini cupcakes (alternately, spread frosting onto cupcakes). Decorate with chocolate sprinkles.

PER SERVING 88 CAL; 5 g FAT (3 g SAT); 1 g PRO; 9 g CARB; 1 g FIBER; 35 mg SODIUM; 20 mg CHOL

Chocolate Chip Bread Pudding

MAKES 9 servings **PREP** 15 minutes
BAKE at 350° for 45 minutes

1	loaf (16 ounces) cinnamon-raisin bread, cut into cubes
1	cup mini semisweet chocolate chips
3	cups chocolate milk
4	large eggs
¼	cup packed dark brown sugar
1	teaspoon vanilla extract
1	tablespoon confectioners' sugar

• Heat oven to 350°. Coat a 9 x 2-inch square baking pan with nonstick cooking spray.

• In a large bowl, toss bread with ¾ cup of the mini chips. In a medium bowl, whisk together chocolate milk, eggs, brown sugar and vanilla.

• Pour milk mixture into bread mixture, then transfer to prepared baking pan, pressing down lightly. Sprinkle with remaining ¼ cup mini chips.

• Bake at 350° for 45 minutes. Dust with confectioners' sugar just before serving.

PER SERVING 409 CAL; 14 g FAT (6 g SAT); 12 g PRO; 60 g CARB; 2 g FIBER; 278 mg SODIUM; 101 mg CHOL

CHOCOLATE CHIP
BREAD PUDDING

SHAMROCK MILKSHAKE
CUPCAKES, PAGE 84

MARCH

73

77

84

COMFORT CLASSICS, SLIMMED DOWN

Simply satisfying—and skinny—slow cooker ideas.

CREAMY CHICKEN
NOODLE SOUP,
PAGE 72

SPINACH-PARMESAN DIP,
PAGE 68

CHAI TEA BASE

Spinach-Parmesan Dip

MAKES 16 servings **PREP** 10 minutes
SLOW COOK on HIGH for 1½ hours or LOW
for 2½ hours

	Nonstick cooking spray
2	packages (10 ounces each) frozen chopped spinach, thawed
1	can (14 ounces) quartered artichoke hearts, drained and coarsely chopped
1	cup chopped onion (1 large)
1	tablespoon Dijon mustard
4	cloves garlic, minced
½	teaspoon dried oregano, crushed
¼	teaspoon cayenne pepper
½	cup light mayonnaise or salad dressing
½	cup fat-free sour cream
¼	cup shredded Parmesan cheese (1 ounce)
¼	cup shredded Italian cheese blend (1 ounce)
1	tablespoon lemon juice

• Coat a 3½- or 4-quart slow cooker with cooking spray; set aside. Squeeze spinach dry, reserving ⅓ cup spinach liquid. In prepared cooker combine spinach, the ⅓ cup liquid, the artichokes, onion, mustard, garlic, oregano and cayenne pepper.

• Cover and cook on HIGH for 1½ hours or LOW for 2½ to 3 hours. Turn off cooker; stir in mayonnaise, sour cream, Parmesan cheese, Italian cheese blend, and lemon juice.

PER SERVING 66 **CAL**; 4 g **FAT** (1 g **SAT**); 3 g **PRO**; 6 g **CARB**; 2 g **FIBER**; 229 mg **SODIUM**; 5 mg **CHOL**

Chai Tea Base

MAKES 14 servings **PREP** 15 minutes **STAND** 10 minutes
SLOW COOK on HIGH for 3 hours or LOW for 6 hours

8	cups water
⅔	cup honey
4	2- to 3-inch sticks cinnamon
2	inches fresh ginger, thinly sliced
½	teaspoon whole cardamom seeds (without pods)
16	whole cloves
16	whole black peppercorns
¼	teaspoon ground nutmeg
12	black tea bags
7	cups low-fat milk

• In a 3½- or 4-quart slow cooker stir together the water and honey until dissolved. Add stick cinnamon, ginger, cardamom seeds, cloves, peppercorns and nutmeg.

• Cover and cook on HIGH for 3 to 4 hours or LOW for 6 to 8 hours. Add tea bags. Cover and let stand for 10 minutes. Strain the mixture through a fine-mesh sieve lined with a double thickness of 100-percent-cotton cheesecloth. Store in the refrigerator for up to 2 weeks.

• For each serving, use ½ cup Chai Tea Base and ½ cup low-fat milk. Heat in a saucepan until steaming.

Iced Chai Prepare as directed, except serve over ice.

PER SERVING 104 **CAL**; 1 g **FAT** (1 g **SAT**); 4 g **PRO**; 20 g **CARB**; 0 g **FIBER**; 59 mg **SODIUM**; 6 mg **CHOL**

Cheesy Noodle Casserole

MAKES 6 servings **PREP** 25 minutes **SLOW COOK** on HIGH for 3½ hours or LOW for 7 hours, plus 20 minutes on HIGH.

- 2½ cups water
- 1 can (10.75 ounces) reduced-fat and reduced-sodium condensed cream of mushroom soup
- 1 can (14.5 ounces) no-salt-added diced tomatoes, undrained
- 1 cup sliced celery (2 stalks)
- 1 cup sliced carrots (2 medium)
- 1 cup chopped onion (1 large)
- 1½ teaspoons dried Italian seasoning, crushed
- 2 cloves garlic, minced
- ¼ teaspoon salt
- ¼ teaspoon black pepper
- 8 ounces dried extra-wide noodles
- 1 package (16 ounces) extra-firm tofu (fresh bean curd), drained, if necessary, and cubed*
- ½ cup shredded reduced-fat cheddar cheese (2 ounces)

• In a 3½- or 4-quart slow cooker whisk together the water and cream of mushroom soup. Stir in tomatoes, celery, carrots, onion, Italian seasoning, garlic, salt and pepper.

• Cover and cook on HIGH for 3½ to 4 hours or LOW for 7 to 8 hours

• Stir in uncooked noodles; cover and cook on HIGH for 20 to 30 minutes more or until tender, stirring once halfway through cooking. Gently stir in tofu cubes. Sprinkle with cheese; cover and let stand until cheese is melted.

*Tip: To drain tofu, place it on a paper towel-lined plate for 15 minutes.

PER SERVING 316 **CAL**; 8 g **FAT** (2 g **SAT**); 17 g **PRO**; 42 g **CARB**; 4 g **FIBER**; 447 mg **SODIUM**; 44 mg **CHOL**

CHEESY NOODLE CASSEROLE

BEEF GYROS

Beef Gyros

MAKES 6 servings **PREP** 25 minutes
SLOW COOK on HIGH for 2 hours or LOW
for 4 hours **STAND** 10 minutes

1	large sweet onion, cut into thin wedges
2	pounds extra-lean ground beef
2	teaspoons dried oregano, crushed
3	cloves garlic, minced
½	teaspoon salt
½	teaspoon black pepper
½	teaspoon paprika
6	oval whole wheat wraps
3	roma tomatoes, sliced
⅓	cup crumbled reduced-fat feta cheese
1	recipe Tzatziki Sauce

• Place onion in a 3½- or 4-quart slow cooker. In a large bowl, combine beef, oregano, garlic, salt, pepper and paprika.

• On waxed paper, shape meat mixture into a 5-inch round loaf. Crisscross three 18 x 2-inch foil strips. Place meat loaf in center of strips. Bringing up foil strips, lift and transfer meat and foil to the slow cooker over the onion. Press the meat away from the side of slow cooker to avoid burning.

• Cover and cook on HIGH for 2 to 2½ hours or on LOW for 4 to 5 hours.

• Using foil strips, carefully lift meat loaf from the slow cooker and transfer to a cutting board. Let stand for 10 minutes before thinly slicing.*

• Divide sliced meat and onion among whole wheat wraps. Top with tomatoes, feta cheese, and Tzatziki Sauce.

Tzatziki Sauce In a medium bowl, stir together 1 carton (6 ounces) plain Greek yogurt; 1 cup shredded, seeded cucumber; 1 tablespoon lemon juice; 1 tablespoon snipped fresh dill weed; 1 teaspoon honey; 1 clove minced garlic; and ¼ teaspoon salt. Serve immediately or cover and chill for up to 4 hours.

***Tip:** Cut the loaf in half crosswise, then place, cut sides down, on the cutting board for easiest slicing.

PER SERVING 386 CAL; 11 g FAT (4 g SAT); 45 g PRO; 32 g CARB; 8 g FIBER; 820 mg SODIUM; 97 mg CHOL

POT ROAST WITH FRUIT AND CHIPOTLE SAUCE

Pot Roast with Fruit and Chipotle Sauce

MAKES 8 servings **PREP** 15 minutes **SLOW COOK** on HIGH for 5 hours or LOW for 10 hours

1	3-pound boneless beef chuck pot roast
2	teaspoons garlic-pepper seasoning
1	package (7 ounces) dried mixed fruit
½	cup water
1	tablespoon finely chopped chipotle peppers in adobo sauce
1	tablespoon cold water
2	teaspoons cornstarch
	Fresh cilantro sprigs (optional)

• Trim fat from meat. If necessary, cut meat to fit into a 3½- or 4-quart slow cooker. Sprinkle both sides of meat with garlic-pepper seasoning. Place meat in cooker. Add fruit, the ½ cup water and the chipotle peppers.

• Cover and cook on HIGH for 5 to 5½ hours or LOW for 10 to 11 hours. Transfer meat and fruit to a serving platter; thinly slice meat. Cover meat and fruit and keep warm.

• For sauce, pour cooking liquid into a bowl or glass measuring cup; skim off fat. In a medium saucepan, combine the 1 tablespoon cold water and the cornstarch; stir into cooking liquid. Cook and stir over medium heat until thickened and bubbly. Cook and stir for 2 minutes more.

• Serve meat and fruit with sauce. If desired, garnish with cilantro.

PER SERVING 275 CAL; 6 g FAT (2 g SAT); 37 g PRO; 17 g CARB; 1 g FIBER; 378 mg SODIUM; 101 mg CHOL

PORK-STUFFED
CABBAGE ROLLS

Pork-Stuffed Cabbage Rolls

MAKES 8 servings   PREP 1 hour 15 minutes   SLOW COOK on HIGH for 3½ hours or LOW for 6½ hours

1	**head (3 pounds) green cabbage, cored**
1	**pound ground pork**
1½	**cups cooked brown rice**
½	**cup chopped onion**
½	**cup golden raisins**
3	**tablespoons canned tomato paste**
4	**cloves garlic, minced**
1	**teaspoon salt**
½	**teaspoon black pepper**
½	**teaspoon caraway seeds, crushed**
1	**can (14½ ounces) no-salt-added diced tomatoes**
1	**can (8 ounces) low-sodium vegetable juice**
1	**can (8 ounces) tomato sauce**
2	**tablespoons reduced-sodium Worcestershire sauce**
2	**teaspoons packed brown sugar**

• Bring a large pot of lightly salted water to a boil. Boil cabbage for 12 to 15 minutes, carefully removing 16 leaves with long-handled tongs as they become pliable. Drain well, then remove tough stems from leaves. Remove remaining cabbage from water and shred 4 cups (discard any remaining cabbage). Place shredded cabbage in bottom of a 5- to 6-quart slow cooker.

• In a large bowl, combine the pork, rice, onion, raisins, tomato paste, garlic, ½ teaspoon of the salt, ¼ teaspoon of the pepper and the caraway. Evenly divide the pork mixture among the 16 cabbage leaves, using a scant ⅓ cup per leaf. Fold sides of leaf over filling and roll up.

• In a medium bowl, combine tomatoes, vegetable juice, tomato sauce, Worcestershire sauce, brown sugar, remaining ½ teaspoon salt and remaining ¼ teaspoon pepper. Pour half of the tomato mixture over shredded cabbage in cooker. Stir to mix. Place cabbage rolls on the shredded cabbage. Top with remaining tomato mixture.

• Cover and cook on HIGH for 3½ to 4 hours or LOW for 6½ to 7½ hours (a cabbage roll in center of cooker should register 160°F on an instant-read thermometer). Carefully remove the cooked cabbage rolls and serve with the shredded cabbage.

PER SERVING 280 **CAL**; 10 g **FAT** (3 g **SAT**); 15 g **PRO**; 36 g **CARB**; 7 g **FIBER**; 634 mg **SODIUM**; 39 mg **CHOL**

Creamy Chicken Noodle Soup

MAKES 8 servings   PREP 25 minutes
SLOW COOK on HIGH for 3 hours or LOW for 6 hours, plus 20 minutes on HIGH

1	**container (32 ounces) reduced-sodium chicken broth**
3	**cups water**
2½	**cups chopped cooked chicken (about 12 ounces)**
1½	**cups sliced carrots (3 medium)**
1½	**cups sliced celery (3 stalks)**
1½	**cups mushrooms, sliced (4 ounces)**
¼	**cup chopped onion**
1½	**teaspoons dried thyme, crushed**
¾	**teaspoon garlic-pepper seasoning**
3	**ounces reduced-fat cream cheese (Neufchâtel), cut up**
2	**cups dried egg noodles**

• In a 5- to 6-quart slow cooker combine chicken broth, the water, chicken, carrots, celery, mushrooms, onion, thyme and garlic-pepper seasoning.

• Cover and cook on HIGH for 3 to 4 hours or on LOW for 6 to 8 hours

• Stir in cream cheese until combined. Stir in uncooked noodles. Cover and cook on HIGH for 20 to 30 minutes more or just until noodles are tender.

PER SERVING 170 **CAL**; 6 g **FAT** (2 g **SAT**); 17 g **PRO**; 11 g **CARB**; 2 g **FIBER**; 401 mg **SODIUM**; 54 mg **CHOL**

Creamy Ham and Potato Chowder

MAKES 6 servings **PREP** 20 minutes **SLOW COOK** on HIGH for 3½ hours

12	ounces tiny yellow potatoes, cut into ¾-inch pieces
1	cup chopped onion (1 large)
2	cans (14.5 ounces) reduced-sodium chicken broth
¼	cup cornstarch
½	teaspoon dried thyme, crushed
¼	teaspoon black pepper
1	can (12 ounces) evaporated fat-free milk (1½ cups)
½	cup diced cooked lean ham
1	cup coarsely shredded carrots (2 medium)
1	cup broccoli florets, steamed
¼	cup shredded cheddar cheese (1 ounce)
2	teaspoons snipped fresh thyme

• In a 4-quart slow cooker combine potatoes and onion. Pour chicken broth over vegetables.

• Cover and cook on HIGH for 3 hours.

• In a medium bowl, combine cornstarch, dried thyme and pepper. Whisk in evaporated milk. Slowly stir the cornstarch mixture, ham and carrots into the hot soup. Cover and cook for 30 minutes more, stirring occasionally.

• Serve soup topped with broccoli, cheese and fresh thyme.

PER SERVING 171 **CAL**; 2 g **FAT** (1 g **SAT**); 11 g **PRO**; 27 g **CARB**; 3 g **FIBER**; 566 mg **SODIUM**; 12 mg **CHOL**

CREAMY HAM AND POTATO CHOWDER

SMOKY BEANS

When pulled pork is on the menu, cook up a batch of these flavorful, low-fat beans (just 2 grams of fat per serving) flavored with a smoked turkey leg.

CHOCOLATE-CHERRY
BREAD PUDDING

Smoky Beans

MAKES 14 servings **PREP** 15 minutes
SLOW COOK on HIGH for 4 hours or LOW for 8 hours

1	**smoked turkey drumstick (about 1 pound)**
2	**cans (15 ounces each) navy or Great Northern beans, rinsed and drained**
1	**can (15 ounces) red beans or pinto beans, rinsed and drained**
1	**can (14.5 ounces) diced tomatoes and green chiles**
1	**cup chicken broth**
1	**medium yellow or red sweet pepper, chopped**
1	**medium onion, chopped**
2	**tablespoons packed brown sugar**
3	**cloves garlic, chopped**
1	**teaspoon dry mustard**
½	**teaspoon dried savory or thyme, crushed**

• In a 5- to 6-quart slow cooker combine the smoked turkey drumstick, beans, diced tomatoes and green chiles, broth, sweet pepper, onion, brown sugar, garlic, dry mustard and savory.

• Cover and cook on HIGH for 4 to 5 hours or on LOW for 8 to 10 hours. Remove turkey drumstick. When cool enough to handle, remove meat from bone and coarsely chop. Discard skin and bone. Stir meat into bean mixture.

PER SERVING 137 CAL; 2 g FAT (1 g SAT); 13 g PRO; 21 g CARB; 5 g FIBER; 492 mg SODIUM; 32 mg CHOL

Chocolate-Cherry Bread Pudding

MAKES 6 servings **PREP** 25 minutes **SLOW COOK** on LOW for 3 hours **COOL** 30 minutes

	Nonstick cooking spray
½	**cup refrigerated or frozen egg product, thawed, or 2 eggs, lightly beaten**
¼	**cup sugar**
¼	**teaspoon almond extract**
⅛	**teaspoon salt**
1	**cup fat-free milk**
3	**cups dried whole wheat bread cubes***
½	**cup chopped bittersweet chocolate (2 ounces)**
⅓	**cup dried tart cherries**
1	**cup warm water**
3	**tablespoons powdered sugar**
2	**tablespoons low-fat Greek yogurt**
1	**teaspoon fat-free milk**
3	**tablespoons sliced almonds, toasted (optional)**

• Lightly coat a 1-quart soufflé dish or casserole** with cooking spray. Tear off an 18 x 12-inch piece of heavy foil; cut in half lengthwise. Fold each piece lengthwise into thirds. Crisscross the foil strips and place the dish in the center of the crisscross; set aside.

• In a medium bowl, combine eggs, sugar, almond extract and salt. Whisk in the 1 cup milk. Gently stir in bread cubes, chocolate and cherries. Pour mixture into prepared dish. Cover dish tightly with foil.

• Pour the warm water into a 3½- to 5-quart slow cooker. Using the ends of the foil strips, transfer dish to cooker. Leave foil strips under dish.

• Cover and cook on LOW for 3 to 3½ hours or until a knife inserted in center comes out clean. Using foil strips, carefully remove dish from cooker; discard foil strips. Cool, uncovered, on a wire rack for 30 minutes before serving.

• Meanwhile, for icing, in a small bowl, combine powdered sugar, yogurt and the 1 teaspoon milk. Drizzle cooled bread pudding with icing. If desired, sprinkle with almonds.

*Tip: To make dried bread cubes, preheat oven to 300°F. Cut whole wheat bread slices (about 3 ounces) into cubes to make 3 cups. Spread cubes in a single layer in a 15 x 10 x 1-inch baking pan. Bake for 10 to 15 minutes or until dry, stirring twice; cool.

**Tip: Before beginning this recipe, check to make sure that the dish or casserole you plan to use fits into your slow cooker.

PER SERVING 189 CAL; 4 g FAT (2 g SAT); 6 g PRO; 34 g CARB; 2 g FIBER; 178 mg SODIUM; 1 mg CHOL

TASTE OF FAME

Feast on what these five celebrities make best.

WHITE PIZZA WITH
ARUGULA, LEMON,
PARMESAN AND RICOTTA

No need for red sauce on this light and lovely pizza. The peppery arugula dressed in lemon juice and olive oil is a fresh and flavorful complement to the creamy ricotta cheese.

White Pizza with Arugula, Lemon, Parmesan and Ricotta

MAKES 6 servings **PREP** 15 minutes **BAKE** at 500° for 15 minutes

3	tablespoons olive oil, plus more to grease pan and brush crust
1	pound pizza dough (homemade or store bought; thawed if frozen)
1	ball (8 ounces) fresh mozzarella, thinly sliced
5	cups packed arugula
½	cup freshly grated Parmesan cheese
2	tablespoons fresh lemon juice (about half a lemon)
¼	teaspoon salt
⅛	teaspoon black pepper
¾	cup ricotta cheese

• Heat oven to 500°. Grease a 17 x 12-inch rimmed baking sheet with olive oil. Drop pizza dough into center of greased sheet, and use fingers to press out and flatten dough so it spreads as close as possible to corners of pan. This may seem difficult, but persist, as a thin crust will be worth it.

• Scatter mozzarella slices over dough and brush exposed edge of crust with olive oil. Bake for 15 minutes, until crust is crispy and cheese is bubbly. (If cheese starts to get too brown, cover center of pizza with foil.)

• While pizza bakes, toss together arugula, Parmesan, the 3 tablespoons oil, the lemon juice, salt and pepper. When pizza is ready, let cool for about 2 minutes and top with salad. Top with 12 spoonfuls of ricotta (1 tablespoon each). Cut into squares and serve.

Tiffani Thiessen

What she's doing now: Playing Elizabeth Burke on USA Network's *White Collar*

What she's best known for: *Saved by the Bell* and *Beverly Hills, 90210*

CARROT GINGER SOUP

Carrot Ginger Soup

MAKES 6 servings PREP 15 minutes COOK 25 minutes

2	tablespoons extra-virgin olive oil
½	cup chopped white onion
4	cups chopped carrots (peeled and cut into ½-inch pieces)
4	cups vegetable broth
1	cup orange juice
1	tablespoon plus 2 teaspoons finely grated peeled fresh ginger
1	tablespoon lemon juice
1	can (14 ounces) coconut milk
½	teaspoon salt
⅛	teaspoon black pepper

• Heat olive oil in a large saucepan over medium heat. Add onion and sauté until translucent, about 5 minutes.

• Add carrots, broth, orange juice, ginger and lemon juice; bring to a boil. Reduce heat and simmer, covered, until carrots are tender, about 20 minutes.

• Remove saucepan from heat. Puree soup with an immersion blender or food processor until very smooth. Return soup to saucepan and stir in coconut milk, salt and pepper. Reheat over medium heat and serve.

Ali Larter

What she's doing now: Playing Crystal Quest on TNT's *Legends*

What she's best known for: *Heroes, Varsity Blues, Final Destination* and *Legally Blonde*

Discover Larter's passion for cooking in *Kitchen Revelry: A Year of Festive Menus from My Home to Yours.*

Old Country Danish Scones

MAKES 26 scones **PREP** 10 minutes **FRY** at 365° for 4 minutes per batch

- **4** **cups all-purpose flour**
- **1** **cup powdered milk**
- **2** **teaspoons salt**
- **2** **tablespoons sugar**
- **4** **teaspoons baking powder**
- **2** **cups warm water**
  Vegetable oil (enough to fill a pan about 4 to 5 inches deep)

• In a large bowl, mix flour, powdered milk, salt, sugar and baking powder. Add the warm water and stir to combine (mixture will be wet). On a well-floured surface, pat out dough until ½ to ¾ inch thick. Cut into pieces of whatever size you'd like your scones to be.

• Fill a pan 4 to 5 inches high with vegetable oil and heat to 365° on a deep-fat fry thermometer. (This should be hot enough so that when you add scones they start to bubble right away and float.) Fry dough pieces in batches until they turn light golden brown, about 3 to 4 minutes per batch. Make sure oil gets back up to 365° before adding more dough.

• Serve with optional toppings. (My grandma always put out an assortment of jellies and jams, honey and heaps of butter.)

Bree Turner

What she's doing now: Playing Rosalee Calvert on NBC's *Grimm*

What she's best known for: *The Ugly Truth* and *Just My Luck*

OLD COUNTRY
DANISH SCONES

LEMON CAPER CHICKEN

Lemon Caper Chicken

MAKES 3 servings **PREP** 15 minutes **COOK** 9 minutes

- 1 **teaspoon kosher salt**
- 1 **teaspoon black pepper**
- 1 **teaspoon lemon pepper**
- 4 **tablespoons all-purpose flour**
- 3 **chicken cutlets**
  Zest and juice of 1 lemon
- 2 **tablespoons olive oil**
- 1 **cup chicken broth**
- 2 **tablespoons capers**
- 3 **cloves garlic, finely minced**
  Splash half-and-half (optional)
  Parsley, for garnish (optional)

• On a flat dish, combine kosher salt, black pepper, lemon pepper and 2 tablespoons of the flour. Coat chicken cutlets in flour mixture and place on a plate. Sprinkle half of the lemon zest over cutlets.

• Heat oil in a large skillet over medium heat. Brown chicken until cooked through, about 7 minutes, turning once. Transfer to a fresh plate.

• In a bowl, whisk lemon juice, chicken broth, capers, garlic and remaining zest until smooth. Pour into skillet with drippings and whisk until combined. Add half-and-half, if desired. Return chicken to pan and heat through, 2 minutes. To serve, spoon sauce over cutlets and garnish with parsley, if desired.

Haylie Duff

What she's doing now: Taping a companion series to her book and blog and promoting her TV movies, *Badge of Honor* and *The Wedding Pact*

What she's best known for: *Napoleon Dynamite, 7th Heaven*

For more of Duff's recipes, pick up *The Real Girl's Kitchen.*

ZUCCHINI SALAD

Ribbons of zucchini lightly dressed in olive oil, lemon, salt and pepper and sprinkled with Parmesan and pine nuts make a simple but beautiful salad.

Zucchini Salad

MAKES 6 servings **PREP** 20 minutes

2½	**pounds zucchini**
3	**tablespoons olive oil**
¼	**cup fresh lemon juice (from 1 lemon)**
¾	**teaspoon sea salt**
½	**teaspoon fresh grated black pepper**
½	**cup shaved Parmesan cheese**
½	**cup toasted pine nuts**

• Use a vegetable peeler to shave zucchini into ribbons. Place in a large bowl.

• Gently toss zucchini with olive oil, lemon juice, salt and pepper. Top with shaved Parmesan and pine nuts. Serve immediately.

Jessica Alba

What she's doing now: Running The Honest Company, which offers toxin-free household goods.

What she's best known for: *Dark Angel, The Fantastic Four*

Check out Alba's book, *The Honest Life,* for tips on how to live naturally.

AN IRISH FEAST

Invite friends over for the wearing of the green, the raising of a glass, the feasting on a tasty St. Patrick's Day spread—and a bit of blarney, too!

CORNED BEEF AND CABBAGE, PAGE 84

CURRANT-ORANGE IRISH
SODA BREAD, PAGE 84

Corned Beef and Cabbage

MAKES 6 servings **PREP** 15 minutes
SLOW COOK on HIGH for 5 hours or LOW for 10 hours

1	3-pound corned beef brisket with spice packet
½	of a small head cabbage, cut into 3 wedges
4	medium carrots, halved lengthwise and cut into 2-inch pieces
2	medium Yukon gold or yellow Finn potatoes, cut into 2-inch pieces
1	medium onion, quartered
½	cup water

• Trim fat from meat. If necessary, cut meat to fit into a 5- to 6-quart slow cooker. Sprinkle spices from packet evenly over meat; rub in with your fingers. Place cabbage, carrots, potatoes and onion in cooker. Add the water. Place meat on top of vegetables.

• Cover and cook on HIGH for 5 to 6 hours or on LOW for 10 to 12 hours.

• Transfer meat to a serving platter; thinly slice across the grain. Using a slotted spoon, transfer vegetables to a serving platter.

Currant-Orange Irish Soda Bread

MAKES 12 servings **PREP** 20 minutes
BAKE at 375°F of 35 minutes

2	cups all-purpose flour
1	to 2 tablespoons sugar
1	teaspoon baking powder
½	teaspoon baking soda
½	teaspoon salt
1	tablespoon finely shredded orange peel
3	tablespoons butter
⅓	cup currants
1	egg, lightly beaten
¾	cup buttermilk

• Heat oven to 375°. Grease a baking sheet; set aside. In a large bowl, stir together flour, sugar, baking powder, baking soda, salt and orange peel. Cut in butter until mixture resembles coarse crumbs. Stir in currants. Make a well in the center of the mixture.

• In a small bowl, combine egg and buttermilk. Add all at once to flour mixture. Stir just until moistened.

• On a lightly floured surface, gently knead dough until dough holds together (about 4 or 5 times). Shape into a 7-inch round loaf.

• Transfer dough to prepared baking sheet. With a sharp knife, make two slashes across the top of the loaf to form an X, cutting all the way to the edge. Bake for 30 to 35 minutes or until golden. Serve warm.

Shamrock Milkshake Cupcakes

MAKES 20 to 22 (2½-inch) cupcakes
PREP 50 minutes **STAND** 30 minutes
BAKE at 350°F for 18 minutes **COOL** 45 minutes

4	egg whites
2	cups all-purpose flour
1	teaspoon baking powder
½	teaspoon baking soda
½	teaspoon salt
1	cup buttermilk or sour milk*
¼	cup green crème de menthe**
½	cup shortening
1¾	cups sugar
1	teaspoon vanilla extract
1	recipe White Chocolate Frosting Green food coloring

• Allow egg whites to stand at room temperature for 30 minutes. Meanwhile, line twenty to twenty-two 2½-inch muffin cups with paper bake cups. In a medium bowl, stir together flour, baking powder, baking soda and salt. In a 2-cup glass measuring cup, combine buttermilk and crème de menthe. Set aside.

• Heat oven to 350°F. In a large mixing bowl, beat shortening on medium to high speed for 30 seconds. Gradually add sugar, about ¼ cup at a time, beating on medium speed until light and fluffy. Beat in vanilla. Add egg whites, one at a time, beating well after each addition. Alternately add flour mixture and buttermilk mixture to shortening mixture, beating on low speed after each addition just until combined.

• Spoon batter into prepared muffin cups, filling each about two-thirds full. Use the back of a spoon to smooth out batter in cups.

• Bake for 15 to 18 minutes or until tops spring back when lightly touched. Cool cupcakes in muffin cups on wire racks for 5 minutes. Remove cupcakes from muffin cups. Cool completely on racks.

• Divide White Chocolate Frosting between two bowls. Tint one portion with green food coloring. Spoon each frosting into a pastry bag fitted with a large star tip. Pipe white and green frostings onto tops of cupcakes to resemble four-leaf clovers.

*Tip: To make 1 cup sour milk, place 1 tablespoon lemon juice or vinegar in a glass measuring cup. Add enough milk to make 1 cup total liquid; stir. Let stand for 5 minutes before using.

**Tip: If you prefer not to use crème de menthe, substitute a mixture of ¼ cup milk, 1 teaspoon mint extract and several drops green food coloring.

White Chocolate Frosting Place 6 ounces chopped white baking chocolate in a large mixing bowl; set aside. In a small saucepan heat ⅓ cup whipping cream just until simmering. Pour over white baking chocolate; let stand, without stirring, for 5 minutes. Stir until smooth; let stand for 15 minutes. Gradually beat 1 cup softened butter into melted white chocolate mixture on medium to high speed, beating until combined. Gradually beat in 1½ to 2 cups powdered sugar until frosting reaches piping or spreading consistency. Makes 3½ cups.

Tender buttermilk white-cake cupcakes are flavored and tinted with crème de menthe liqueur and topped with white chocolate frosting in the shape of a four-leaf clover in these St. Paddy's Day treats.

SHAMROCK MILKSHAKE
CUPCAKES

HERB-CRUSTED RACK OF LAMB,
PAGE 103

APRIL

95

107

113

HEALTHY FAMILY DINNERS

At less than $3 a serving, you can bank on this week's worth of budget-friendly meals.

DOUBLE-DUTY POT ROAST

SUNDAY

Double-Duty Pot Roast

MAKES 6 servings, plus leftovers **PREP** 15 minutes
SLOW COOK on HIGH for 6 hours or LOW for 8 hours **COOK** 1 minute

1	**large onion, chopped**
3	**cloves garlic, chopped**
2	**ribs celery, chopped**
1	**large carrot, chopped**
1	**bottom round pot roast (about 4 pounds)**
1	**teaspoon salt**
1	**teaspoon dried thyme**
½	**teaspoon black pepper**
4	**cups beef broth**
¼	**cup tomato paste**
2	**tablespoons reduced-sodium Worcestershire sauce**
6	**tablespoons cornstarch**
1	**package (12 ounces) whole-grain noodles, cooked per package directions**
	Sautéed red cabbage and apples (optional)

• Coat a 4½-quart slow cooker with nonstick cooking spray.

• Add onion, garlic, celery and carrot.

Season pot roast with salt, thyme and pepper; place on top of vegetables.

• Combine broth, tomato paste and Worcestershire sauce; pour over roast. Cover and cook on HIGH for 6 hours or LOW for 8 hours.

• Remove roast and cut in half. Cool half, wrap in plastic and refrigerate for Curried Beef on Tuesday (page 90).

• Strain liquid into a medium saucepan and bring to a simmer. Combine cornstarch with 3 tablespoons water and stir into liquid. Cook, stirring continuously until thickened, about 1 minute. Cool half and refrigerate for Curried Beef.

• Serve remaining pot roast and gravy with cooked noodles and, if desired, sautéed red cabbage and apples.

PER SERVING 498 CAL; 15 g FAT (5 g SAT); 41 g PRO; 46 g CARB; 2 g FIBER; 564 mg SODIUM; 138 mg CHOL

MONDAY

Shrimp Marinara

MAKES 6 servings **PREP** 20 minutes
COOK 34 minutes

2	**tablespoons olive oil**
6	**cloves garlic, sliced**
2	**cans (28 ounces each) crushed tomatoes**
1	**can (14.5 ounces) no-salt-added diced tomatoes**
2	**teaspoons sugar**
2	**teaspoons dried oregano**
1	**teaspoon salt**
½	**teaspoon red pepper flakes**
1	**pound medium shrimp, peeled and deveined**
1	**cup frozen green peas, thawed**
2	**packages (13.25 ounces each) whole wheat penne**
½	**cup fresh basil leaves, torn (optional)**
	Sautéed broccoli rabe (optional)

• Heat oil in a large pot over medium-high heat; add garlic and cook for 1 to 2 minutes, until golden. Stir in crushed tomatoes, diced tomatoes, sugar, oregano, salt and red pepper flakes. Bring to a boil; reduce heat to medium and simmer, with lid ajar, for 30 minutes. Stir occasionally.

• Spoon half the sauce, about 3½ cups, into a container and cool. Cover and refrigerate for Baked Penne on Wednesday (page 90).

• Stir shrimp and peas into remaining sauce. Cook for 2 minutes or until shrimp are cooked through.

• Meanwhile, cook penne following package directions. Cool half the penne, about 6 cups, and place in a plastic bag. Refrigerate for Baked Penne.

• To serve, toss remaining penne with shrimp sauce and, if desired, basil. Serve with sautéed broccoli rabe, if desired.

PER SERVING 410 CAL; 5 g FAT (1 g SAT); 27 g PRO; 62 g CARB; 10 g FIBER; 552 mg SODIUM; 115 mg CHOL

SHRIMP MARINARA

WEDNESDAY

Baked Penne

MAKES 6 servings   **PREP** 15 minutes
BAKE at 350° for 45 minutes

3	**tablespoons unseasoned bread crumbs**
6	**cups cooked whole wheat penne (page 88)**
3½	**cups marinara sauce (page 88)**
2	**cups shredded reduced-fat mozzarella**
½	**cup diced ham**
6	**eggs, lightly beaten**
3	**tablespoons grated Parmesan cheese**
	Tossed salad (optional)

• Heat oven to 350°. Coat a 3-quart casserole with nonstick cooking spray and sprinkle bottom and sides with bread crumbs.

• In a large bowl, combine penne, 3 cups of the marinara sauce, 1½ cups of the mozzarella, the ham and eggs. Spoon into prepared casserole and sprinkle remaining ½ cup mozzarella over top. Bake at 350° for 30 minutes. Sprinkle Parmesan over casserole and bake an additional 15 minutes.

• Cut into portions and serve with remaining ½ cup marinara sauce, warmed, and, if desired, a tossed salad.

PER SERVING 376 **CAL**; 10 g **FAT** (3 g **SAT**); 23 g **PRO**; 47 g **CARB**; 6 g **FIBER**; 806 mg **SODIUM**; 170 mg **CHOL**

TUESDAY

Curried Beef and Biscuits

MAKES 6 servings   **PREP** 15 minutes   **COOK** 16 minutes   **BAKE** at 350° for 30 minutes

1	**tablespoon olive oil**
1	**large onion, thinly sliced**
1	**large baking potato (12 ounces), peeled and diced**
1	**red sweet pepper, seeded and thinly sliced**
1	**teaspoon garam masala**
½	**teaspoon ground cumin**
½	**teaspoon ground ginger**
4	**cups cubed cooked pot roast (page 88)**
2	**cups gravy (page 88)**
6	**refrigerated country-style biscuits (from a 12-ounce package)**
	Steamed green beans (optional)

• Heat oven to 350°.

• Heat oil in a large cast-iron or ovenproof skillet over medium-high heat. Add onion and potato; cook for 15 minutes, stirring occasionally. Add red pepper, garam masala, cumin and ginger; cook for 1 minute, stirring occasionally.

• Spoon in pot roast and gravy. Cover and bake at 350° for 15 minutes, until bubbly. Arrange biscuits on top and bake, uncovered, an additional 15 minutes or until biscuits are golden brown.

• Serve warm with steamed green beans, if desired.

PER SERVING 410 **CAL**; 15 g **FAT** (5 g **SAT**); 35 g **PRO**; 32 g **CARB**; 2 g **FIBER**; 739 mg **SODIUM**; 72 mg **CHOL**

BAKED PENNE

CHICKEN FAJITAS

THURSDAY

Chicken Fajitas

MAKES 4 servings **PREP** 20 minutes
BROIL 6 minutes **COOK** 10 minutes

4	thin-cut boneless, skinless chicken breasts (about 4 ounces each)
2	tablespoons McCormick Perfect Pinch Mexican seasoning
1	tablespoon canola oil
1	large sweet onion, cut into ¼-inch slices
1	green bell pepper, seeded and cut into ¼-inch slices
1	small zucchini, cut into matchsticks
1	small yellow squash, cut into matchsticks
½	teaspoon salt
8	corn tortillas
1	pouch Minute Rice Multigrain Medley, cooked per package directions
½	cup reduced-fat sour cream
1	lime, cut into wedges

• Heat broiler. Coat broiler pan with nonstick cooking spray.

• Season chicken on both sides with 4 teaspoons of the Mexican seasoning. Broil 3 minutes, turn and broil 3 minutes more or until internal temperature reaches 165°. Place chicken on a cutting board and keep warm.

• Meanwhile, heat oil in a large nonstick skillet over medium-high heat. Add onion; cook for 5 minutes, stirring occasionally. Stir in green pepper, zucchini, summer squash, salt and remaining 2 teaspoons of the Mexican seasoning; cook an additional 5 minutes, stirring occasionally.

• Slice chicken breasts and wrap in tortillas with vegetables. Serve with rice, sour cream and lime wedges for squeezing over fajitas.

PER SERVING 438 **CAL**; 12 g **FAT** (3 g **SAT**); 31 g **PRO**; 51 g **CARB**; 6 g **FIBER**; 712 mg **SODIUM**; 78 mg **CHOL**

HOISIN-GLAZED PORK, BOK CHOY AND SNAP PEAS

FRIDAY

Hoisin-Glazed Pork, Bok Choy and Snap Peas

MAKES 4 servings **PREP** 20 minutes **COOK** 11 minutes

4	teaspoons vegetable oil
4	boneless pork chops (about 4 ounces each), cut into ½-inch slices against the grain
2	tablespoons hoisin sauce
1	bunch bok choy (about 1 pound), trimmed and cut into 1-inch pieces
½	pound sugar snap peas, trimmed
1	cup reduced-sodium beef broth
2	tablespoons cornstarch
1	tablespoon light soy sauce
3	cups cooked jasmine rice

• Heat 2 teaspoons of the oil in a large nonstick skillet over medium-high heat. Add pork and stir-fry for 2 minutes; remove to a bowl and toss with hoisin sauce. Keep warm.

• Add remaining 2 teaspoons vegetable oil and bok choy to skillet; stir-fry for 2 minutes. Add snap peas and stir-fry for 5 minutes or until vegetables are tender.

• Combine broth, cornstarch and soy sauce; add to skillet and simmer for 2 minutes, until thickened.

• Spoon stir-fried vegetables and pork over cooked rice.

PER SERVING 373 **CAL**; 12 g **FAT** (3 g **SAT**); 30 g **PRO**; 35 g **CARB**; 4 g **FIBER**; 728 mg **SODIUM**; 62 mg **CHOL**

SLOW COOKER SURPRISES

Here are 8 novel ideas: Think stuffed artichokes, zucchini gratin—even veggie lasagna.

STUFFED ARTICHOKES

Stuffed Artichokes

MAKES 5 servings PREP 25 minutes
SLOW COOK on HIGH for 4 hours

5	globe artichokes
⅔	cup seasoned bread crumbs
¼	cup grated Parmesan cheese, plus more for garnish
¼	cup pine nuts, chopped
1	tablespoon chopped fresh parsley
1	clove garlic, grated
1	teaspoon fresh lemon zest plus 1 tablespoon lemon juice
2	tablespoons unsalted butter, melted
⅓	cup white wine

• With a sharp knife, cut top third off each artichoke. Trim stems to ¼ to ½ inch. With scissors or kitchen shears, snip off pointed tips of remaining leaves. Gently pry open leaves of artichokes.

• In a large bowl, combine bread crumbs, Parmesan, pine nuts, parsley, garlic, lemon zest and juice, and butter. Stir until well combined.

• Hold one of the artichokes over bowl with stuffing mixture. With a large spoon, press stuffing into center of artichoke and into spaces in between leaves, packing as tightly as possible. Repeat with all artichokes.

• Combine wine with 1 cup water in a 5-quart slow cooker. Place artichokes in slow cooker and cook on HIGH for 4 hours. Use a large spoon to carefully remove artichokes to a platter. Garnish with additional Parmesan. To eat, pull a leaf from artichoke and scrape between teeth to remove stuffing and soft part of leaf at base.

PER SERVING 242 CAL; 11 g FAT (4 g SAT); 10 g PRO; 30 g CARB; 10 g FIBER; 493 mg SODIUM; 16 mg CHOL

EASY BOLOGNESE

Easy Bolognese

MAKES 4 servings, plus enough sauce for another meal PREP 15 minutes COOK 5 minutes
SLOW COOK on HIGH for 5½ hours

6	ounces turkey bacon, chopped
3	medium shallots, chopped
2	ribs celery, chopped
2	medium carrots, finely chopped
3	cloves garlic, sliced
1	can (28 ounces) crushed San Marzano tomatoes
1	can (8 ounces) tomato sauce
⅓	cup dry red wine
½	teaspoon black pepper
¼	teaspoon salt
1	pound lean ground beef
1	small package (8 ounces) pappardelle
½	cup heavy cream
6	tablespoons grated Parmesan cheese

• Place turkey bacon in a medium nonstick skillet over medium to medium-high heat. Cook 5 minutes, until lightly browned.

• Combine turkey bacon, shallots, celery, carrots, garlic, crushed tomatoes, tomato sauce, red wine, pepper and salt in slow cooker. Crumble in ground beef and gently stir together.

• Cover and cook on HIGH for 5½ hours.

• Just before serving, bring a large pot of salted water to a boil. Cook pasta per package directions for al dente. Drain and transfer to a serving bowl. Stir heavy cream and 3 tablespoons of the Parmesan into sauce in slow cooker. Place half the sauce (3 cups) in a resealable container, cool and freeze for another meal. Spoon remaining 3 cups sauce over pasta. Sprinkle with remaining 3 tablespoons Parmesan.

PER SERVING 470 CAL; 16 g FAT (8 g SAT); 27 g PRO; 54 g CARB; 6 g FIBER; 803 mg SODIUM; 146 mg CHOL

SEAFOOD AND SPRING
VEGGIE CHOWDER

Seafood and Spring Veggie Chowder

MAKES 5 servings **PREP** 24 minutes
SLOW COOK on HIGH for 4 hours 30 minutes or
LOW for 6 hours 45 minutes plus 15 minutes

- **2** leeks, white and light-green parts only, sliced and cleaned well
- **2** medium carrots, peeled and sliced in half-moons
- **1** large rib celery, diced
- **1** pound russet potatoes, peeled and diced
- **2** cups milk
- **2** cups reduced-sodium vegetable broth
- **1** teaspoon Old Bay seasoning
- **½** teaspoon garlic powder
  Pinch ground nutmeg
- **1** bunch pencil-thin asparagus, trimmed and cut into ¼- to ½-inch pieces
- **½** pound peeled, deveined shrimp, cut in half
- **½** pound small bay scallops (thawed, if frozen)
- **½** pound lump crabmeat or imitation crab (surimi), torn into small pieces
- **3** tablespoons instant potato flakes
  Salt and pepper to taste (optional)

• Coat a 3½- or 4-quart slow cooker bowl with nonstick cooking spray. Add leeks, carrots, celery and potatoes. Stir in milk, vegetable broth, Old Bay seasoning, garlic powder and nutmeg. Cover and cook on HIGH for 4½ hours or LOW for 6 hours 45 minutes.

• Uncover and stir in asparagus, shrimp, scallops, crab and potato flakes. Re-cover and cook for an additional 15 minutes (on either HIGH or LOW; see Note). Season to taste with salt and pepper, if desired.

Note: Seafood cooks very quickly and can easily get tough. Make sure that shrimp and scallops are opaque yet tender and crab is heated through.

PER SERVING 330 CAL; 5 g FAT (2 g SAT); 29 g PRO; 44 g CARB; 5 g FIBER; 957 mg SODIUM; 103 mg CHOL

LASAGNA PRIMAVERA

Lasagna Primavera

MAKES 6 servings **PREP** 20 minutes **COOK** 6 minutes **SLOW COOK** on LOW for 4 hours
LET STAND 30 minutes

- **2** tablespoons olive oil
- **1** package (8 ounces) shredded carrots
- **1** package (8 ounces) sliced mushrooms
- **1** package (5 ounces) mixed baby kale, coarsely chopped
- **1** can (12 ounces) evaporated milk
- **1** envelope (1.6 ounces) Alfredo mix (such as Knorr)
- **2** cloves garlic, sliced
- **¼** teaspoon salt
- **¼** teaspoon black pepper
- **1** cup fresh basil leaves, chopped
  Pinch ground nutmeg
- **1** container (15 ounces) part-skim ricotta
- **3** cups shredded part-skim mozzarella
- **12** traditional lasagna noodles
- **2** tablespoons grated Parmesan cheese

• Line a 4½- or 5-quart slow cooker with a slow cooker liner. Coat liner with nonstick cooking spray.

• Heat oil in a large skillet over medium heat. Add carrots, mushrooms and kale and cook, stirring, for 4 minutes.

• In a small bowl, whisk together evaporated milk and Alfredo mix. Add to skillet along with garlic, salt and pepper. Bring to a simmer and cook for 2 minutes. Remove from heat and stir in basil and nutmeg.

• Meanwhile, in a small bowl, blend ricotta with 1 cup of the shredded mozzarella.

• Begin layering: Break 3 of the noodles into thirds and spread over bottom of slow cooker. Top with half of the vegetable mixture (about 2 cups). Continue layering with 3 more noodles (in thirds), then ricotta mixture.

• Top ricotta mixture with 3 more noodles (in thirds), and remaining vegetable mixture. Finish layering with remaining three noodles (in thirds), then scatter noodles with remaining 2 cups shredded mozzarella and the grated Parmesan.

• Cover and cook on LOW for 4 hours. Uncover and lift lasagna from crock with slow cooker liner.

• Let lasagna stand for 30 minutes, then cut into 6 pieces and serve.

PER SERVING 563 CAL; 27 g FAT (14 g SAT); 35 g PRO; 48 g CARB; 3 g FIBER; 1,036 mg SODIUM; 81 mg CHOL

FENNEL AND ZUCCHINI GRATIN

Fennel and Zucchini Gratin

MAKES 6 servings PREP 25 minutes SLOW COOK on HIGH for 5½ hours or LOW for 8 hours

1½	cups brown rice (uncooked)
1¼	pounds zucchini, trimmed and cut diagonally into ¼-inch slices
¼	teaspoon salt
¼	teaspoon black pepper
4	tablespoons seasoned dry bread crumbs
1	fennel bulb (about 1¼ pounds), trimmed and thinly sliced
1	package (14 ounces) uncooked mild chicken sausage
2	cups shredded Gruyère or Jarlsberg cheese
2	tablespoons cornstarch
1	cup low-sodium chicken broth
1	tablespoon Dijon mustard

• Coat a 5½- or 6-quart slow cooker bowl with nonstick cooking spray. Scatter uncooked rice over bottom. In a medium bowl, toss zucchini with ⅛ teaspoon each of the salt and pepper and 2 tablespoons of the bread crumbs. Layer half the zucchini over rice.

• In a second medium bowl, toss sliced fennel with remaining ⅛ teaspoon each of the salt and pepper and remaining 2 tablespoons bread crumbs. Layer half over zucchini.

• Remove half the sausage links from their casings and crumble over fennel layer. In a small bowl, toss cheese with cornstarch and scatter half over sausage.

• Repeat layering with remaining zucchini, fennel, sausage and cheese. Whisk together chicken broth and mustard and pour into slow cooker. Cover and cook on HIGH for 5½ hours or LOW for 7½ to 8 hours. (Keep an eye on slow cooker for last half hour; if edges of gratin begin to get overly brown, stop cooking.)

PER SERVING 543 CAL; 22 g FAT (10 g SAT); 33 g PRO; 54 g CARB; 7 g FIBER; 1,057 mg SODIUM; 111 mg CHOL

Potato-Topped Beef Stew

MAKES 5 servings PREP 15 minutes
COOK 5 minutes SLOW COOK on HIGH for 5 hours or LOW for 7 hours

2	tablespoons vegetable oil
1½	pounds beef chuck for stew
3	tablespoons all-purpose flour
½	teaspoon salt
¼	teaspoon black pepper
1	package (8 ounces) cremini mushrooms, cleaned and quartered
1	medium onion, diced
2	carrots, peeled and cut into ½-inch slices
2	cloves garlic, chopped
½	cup reduced-sodium beef broth
½	cup red wine
1	cup thawed frozen peas
3	tablespoons snipped chives
1	package (24 ounces) prepared mashed potatoes

• Heat oil in a large skillet over medium-high heat. Toss beef with 2 tablespoons of the flour, ¼ teaspoon of the salt and the pepper. Add beef to skillet and brown on all sides, 5 minutes. Remove from heat.

• Meanwhile, coat a 4-quart slow cooker bowl with nonstick cooking spray. Add mushrooms, onion, carrots and garlic. Season with remaining ¼ teaspoon salt. Stir in broth and wine, then browned beef. Cover and cook on HIGH for 5 hours or LOW for 7 hours.

• Scoop ½ cup liquid from slow cooker and whisk in remaining 1 tablespoon flour. Stir back into slow cooker along with thawed peas and 1 tablespoon of the chives. Cover cooker and keep warm.

• Heat potatoes per package directions. Stir in remaining 2 tablespoons chives and ¼ cup warm water. Spread potatoes over filling and serve.

PER SERVING 503 CAL; 10 g FAT (7 g SAT); 35 g PRO; 38 g CARB; 6 g FIBER; 886 mg SODIUM; 76 mg CHOL

BEER-BRAISED
CORNED BEEF
AND CABBAGE

Beer-Braised Corned Beef and Cabbage

MAKES 6 servings **PREP** 15 minutes
SLOW COOK on HIGH for 4½ hours or on LOW
for 7 hours plus 1½ hours on HIGH

1	**teaspoon peppercorns**
1	**cinnamon stick**
12	**whole cloves**
1	**bottle (12 ounces) lager or pilsner beer**
2½	**pounds flat corned beef brisket, trimmed of excess fat**
2½	**pounds baby potatoes, large potatoes halved**
1	**head green cabbage, cut into wedges**
3	**tablespoons unsalted butter**
2	**tablespoons chopped parsley**

• Place peppercorns, cinnamon stick, cloves and beer in a 6-quart slow cooker. Add 1 cup water. Top with corned beef brisket. Add potatoes to slow cooker (around sides of brisket where possible). Cover and cook on HIGH for 4½ hours or LOW for 7 hours.

• Uncover and add cabbage to slow cooker. If cooking on LOW, increase temperature to HIGH. Re-cover and cook for 1½ hours.

• To serve, lift cabbage wedges carefully from slow cooker and place on a platter. With a slotted spoon, remove potatoes from slow cooker to a bowl. Toss with butter and parsley. Remove brisket from cooker and slice against the grain into ¼-inch-thick slices (you may want to halve this crosswise first). Serve brisket with potatoes and cabbage.

PER SERVING 531 **CAL**; 28 g **FAT** (13 g **SAT**); 20 g **PRO**; 4 g **CARB**; 7 g **FIBER**; 782 mg **SODIUM**; 15 mg **CHOL**

Fruit Compote

MAKES 6 servings **PREP** 15 minutes **SLOW COOK** on HIGH for 3 hours
BAKE at 375° for 15 minutes **COOL** 15 minutes

COMPOTE

2	**pounds fresh strawberries, hulled, larger berries halved**
12	**ounces fresh or frozen diced rhubarb (do not thaw; see Note)**
1	**pint fresh raspberries**
¾	**cup packed light brown sugar**
¼	**cup quick-cooking tapioca**
2	**tablespoons fresh lemon juice**
½	**teaspoon ground cardamom** Vanilla ice cream (optional)

TOPPING

1	**cup all-purpose flour**
½	**cup rolled oats**
¾	**cup packed light brown sugar**
¼	**teaspoon ground cinnamon** Pinch of salt
6	**tablespoons unsalted butter, cut up**

• **Compote.** Coat the bowl of a 4-quart slow cooker with nonstick cooking spray. Add strawberries, rhubarb, raspberries, brown sugar, tapioca, lemon juice and cardamom. Stir to combine.

• Cover and cook on HIGH for 3 hours.

• **Topping.** Meanwhile, heat oven to 375°. In a medium bowl, combine flour, oats, brown sugar, cinnamon and salt. Cut in butter with a pastry blender or your hands until crumbs the size of small peas form. Crumble onto a large baking sheet. Bake at 375° for 15 minutes or until browned and set. Break apart into small pieces.

• Uncover slow cooker and let cool 15 minutes. Spoon into bowls and top each with a scoop of ice cream, if desired, and some of the topping. Serve slightly warm.

Note: If you cannot find fresh or frozen rhubarb, swap in 2 Granny Smith apples, peeled, cored and diced. Reduce brown sugar to ½ cup.

PER SERVING 386 **CAL**; 10 g **FAT** (5 g **SAT**); 4 g **PRO**; 74 g **CARB**; 5 g **FIBER**; 21 mg **SODIUM**; 44 mg **CHOL**

HAPPY EASTER

A delicious do-ahead menu.

HERB-CRUSTED RACK
OF LAMB

Herb-Crusted Rack of Lamb

MAKES 2 lamb racks (16 ribs)
PREP 15 minutes   **COOK** 4 minutes
ROAST at 450° for 25 minutes
LET REST 10 minutes

¼	**cup fresh mint, finely chopped**
¼	**cup fresh parsley, finely chopped**
1	**tablespoon fresh thyme, finely chopped**
1	**tablespoon lemon zest**
2	**cloves garlic, finely chopped**
⅓	**cup plain bread crumbs**
3	**tablespoons olive oil**
½	**teaspoon salt**
¼	**teaspoon black pepper**
2	**lamb racks (1¼ pounds each), frenched***

• Heat oven to 450°. In a bowl, combine mint, parsley, thyme, lemon zest, garlic, bread crumbs, 2 tablespoons of the olive oil, ¼ teaspoon of the salt and ⅛ teaspoon of the pepper. Set aside. Season lamb racks with remaining ¼ teaspoon salt and ⅛ teaspoon pepper.

• Heat remaining 1 tablespoon olive oil in a large pan over medium-high heat. When pan is hot, sear lamb for 2 minutes per side (4 minutes total), using tongs to turn. Place lamb on a rimmed baking sheet fitted with a wire rack. Cool slightly (a few minutes), then firmly pat herb mixture on top of each lamb rack.

• Roast lamb at 450° for 20 to 25 minutes, until internal temperature reaches 135°. Let rest for 10 minutes; temperature will increase about 10 degrees to medium-rare. Slice ribs and serve.

*Note: The term "frenched" means to have the fat and cartilage scraped off of the ends of the bones to create an attractive presentation.

PER RIB 237 **CAL**; 20 g **FAT** (9 g **SAT**); 12 g **PRO**; 2 g **CARB**; 0 g **FIBER**; 138 mg **SODIUM**; 48 mg **CHOL**

Chilled Pea Soup

MAKES 8 servings   **PREP** 5 minutes   **COOK** 9 minutes

1	**tablespoon olive oil**
1	**cup diced sweet onion**
2	**cloves garlic, chopped**
4	**cups reduced-sodium chicken broth**
2	**bags (14.4 ounces each) frozen peas**
1	**cup fresh mint, plus more for garnish**
¼	**cup fresh parsley**
2	**tablespoons fresh lemon juice**
1	**teaspoon salt**
¼	**teaspoon freshly cracked black pepper**
	Greek yogurt or crème fraîche for garnish (optional)

• Heat oil in a large pot over medium heat. Stir in onion and cook for 3 to 5 minutes, until softened. Add garlic and cook for 1 minute. Pour in chicken broth and peas; bring to a boil. Reduce heat to a simmer and cook for 3 minutes. Stir in mint and parsley.

• Transfer mixture to a bowl. Stir in lemon juice, salt and pepper. Pour into a blender; blend until smooth. Cool, then refrigerate until chilled.

• Serve chilled. Garnish with mint and, if desired, yogurt or crème fraîche.

PER SERVING 130 **CAL**; 2 g **FAT** (0 g **SAT**); 8 g **PRO**; 21 g **CARB**; 6 g **FIBER**; 416 mg **SODIUM**; 0 mg **CHOL**

WATERCRESS, ARUGULA AND
ASPARAGUS SALAD

Watercress, Arugula and Asparagus Salad

MAKES 8 servings **PREP** 15 minutes
COOK 1 minute

2	**tablespoons olive oil**
2	**tablespoons white wine vinegar**
2	**teaspoons grainy mustard (such as Maille Old Style whole-grain Dijon)**
¼	**cup finely diced shallots**
½	**teaspoon salt**
⅛	**teaspoon black pepper**
1	**pound asparagus, trimmed and sliced into 1-inch pieces**
10	**cups (4 ounces) watercress, roughly chopped**
10	**cups (4 ounces) arugula**
8	**radishes, thinly sliced**

• In a small bowl, whisk olive oil, vinegar and mustard. Stir in shallots, ¼ teaspoon of the salt and the pepper.

• Bring a pot of lightly salted water to a boil. Add asparagus; cook for 1 minute. Drain and run under cold water to cool.

• In a large bowl, toss asparagus with watercress, arugula and radishes. Right before serving, stir in remaining ¼ teaspoon salt and the dressing.

PER SERVING 47 **CAL**; 4 g **FAT** (1 g **SAT**); 2 g **PRO**; 3 g **CARB**; 1 g **FIBER**; 174 mg **SODIUM**; 0 mg **CHOL**

Cauliflower-Potato Mash

MAKES 8 servings **PREP** 15 minutes **COOK** 10 minutes

1	head cauliflower, cored and cut into florets
1½	pounds baking potatoes, peeled and cut into 1-inch cubes
1	clove garlic, chopped
2	cups milk
3	tablespoons unsalted butter
1¼	teaspoons salt
¼	teaspoon black pepper
	Fresh parsley (optional)

• Bring cauliflower, potatoes, garlic and milk to a boil in a lidded pot. Reduce heat, cover and simmer for 10 minutes, until vegetables are fork-tender. Drain, reserving milk. Return vegetables to pot. Stir in butter and half the milk; mash until smooth. (If too thick, pour in more milk.) Stir in salt and pepper. Garnish with parsley, if desired.

PER SERVING 150 **CAL**; 5 g **FAT** (3 g **SAT**); 5 g **PRO**; 22 g **CARB**; 3 g **FIBER**; 411 mg **SODIUM**; 16 mg **CHOL**

CAULIFLOWER-POTATO MASH

LEMON-THYME CAKE

Lemon-Thyme Cake

MAKES 18 servings **PREP** 15 minutes **BAKE** at 350° for 1 hour

3	cups all-purpose flour
1	teaspoon baking powder
1	teaspoon baking soda
½	teaspoon salt
2	sticks (1 cup) unsalted butter, softened
2	cups granulated sugar
5	eggs
¼	cup plus 2 tablespoons lemon juice
2	tablespoons lemon zest
3	tablespoons fresh thyme, roughly chopped, plus sprigs for garnish (optional)
1	teaspoon vanilla extract
1	cup buttermilk
2	cups confectioners' sugar
¼	cup heavy cream

• Heat oven to 350°. Butter and flour a 12-cup Bundt pan, making sure to cover every crease so the cake will release after it is baked.

• In a bowl, whisk together flour, baking powder, baking soda and salt. In a separate larger bowl, beat butter and granulated sugar on high speed for 2 to 3 minutes, until fluffy. Beat in eggs 1 at a time. Whisk in ¼ cup of the lemon juice, the zest, thyme and vanilla. On low speed, beat in half the flour mixture, then the buttermilk, followed by remaining flour mixture. Pour batter into prepared Bundt pan, tapping it on the counter to release air bubbles.

• Bake at 350° for 50 minutes to 1 hour, until a toothpick inserted in center of cake comes out clean.

• Cool in Bundt pan for exactly 10 minutes. Loosen edges with a paring knife, then turn out onto a cake stand or plate, gently shaking to remove. Allow cake to cool completely.

• In a bowl, beat confectioners' sugar, cream and remaining 2 tablespoons lemon juice on low until combined. Drizzle over cake with a spoon. Garnish with thyme sprigs, if desired.

PER SERVING 337 **CAL**; 13 g **FAT** (7 g **SAT**); 5 g **PRO**; 53 g **CARB**; 1 g **FIBER**; 193 mg **SODIUM**; 89 mg **CHOL**

SPRING SWEETS

Celebrate the Easter holiday with these charming treats.

EGG COOKIE ORNAMENTS

BUNNY SURPRISE CONES

COCONUT CHICKS

BROWNIE BIRD NESTS

Bunny Surprise Cones

MAKES 24 servings **PREP** 20 minutes
BAKE at 350° for 18 minutes
ASSEMBLY 30 minutes

1	box (15.25 ounces) yellow cake mix
3	large eggs
⅓	to ½ cup vegetable oil
1	box (3 ounces) wafer ice cream cones
2	cans (16 ounces each) white frosting
1½	cups assorted jelly beans or M&M's
1	package Wilton small candy eyeballs
24	small round pink candy beads (check Michaels or stores where baking supplies are sold)
24	marshmallows
	Pink sparkling sugar

• Heat oven to 350°. Prepare cake mix with eggs, oil and 1 cup water per package directions. Transfer to a large resealable plastic bag.

• Coat 2 mini muffin pans with nonstick cooking spray. Fill each cup almost to top. Bake at 350° for 16 to 18 minutes. Remove cakes from pan, re-coat, re-fill and bake a second batch. Cool cakes.

• Trim cakes level. Transfer frosting to a large pastry bag. Snip tip to create a ¼-inch opening. Pour 1 tablespoon jelly beans or M&M's into bottom of each cone (see Note). Place 1 cake into an ice cream cone, pressing lightly to fit. Squeeze a little frosting onto cake in cone and place another cake, trimmed side down, into cone. Repeat with all jelly beans or M&M's, cakes and cones.

• Pipe or spread frosting onto cakes to cover. Add candy eyes and pink beads for noses.

• Cut marshmallows in half diagonally and dip cut edges into sparkling sugar. Press into bunnies (to resemble ears).

Note: The candies in the bottom of each cone are not just for fun; they help keep the bunnies from tipping over.

Brownie Bird Nests

MAKES 16 servings **PREP** 5 minutes
BAKE at 325° for 25 minutes

⅓	cup unsalted butter, melted
1	large egg
¼	cup milk
1	box (20 ounces) brownie mix
48	Jordan almonds or malted milk eggs

• Heat oven to 325°. In a large bowl, whisk butter, egg and milk. Stir in brownie mix just until combined.

• Coat 16 muffin tin cups with nonstick cooking spray and divide brownie batter evenly among prepared cups. Bake at 325° for 25 minutes. Cool in pans on a wire rack for 15 minutes, then run a thin knife or spatula around brownie edges and remove from pans.

• Gently press centers of brownies to make an indent. Place 3 almonds in each brownie nest.

Coconut Chicks

MAKES 24 servings **MICROWAVE** 25 seconds
ASSEMBLY 45 minutes

3½	cups sweetened flake coconut
	Lemon yellow gel food color
24	store-bought doughnut holes
1	can (16 ounces) white or yellow frosting
32	mini chocolate chips
	Dot candies, orange slice candies or Mike & Ike candies

• Place coconut in a large resealable plastic bag. Add enough food color to tint to desired shade of yellow. Using bag, knead color into coconut until evenly distributed. Pour coconut into a shallow dish.

• Spoon ¼ cup of the frosting into a piping bag. Place remaining frosting (in can) in microwave and heat for 15 seconds. Stir until thin enough to coat doughnut holes, about the consistency of honey. Microwave 5 to 10 seconds more, if needed.

• Spear 1 doughnut hole on a fork. Dip in frosting to coat. Tap fork gently against frosting can until excess has dripped off.

• Push doughnut hole off fork into coconut. Gently roll to coat. Transfer to wax-paper-lined sheet. Repeat with all doughnut holes.

• Snip piping bag. Pipe frosting to affix chocolate chips for eyes. Cut candies into triangles to resemble beaks.

Egg Cookie Ornaments

MAKES 28 servings **PREP** 10 minutes
BAKE at 350° for 13 minutes per batch
DECORATE 1 hour

1	package (16.5 ounces) refrigerated sugar cookie dough
½	cup all-purpose flour
1	box (1 pound) confectioners' sugar
3	tablespoons powdered egg whites or meringue powder
	Bright orange and mint green gel food colors
	Assorted sparkling sugars (optional)

• Heat oven to 350°. Place cookie dough in a large bowl. Add flour and knead in until incorporated.

• Roll out dough to ⅛-inch thickness. Cut out cookies with a 2¾-inch egg-shaped cookie cutter, re-rolling and re-cutting scraps. Transfer cutouts to 2 large cookie sheets. With a drinking straw or chopstick, make a hole in top of each cookie (so you can thread a ribbon through it). Bake at 350° for 13 minutes, until set and just beginning to brown.

• Prepare icing: Combine confectioners' sugar, powdered egg whites and 6 tablespoons water in a large bowl. Beat with a mixer on low for 30 seconds, then on high for 4 minutes. Divide about 1¼ cups icing between 2 smaller bowls. Tint 1 bowl orange and 1 green.

• Spread cookies with white icing (thinning with water if needed). Decorate cookies with colored icings. Add sparkling sugars, if desired.

SET THE SEDER TABLE

Cookbook author Jamie Geller offers 5 kosher recipes perfect for Passover.

BALSAMIC LONDON BROIL

Balsamic London Broil

KOSHER STATUS meat
MAKES 8 to 10 servings **PREP** 10 minutes
MARINATE 3 to 6 hours **ROAST** at 400° for 50 minutes **LET REST** 5 minutes

- 2½ **pounds London broil**
- 5 **cloves garlic, minced**
- ¾ **cup balsamic vinegar**
- ¼ **cup plus 1 tablespoon olive oil**
- 2 **medium red onions**
- 2 **medium yellow onions**
- 8 **medium shallots**
  Kosher salt
  Freshly ground black pepper

• Combine meat with garlic, vinegar and ¼ cup of the olive oil in a large resealable plastic bag. Marinate in refrigerator for 3 to 6 hours.

• Heat oven to 400°. Remove meat from refrigerator so it can come to room temperature.

• Cut onions into quarters and halve shallots. On a large rimmed baking sheet, toss together onions, shallots and remaining 1 tablespoon olive oil. Season with salt and pepper and roast at 400° until tender, 40 to 50 minutes.

• After veggies have been roasting for 20 minutes, pour off and discard marinade from meat. Pat meat dry and season it all over with salt and pepper. Heat a large ovenproof skillet over medium-high heat and sear meat until nicely browned, about 5 minutes per side. Transfer skillet to oven and cook alongside vegetables until an instant-read thermometer inserted into meat reads 130° for medium-rare, 12 to 18 minutes. Remove meat and veggies from oven. Let meat rest for 5 minutes before slicing.

Crystal Clear Chicken Soup with Julienned Vegetables and Angel Hair

KOSHER STATUS meat
MAKES 6 quarts; 24 servings **PREP** 15 minutes
COOK 4 hours **REFRIGERATE** overnight

STOCK BASE

- 1 **chicken (about 3½ pounds), cut into 8 pieces**
- 2 **bone-in chicken breasts (about 1½ pounds)**
- 4 **or 5 beef marrow bones (about 2 pounds)**
- 5 **medium carrots, quartered**
- 2 **large parsnips, quartered**
- 2 **small turnips, quartered**
- 2 **medium parsley roots, quartered, or sub in a combo of more parsnips and turnips**
- 1 **large green bell pepper, halved, ribs and seeds removed**
- 1 **large onion**
- 3 **tablespoons kosher salt**
- 20 **fresh parsley sprigs**
- ½ **head cauliflower, broken into florets**
- 7 **cloves garlic**
- 20 **black or white peppercorns**
- 4 **whole allspice**

SOUP

- 1 **large zucchini, cut into ⅛-inch julienne**
- 1 **large carrot, peeled, cut into ⅛-inch julienne**
- 1 **large daikon radish, peeled, cut into ⅛-inch julienne**
- 1 **pound Passover noodles, cooked and drained, at room temperature**

• Place chicken, marrow bones, carrots, parsnips, turnips, parsley roots, green pepper, onion and 1 tablespoon of the salt in a 12-quart stockpot. Cover with 6 quarts cold water and bring to a boil over high heat. Skim and discard foam that forms at the top when it comes to a boil.

• Add remaining 2 tablespoons salt, the parsley, cauliflower, garlic, peppercorns and allspice and return to a boil. Simmer, covered, over low heat for 1 hour. Remove the 4 chicken breasts and allow them to cool slightly. Remove meat from bones. Shred or chop meat and store it in fridge to serve in soup or for another use. Return bones to pot. Continue simmering, covered, over low heat, for at least 2 hours more.

• Strain entire contents of pot through a colander lined with cheesecloth. Discard all solids or save them for another use. Chill broth overnight.

• To serve soup, remove surface fat and pour broth into a large pot. Bring to a simmer over low heat and cook until warm, 10 to 15 minutes. Add zucchini, carrot, daikon and, if desired, reserved chicken. Simmer 5 minutes to cook vegetables and heat chicken. Be careful to keep soup over low heat; bringing soup to a boil can make it cloudy. Season to taste with salt.

• Place ¼ cup Passover noodles in each soup bowl and ladle hot soup over pasta. Serve immediately.

• This soup can be frozen after surface fat is removed. You can freeze breast meat separately if you want to use it for other dishes.

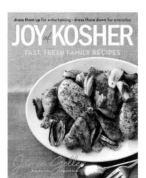

From *Joy of Kosher: Fast, Fresh Family Recipes* by Jamie Geller. Copyright © 2013 by Jamie Geller. Reprinted by permission of William Morrow Cookbooks, an imprint of HarperCollins Publishers.

WILTED SPINACH WITH
CRISPY GARLIC CHIPS

DADDY'S DEEP-DISH
POTATO KUGEL

Wilted Spinach with Crispy Garlic Chips

KOSHER STATUS pareve **MAKES** 6 servings **PREP** 5 minutes **COOK** 12 minutes

8	cloves garlic, thinly sliced
½	cup plus 2 tablespoons olive oil
3	bags (5 ounces each) baby spinach
½	teaspoon kosher salt
	Freshly ground black pepper

• Line a plate with paper towels.

• Place garlic and ½ cup of the olive oil in a small saucepan and bring to a simmer over medium-high heat. Reduce heat to medium-low and cook until garlic is lightly browned and crispy, 5 to 8 minutes, taking care not to burn it. Transfer garlic with a fork or slotted spoon to prepared plate; set aside to drain.

• Heat remaining 2 tablespoons olive oil in a large sauté pan over medium-high heat. Add spinach and cook, stirring continually, until wilted and warm, 2 to 4 minutes. Season with salt and pepper to taste.

• Transfer spinach to a serving plate and garnish with crispy garlic chips.

Daddy's Deep-Dish Potato Kugel

KOSHER STATUS pareve
MAKES 6 to 8 servings **PREP** 15 minutes
BAKE at 400° for 1 hour 40 minutes

1	tablespoon plus 1 teaspoon canola oil
3¾	pounds russet potatoes (about 7 large)
7	large eggs
1½	teaspoons kosher salt
½	teaspoon freshly ground black pepper

• Heat oven to 400°.

• Brush an 8-inch square glass baking dish with 1 teaspoon of the canola oil. Wipe oil all over the bottom of dish and up the sides using a paper towel. Set aside.

• Peel potatoes and rinse in cold water. Grate potatoes into a large bowl on smallest side of a box grater. Pour off all water. Add eggs, remaining 1 tablespoon oil, the salt and pepper. Mix really well by hand, breaking up yolks, until everything is thoroughly combined and batter is smooth. Pour into prepared dish and bake at 400° until top is crispy and deep golden brown and a toothpick comes out clean, 1 hour 30 minutes to 1 hour 40 minutes.

• Check kugel at the 45-minute, 1-hour and 1-hour-15-minute marks. If your kugel has risen in the center, use a fork to poke holes in it, then use the back of the fork to pat down and flatten it. You want a perfectly flat top. If your kugel doesn't rise, don't worry; this is a good thing.

• Remove kugel from oven. Using a knife, separate kugel from walls of baking dish, being careful not to break kugel and paying special attention to corners. Place a square serving platter over kugel and invert kugel onto platter. It's best to cut kugel into squares at the table, to order, so it does not dry out.

OLIVE OIL DARK CHOCOLATE MOUSSE

Olive Oil Dark Chocolate Mousse

KOSHER STATUS pareve **MAKES** 6 servings **PREP** 20 minutes
MICROWAVE 1½ minutes **REFRIGERATE** overnight

10	ounces high-quality 72% cacao bittersweet chocolate, finely chopped, or chocolate chips
8	large eggs, separated, at room temperature
¾	cup sugar
½	cup extra-virgin olive oil
1	teaspoon instant coffee granules dissolved in 2 tablespoons boiling water
¼	teaspoon kosher salt
	Grated zest of 1 small orange (optional)

• Place chocolate in a microwave-safe bowl and melt in microwave, stirring after each 10-second increment, until smooth, about 1½ minutes. Let cool slightly.

• Place egg yolks and ½ cup of the sugar in a medium bowl and whisk until pale yellow. Whisk in olive oil, coffee, salt and, if desired, orange zest until combined. Add melted chocolate and whisk until smooth.

• Beat egg whites in the bowl of a stand mixer or with a hand mixer until soft peaks form. Gradually sprinkle in remaining ¼ cup sugar and beat just until stiff peaks form. Add a generous spoonful of the egg white mixture to chocolate mixture. Stir firmly until completely incorporated. Pour chocolate mixture into bowl of egg whites. Gently fold with a large spoon or rubber spatula until completely combined.

• Divide mousse into 6 dishes and cover with plastic wrap. Refrigerate overnight.

MINI BLUEBERRY PIES,
PAGE 127

MAY

123

128

132

HEALTHY FAMILY DINNERS

7 take-out classics that you can make easily (and much healthier) at home.

PANKO FRIED FISH
AND SMOKY CHIPS

**DOUBLE-DECKER
TERIYAKI BURGERS**

Panko Fried Fish and Smoky Chips

MAKES 4 servings **PREP** 10 minutes
BAKE at 450° for 20 minutes **COOK** 6 minutes

1	pound (from a 2-pound bag) frozen straight-cut fries
1	teaspoon smoked paprika
4	tilapia fillets (about 4 ounces each)
½	teaspoon salt
¼	teaspoon black pepper
2	egg whites, lightly beaten
1	cup whole wheat panko
3	tablespoons canola oil
	Lemon wedges for squeezing
	Ketchup and tartar sauce (optional)

• Heat oven to 450°. Place fries on an ungreased baking sheet in single layer. Bake at 450° for 10 minutes. Sprinkle with smoked paprika and bake for an additional 8 to 10 minutes, until crispy, turning once.

• Meanwhile, season tilapia with ¼ teaspoon of the salt and the pepper. Dip in egg whites and coat with panko.

• Heat oil in a large nonstick skillet over medium-high heat. Add tilapia and cook for 2 to 3 minutes per side, until golden.

• Sprinkle tilapia with remaining ¼ teaspoon salt. Serve with fries and lemon wedges. Accompany with ketchup and tartar sauce, if desired.

PER SERVING 399 **CAL**; 15 g **FAT** (1 g **SAT**); 30 g **PRO**; 39 g **CARB**; 3 g **FIBER**; 763 mg **SODIUM**; 57 mg **CHOL**

Double-Decker Teriyaki Burgers

MAKES 4 servings **PREP** 20 minutes **REFRIGERATE** 1 hour **GRILL** 9 minutes

1	cup shredded broccoli slaw
2	tablespoons reduced-fat mayonnaise
1	tablespoon rice vinegar
¼	teaspoon sugar
1	pound 95% lean ground beef
4	ounces shiitake mushrooms, stems removed, finely chopped
2	scallions, trimmed and chopped
2	tablespoons reduced-sodium teriyaki sauce
1	tablespoon finely chopped fresh ginger
4	canned pineapple slices in juice, drained and patted dry
4	slices (1 ounce each) reduced-fat Muenster or mozzarella cheese
4	sesame-seeded hamburger buns

• In a small bowl, combine broccoli slaw, mayonnaise, vinegar and sugar. Refrigerate until serving.

• In a medium bowl, combine ground beef, mushrooms, scallions, teriyaki sauce and ginger. Form into 8 patties, about 3 inches in diameter; refrigerate for 1 hour.

• Generously coat stovetop grill pan with nonstick cooking spray. Heat pan over medium-high heat. Grill pineapple slices for 2 minutes per side. Remove to a plate and keep warm. Coat pan again with nonstick cooking spray and add burgers; grill for 3 minutes. Turn and place a slice of cheese on 4 of the burgers; grill 2 more minutes. Top cheese-covered burgers with remaining burgers.

• To serve, place ¼ cup broccoli slaw mixture on each bun bottom and top with double burger, a pineapple slice and top half of bun.

PER SERVING 412 **CAL**; 12 g **FAT** (5 g **SAT**); 35 g **PRO**; 41 g **CARB**; 3 g **FIBER**; 748 mg **SODIUM**; 73 mg **CHOL**

TURKEY NACHOS SUPREME

Turkey Nachos Supreme

MAKES 4 servings **PREP** 15 minutes
BAKE at 425° for 10 minutes and at 350° for
15 minutes **COOK** 6 minutes

2	packages (6.9 ounces each) corn tortillas, cut into 6 wedges each
1	tablespoon vegetable oil
8	ounces 93% lean ground turkey, crumbled
½	green bell pepper, seeds removed and chopped
1	can (8 ounces) reduced-sodium tomato sauce
1	package (1 ounce) reduced-sodium taco seasoning mix
1	can (15 ounces) no-salt-added black beans, drained and rinsed
½	cup jarred salsa
4	scallions, trimmed and thinly sliced
½	cup shredded reduced-fat Monterey Jack cheese
2	plum tomatoes, seeds removed and sliced
⅓	cup fresh cilantro leaves
	Lime wedges for squeezing

• Heat oven to 425°. Spread tortilla wedges on 2 baking sheets. Bake at 425° for 5 minutes. Flip over. Spray with nonstick cooking spray and bake for 4 to 5 minutes more, until crispy.

• Heat oil in a large skillet over medium-high heat. Add ground turkey and green pepper, stirring occasionally. Cook for 2 minutes, until turkey is no longer pink. Stir in tomato sauce and ⅓ cup water. Reserve 1 teaspoon of the taco seasoning mix and add remainder to skillet. Cook for 4 minutes, stirring occasionally.

• Reduce oven temperature to 350°. Line bottom and sides of a 13 x 9 x 2-inch baking dish with tortilla chips. Spoon turkey mixture, beans and salsa evenly over chips. Top with scallions and Monterey Jack. Bake at 350° for 15 minutes, until heated through and cheese is melted.

• To serve, scatter tomatoes and cilantro over nachos. Serve with lime wedges for squeezing.

PER SERVING 500 **CAL**; 18 g **FAT** (3 g **SAT**); 25 g **PRO**; 66 g **CARB**; 11 g **FIBER**; 768 mg **SODIUM**; 43 mg **CHOL**

CHILI-CHEESE CONEYS

Chili-Cheese Coneys

MAKES 8 servings **PREP** 15 minutes **COOK** 12 minutes **BROIL** 2 minutes

1	tablespoon vegetable oil
1	small zucchini, diced
½	medium onion, chopped
½	green bell pepper
3	cloves garlic, chopped
1	can (15 ounces) red beans, drained and rinsed
1	can (8 ounces) no-salt-added tomato sauce
1	tablespoon chili powder
1	teaspoon ground cumin
8	reduced-fat-and-sodium frankfurters (such as Boar's Head light skinless beef frankfurters)
8	top-sliced hot dog rolls
1	cup shredded reduced-fat cheddar cheese
	Chopped onion and diced cucumber (optional)

• Heat oil in a medium saucepan over medium-high heat. Add zucchini, onion, green pepper and garlic; cook for 3 minutes, stirring occasionally. Stir in beans, tomato sauce, chili powder and cumin. Simmer, covered, for 5 minutes, stirring occasionally. Set aside.

• Heat broiler to high; set rack 6 inches from heat source. Heat a large nonstick skillet over medium-high heat. Add frankfurters and cook, turning frequently, for 3 to 4 minutes, or until browned and heated through. Place frankfurters in rolls and place on large broiler pan. Spoon ¼ cup of the chili over each and sprinkle with 2 tablespoons cheddar. Reserve remaining 2 cups chili for another meal.

• Broil on high for 1 to 2 minutes or until cheddar is melted. Top with chopped onion and diced cucumber, if desired.

PER SERVING 313 **CAL**; 13 g **FAT** (5 g **SAT**); 17 g **PRO**; 31 g **CARB**; 3 g **FIBER**; 698 mg **SODIUM**; 35 mg **CHOL**

CHICKEN KORMA

Chicken Korma

MAKES 4 servings PREP 15 minutes LET STAND 15 minutes COOK 13 minutes

¼	cup unsalted cashews
2	tablespoons canola oil
1	large onion, sliced
1	tablespoon fresh ginger, chopped
2	cloves garlic, chopped
2	teaspoons curry powder
1	teaspoon turmeric
1¼	pounds boneless, skinless chicken breasts, cut into 1-inch pieces
½	cup reduced-sodium chicken broth
¼	cup tomato sauce
¾	teaspoon salt
½	cup low-fat plain Greek yogurt
2	teaspoons cornstarch
3	cups cooked basmati rice
	Naan bread (optional)
	Crispy Green Beans (see recipe, right) (optional)

• Place cashews in a small bowl and add ¼ cup boiling water. Let stand for 15 minutes.

• Heat oil in a large nonstick skillet over medium-high heat. Add onion, ginger and garlic; cook for 3 minutes, stirring occasionally. Stir in curry and turmeric and cook for 30 seconds. Add chicken and cook for 3 minutes, stirring occasionally.

• Stir in broth, tomato sauce and salt; simmer for 3 minutes, stirring occasionally.

• Meanwhile, in a food processor, blend cashews with soaking water and yogurt until smooth. Add to skillet and simmer for 2 minutes. Blend cornstarch with 1 tablespoon water and stir into skillet. Cook for 1 minute, until thickened.

• Serve chicken with cooked rice and, if desired, naan and Crispy Green Beans.

Crispy Green Beans Microwave 1 package (12 ounces) steam-in-bag fresh green beans for 3 minutes. Heat 1 tablespoon canola oil in a large nonstick skillet over medium-high heat. Add green beans, 1 tablespoon chopped garlic and ⅛ teaspoon salt. Cook, stirring frequently, for 5 minutes or until dark and crisp.

PER SERVING 496 CAL; 16 g FAT (3 g SAT); 36 g PRO; 53 g CARB; 2 g FIBER; 669 mg SODIUM; 80 mg CHOL

CHEESE-STUFFED-CRUST PIZZA

CRISPY CHICKEN LETTUCE WRAPS

Cheese-Stuffed-Crust Pizza

MAKES 16 squares **PREP** 15 minutes
COOK 5 minutes **BAKE** at 450° for 18 minutes

1	tablespoon vegetable oil
1½	cups sliced mushrooms
1	yellow sweet pepper, seeded and sliced
½	red onion, sliced
1	refrigerated thin-crust pizza crust (11 ounces)
6	ounces cheddar-mozzarella cheese sticks
½	cup marinara sauce
½	teaspoon dried oregano
1	cup reduced-fat shredded mozzarella cheese
1	ounce sliced turkey pepperoni
1	cup grape tomatoes, halved

• Heat oven to 450°.

• Heat oil in a large nonstick skillet over medium-high heat. Add mushrooms, yellow pepper and onion; cook for 5 minutes, stirring occasionally. Place on a plate and blot with a paper towel. Set aside.

• Meanwhile, unroll dough onto a baking sheet. With a floured rolling pin, roll into a 15 x 15-inch square. Place cheese sticks along the edges, cutting sticks as necessary. Roll 1 inch of dough over cheese and gently seal with a fork. Bake at 450° for 8 minutes. Remove from oven. Spread sauce evenly over pizza and sprinkle with oregano. Scatter mozzarella over pizza and top with vegetables, pepperoni and tomatoes. Bake at 450° for 8 to 10 minutes, until pizza is crisp and golden brown.

• Cool for 5 minutes. Cut into 16 squares.

PER SQUARE 143 **CAL**; 5 g **FAT** (3 g **SAT**); 9 g **PRO**; 16 g **CARB**; 1 g **FIBER**; 343 mg **SODIUM**; 15 mg **CHOL**

Crispy Chicken Lettuce Wraps

MAKES 4 servings **PREP** 20 minutes **COOK** 12 minutes

2	tablespoons canola oil
1	pound boneless, skinless chicken thighs, cut into ½-inch pieces
8	ounces cremini mushrooms, chopped
1	red sweet pepper, seeded and chopped
3	scallions, chopped
2	cloves garlic, chopped
½	teaspoon Chinese five-spice powder
¼	teaspoon red pepper flakes
1	can (8 ounces) chopped water chestnuts, drained
¼	cup chicken broth
2	tablespoons reduced-sodium soy sauce
1	tablespoon hoisin sauce
1	head Boston lettuce, separated into 16 leaves
½	cup crispy rice noodles
	Duck sauce (optional)

• Heat oil in a large skillet over medium-high heat. Add chicken and stir-fry for 6 minutes; remove to a plate.

• Add mushrooms, red sweet pepper, scallions, garlic, five-spice powder and red pepper flakes. Stir-fry for 3 minutes or until mushrooms and peppers are tender. Stir in water chestnuts, broth, soy sauce and hoisin sauce. Bring to a simmer; add chicken and cook for 3 minutes, stirring occasionally.

• To serve, spoon chicken mixture into lettuce leaves and sprinkle with some rice noodles. If desired, serve with duck sauce for dipping.

PER SERVING 374 **CAL**; 16 g **FAT** (3 g **SAT**); 30 g **PRO**; 30 g **CARB**; 5 g **FIBER**; 769 mg **SODIUM**; 110 mg **CHOL**

POP CULTURE

Why should lollipops have all the fun? Here are five scrumptious sweets, all on a stick.

SHORTCUT STRAWBERRY
SHORTCAKE PUSH POPS,
PAGE 128

Brownie Pops

MAKES 20 pops **PREP** 30 minutes
MICROWAVE 2½ minutes **BAKE** at 350° for
18 minutes per batch **LET COOL** 10 minutes

- **3** ounces unsweetened chocolate, chopped
- **½** cup (1 stick) unsalted butter
- **1** cup all-purpose flour
- **½** teaspoon baking powder
- **⅛** teaspoon salt
- **1** cup sugar
- **2** large eggs
- **1** teaspoon vanilla extract
- **20** lollipop sticks
- **1** cup white chocolate chips
- **1** tablespoon vegetable oil
- **1** cup toasted sweetened flake coconut
- **½** cup chopped toasted sliced almonds

• Heat oven to 350°. Coat 1 or 2 Wilton brownie pops silicone mold pan(s) with nonstick cooking spray. Place pan(s) on top of a baking sheet.

• Combine unsweetened chocolate and butter in a 1-cup glass measuring cup. Microwave, stirring often, until smooth, 60 to 90 seconds.

• Combine flour, baking powder and salt in a small bowl.

• Combine sugar, eggs, vanilla and chocolate mixture in a medium bowl. Stir in flour mixture.

• Scoop 1 tablespoon batter into each pop mold. Transfer with baking sheet to oven. Bake at 350° for 10 minutes. Remove pan from oven, insert a lollipop stick into each brownie, return to oven and continue baking until firm, about 8 minutes more. Cool for 10 minutes.

• Remove pops, re-coat pan(s) and repeat to make more brownie pops.

• Combine white chocolate chips with oil in a 2-cup glass measuring cup. Microwave, stirring until smooth, about 60 seconds. Dunk top of each brownie in melted chocolate, shake off excess and sprinkle with toasted coconut or chopped almonds. Place on a wax-paper-lined baking sheet.

PER POP 181 **CAL**; 11 g **FAT** (6 g **SAT**); 2 g **PRO**; 21 g **CARB**; 1 g **FIBER**; 44 mg **SODIUM**; 34 mg **CHOL**

Mini Blueberry Pies

MAKES 16 servings **PREP** 15 minutes
COOK 7 minutes **REFRIGERATE** 20 minutes
BAKE at 425° for 11 minutes

1	cup blueberries
3	tablespoons sugar
2	teaspoons cornstarch
1	box (14.1 ounces) refrigerated piecrust
16	wooden pop sticks
1	large egg, beaten with 1 tablespoon water
	Sugar

• In a small saucepan, combine ¾ cup of the blueberries, the 3 tablespoons sugar and the cornstarch. Stir in ¼ cup water. Cook over medium heat for 5 to 7 minutes or until berries have popped and mixture has thickened. Remove from heat and stir in remaining ¼ cup blueberries. Cover and refrigerate for 20 minutes.

• Heat oven to 425°. Unroll one of the piecrusts on a cutting board. Cut out circles with a 2½-inch cookie cutter. Gather together scraps, re-roll and cut out circles (you should have 16 total). Repeat with second piecrust.

• Divide 16 of the rounds between 2 cookie sheets. Gently press a pop stick into each round. Spoon a heaping teaspoon of the blueberry filling in center of each round. Brush edges with egg mixture and place a second round on top. Seal edges with a fork, brush tops with egg mixture and sprinkle pies with a little sugar. Cut small vent holes into each pie.

• Bake at 425° for 10 to 11 minutes. Remove with a thin spatula to a wire rack. Cool slightly and serve.

PER SERVING 131 **CAL**; 7 g **FAT** (3 g **SAT**); 1 g **PRO**; 16 g **CARB**; 0 g **FIBER**; 97 mg **SODIUM**; 18 mg **CHOL**

RICE KRISPIE TREATS

Rice Krispie Treats

MAKES 24 servings **YIELD** 24 pops **PREP** 30 minutes **MICROWAVE** 2 ½ minutes

1	bag (10 ounces) marshmallows
3	tablespoons unsalted butter
6	cups Rice Krispies cereal
4	ounces semisweet chocolate, chopped
1	teaspoon vegetable oil
24	ice cream sticks
	Jumbo rainbow nonpareils or sprinkles

• Line a 13 x 9 x 2-inch baking pan with foil. Coat foil and a spatula with nonstick cooking spray.

• Combine marshmallows and butter in a large glass bowl and microwave until melted, about 1 minute. Stir with coated spatula until smooth. Add cereal and stir until well combined. Transfer mixture to prepared pan. With greased hands, evenly pat mixture into pan, pressing firmly. Let cool up to 5 minutes.

• Combine chocolate and vegetable oil in a medium glass bowl and microwave, stirring often, until smooth, about 60 to 90 seconds.

• Cut Rice Krispie bar into 24 pieces. Insert an ice cream stick into bottom of each piece. Dip into melted chocolate. Gently tap bottom of stick a few times so that chocolate drips down. Sprinkle with nonpareils. Place on a wax-paper-lined baking sheet.

PER SERVING 113 **CAL**.; 3 g **FAT** (2 g **SAT**); 1 g **PRO**; 21 g **CARB**; 0 g **FIBER**; 72 mg **SODIUM**; 4 mg **CHOL**

Shortcut Strawberry Shortcake Push Pops

MAKES 12 shortcakes **PREP** 10 minutes
REFRIGERATE 1 hour

2¼	**cups diced strawberries**
1	**tablespoon plus 2 teaspoons sugar**
¾	**cup heavy cream**
½	**teaspoon vanilla extract**
¾	**of an angel food cake (found in bakery section)**
12	**push-up pops (such as Wilton or Nordic Ware)**

• Combine strawberries and 1 tablespoon of the sugar in a medium bowl. Whip heavy cream, remaining 2 teaspoons sugar and vanilla to medium peaks. Spoon cream into a resealable plastic bag; snip off a corner for piping.

• Cut cake into scant ½-inch thick slices (you will need 24 slices).

• Place 1 tablespoon strawberries on bottom of each push-up pop mold. Press a slice of cake on top of strawberries, compressing to fit. Add another 1 tablespoon strawberries. Pipe a thin layer of cream on top. Repeat layers (cake, berries, cream) to fill molds. Chill 1 hour before serving.

PER SHORTCAKE 111 **CAL**; 6 g **FAT** (3 g **SAT**); 1 g **PRO**; 14 g **CARB**; 1 g **FIBER**; 130 mg **SODIUM**; 20 mg **CHOL**

Berry Cheesecake Pops

MAKES 24 servings **PREP** 20 minutes
BAKE at 350° for 45 minutes
REFRIGERATE overnight **MICROWAVE** 2 minutes
FREEZE 30 minutes **DECORATE** 45 minutes

2	**packages (8 ounces each) cream cheese, softened**
⅓	**cup sugar**
¼	**cup mixed berry, strawberry or seedless raspberry preserves**
¼	**cup sour cream**
2	**tablespoons cornstarch**
1	**teaspoon vanilla extract**
⅛	**teaspoon salt**
2	**large eggs**
1	**bag (12 ounces) Wilton White Candy Melts**
24	**lollipop sticks**
⅔	**cup cornflake crumbs**
2	**ounces semisweet chocolate, chopped**

• Heat oven to 350°. Coat an 8-inch square baking dish with nonstick cooking spray.

• In a large bowl, beat cream cheese, sugar and preserves until smooth. Stir in sour cream and scrape down sides of bowl. Add cornstarch, vanilla and salt. Blend on low speed. Add eggs, one at a time, blending well after each. Pour into prepared pan, spreading level.

• Bake at 350° for 45 minutes, until set in the center. Cool on a wire rack, then refrigerate overnight.

• Use a small scoop to shape cheesecake into 1-inch balls (start at center of pan; don't use browned edges if possible). Roll cheesecake balls between your hands and place on a wax-paper-lined baking sheet.

• Melt white candy in microwave, per package directions, about 1 minute. Dip each stick into melted candy and insert into cake balls. Freeze for 30 minutes.

• Re-melt candy if needed. Have cornflake crumbs ready in a small bowl. Remove half of the cheesecake pops from freezer. Dip to coat in white candy, shaking off excess. Dip bottom halves of pops in cornflake crumbs to resemble a crust. Place upright on wax paper.

• Melt semisweet chocolate in microwave for 1 minute. Stir until smooth and transfer to a small resealable plastic bag. Remove remaining pops from freezer and dip in white candy to coat. Shake off excess and let dry on wax paper. Snip a small corner from bag of chocolate. While spinning a pop in one hand, drizzle chocolate in a thin spiral. Refrigerate pops until serving.

PER SERVING 171 **CAL**; 11 g **FAT** (8 g **SAT**); 2 g **PRO**; 15 g **CARB**; 0 g **FIBER**; 97 mg **SODIUM**; 40 mg **CHOL**

FORK IN THE ROAD

Homemade takes on food-truck faves.

KOREAN TACOS

Korean Tacos

MAKES 8 tacos   **PREP** 20 minutes
MARINATE 1 hour   **REFRIGERATE** 30 minutes
COOK 9 minutes   **LET REST** 5 minutes

1	**pound boneless rib-eye steaks (about 2 steaks), ½ inch thick**
¼	**cup plus 1 tablespoon rice vinegar**
¼	**cup low-sodium soy sauce**
¼	**cup canola oil**
3	**tablespoons sugar**
1	**tablespoon plus 1 teaspoon Sriracha**
2	**teaspoons sesame oil**
½	**cup thinly sliced yellow onion**
3	**cloves garlic, sliced**
1	**2-inch piece of ginger, peeled and thinly sliced**
¼	**teaspoon salt**
½	**English cucumber, cut into matchsticks (about 1½ cups)**
8	**6-inch flour tortillas, warmed Sliced radishes and sesame seeds (optional)**

• Place steaks in a large resealable plastic bag. In a bowl, whisk together ¼ cup of the vinegar, the soy sauce, canola oil, 2 tablespoons of the sugar, 1 tablespoon of the Sriracha and 1 teaspoon of the sesame oil. Stir in onion, garlic and ginger. Pour into bag, making sure steak is covered. Marinate in refrigerator for 1 hour.

• In a separate bowl, whisk together remaining 1 tablespoon each vinegar and sugar, and remaining 1 teaspoon each Sriracha and sesame oil. Stir in salt and cucumber. Cover bowl with plastic wrap and refrigerate for 30 minutes.

• Heat a large sauté pan over medium-high heat. Remove steaks from marinade (save marinade) and pat dry with paper towels. Cook for 2 to 3 minutes per side, until medium-rare. Set aside to rest 5 minutes. Add marinade to pan. Bring to a boil; cook 3 minutes, until sauce has thickened.

• Thinly slice steaks; toss in pan with sauce. Serve on tortillas with pickled cucumbers and, if desired, radishes, sesame seeds and additional Sriracha.

PER TACO 314 **CAL**; 19 g **FAT** (5 g **SAT**); 14 g **PRO**; 22 g **CARB**; 1 g **FIBER**; 675 mg **SODIUM**; 37 mg **CHOL**

MEATBALL BAHN MI

Meatball Bahn Mi

MAKES 6 sandwiches   **PREP** 20 minutes   **BAKE** at 375° for 20 minutes

1	**pound ground pork**
1	**egg**
3	**scallions, sliced**
2	**cloves garlic, minced**
½	**cup plain bread crumbs**
⅓	**cup fresh cilantro, chopped**
2	**tablespoons packed light brown sugar**
2	**tablespoons fresh lime juice**
1	**tablespoon fish sauce**
1	**tablespoon low-sodium soy sauce**
1	**teaspoon Sriracha, plus more for topping**
1½	**French baguettes, sliced into 6 pieces**
6	**tablespoons light mayonnaise Grated carrot, sliced cucumber and fresh cilantro**

• Heat oven to 375°. In a large bowl, combine pork, egg, scallions, garlic, bread crumbs, cilantro, brown sugar, lime juice, fish sauce, soy sauce and the 1 teaspoon Sriracha. Form into 24 meatballs. Place meatballs on a rimmed baking sheet coated with nonstick cooking spray and bake at 375° for 20 minutes.

• Slice baguette pieces lengthwise and spread 1 tablespoon mayonnaise on bottom half of each. Top with grated carrot, sliced cucumber and cilantro, then place 4 meatballs on each. Finish with Sriracha. Serve warm.

PER SANDWICH 566 **CAL**; 24 g **FAT** (7 g **SAT**); 26 g **PRO**; 62 g **CARB**; 3 g **FIBER**; 1,150 mg **SODIUM**; 95 mg **CHOL**

SHRIMP DUMPLINGS WITH
MISO DIPPING SAUCE

Shrimp Dumplings with Miso Dipping Sauce

MAKES 8 servings (48 dumplings) **PREP** 1 hour **COOK** 12 minutes

2	**tablespoons white miso paste**
2	**teaspoons rice vinegar**
6	**large scallions, sliced**
1	**teaspoon wasabi**
1	**tablespoon low-sodium soy sauce**
1	**pound uncooked peeled and deveined shrimp, finely chopped**
1	**can (8 ounces) water chestnuts, drained and finely chopped**
4	**teaspoons grated fresh ginger**
1	**package (12 ounces) wonton wrappers**
2	**egg whites, lightly beaten**

• In a small bowl, whisk together miso paste, rice vinegar and 1/2 cup water until smooth. Stir in 2 of the sliced scallions. Cover; set aside until serving.

• In a separate bowl, whisk together wasabi and soy sauce until smooth. Stir in remaining scallions, the shrimp, water chestnuts and ginger. Bring a large pot of lightly salted water to a boil. Place 1 wonton wrapper on a dry surface. Add 2 teaspoons filling to center and brush edges with egg whites. Bring together corners and press firmly to seal (see folding instructions on package). Repeat with remaining wrappers. (Cover wrappers and dumplings with damp towels while prepping.)

• Add 12 dumplings to boiling water. Cook for 3 minutes; dumplings will float to surface. Repeat 3 more times, until all dumplings are cooked. Serve hot with miso dipping sauce.

PER SERVING 207 **CAL**; 2 g **FAT** (0 g **SAT**); 18 g **PRO**; 29 g **CARB**; 3 g **FIBER**; 559 mg **SODIUM**; 93 mg **CHOL**

CHICKEN YAKITORI

Chicken Yakitori

MAKES 8 skewers PREP 30 minutes MARINATE 30 minutes COOK 3 minutes GRILL 6 minutes

8	10-inch wooden skewers
¼	cup low-sodium soy sauce
¼	cup mirin
¼	cup rice vinegar
2	teaspoons sugar
1½	pounds boneless, skinless chicken thighs, cut into 1-inch chunks
1	large bunch scallions, cut into 2-inch pieces

• Soak skewers in a bowl of water until ready to use. In a large bowl, combine 2 tablespoons each of the soy sauce, mirin and rice vinegar and 1 teaspoon of the sugar. Stir in chicken, cover and marinate in refrigerator for 30 minutes.

• In a small saucepan over medium-high heat, add remaining 2 tablespoons each soy sauce, mirin and rice vinegar, and remaining 1 teaspoon sugar. Stir to combine. Bring to a boil. Simmer for 3 minutes, until thickened. Divide glaze between 2 small bowls.

• Heat grill or grill pan to medium-high. Thread skewers, alternating 1 or 2 pieces of chicken with 1 piece of scallion. (Makes 8 skewers.) Lightly coat grill or grill pan with oil or cooking spray. Grill skewers for 3 minutes, brushing tops with glaze in a bowl. Flip skewers and brush with glaze from second bowl. Grill for 3 more minutes, until chicken is cooked through.

PER SKEWER 131 CAL; 3 g FAT (1 g SAT); 17 g PRO; 4 g CARB; 0 g FIBER; 378 mg SODIUM; 71 mg CHOL

MIDDLE EASTERN LAMB
AND RICE

Middle Eastern Lamb and Rice

MAKES 4 servings   **PREP** 20 minutes   **MARINATE** 1 hour   **COOK** 20 minutes

LAMB

3	tablespoons olive oil
¼	cup lemon juice
½	teaspoon ground cumin
½	teaspoon salt
¼	teaspoon black pepper
⅓	cup chopped fresh cilantro
2	cloves garlic, chopped
1	tablespoon chopped fresh oregano
1	pound lamb steak, cubed into ½-inch pieces

YOGURT SAUCE

3	tablespoons plain Greek yogurt
3	tablespoons light mayonnaise
1	tablespoon lemon juice
½	teaspoon sugar
2	tablespoons chopped fresh parsley

RICE

1	teaspoon olive oil
¼	teaspoon ground cumin
¼	teaspoon ground turmeric
1	cup uncooked basmati rice
2	cups low-sodium chicken broth
½	teaspoon salt
	Tomato slices, chopped iceberg lettuce and harissa hot pepper sauce (for topping)

• **Lamb.** In a large bowl, whisk together olive oil, lemon juice, cumin, salt and pepper. Stir in cilantro, garlic and oregano. Stir in lamb. Cover with plastic wrap and refrigerate for 1 hour.

• **Yogurt Sauce.** In a bowl, stir together yogurt, mayonnaise, lemon juice, sugar and 1 tablespoon water until smooth. Stir in parsley. Cover and refrigerate until serving.

• **Rice.** Meanwhile, in a medium lidded pot, heat oil over medium heat. Stir in cumin, turmeric and rice; cook for 1 minute. Pour in chicken broth and salt. Cover and bring to a boil. Reduce heat to a simmer and cook about 15 minutes, until liquid is absorbed. Let stand for 5 minutes, covered, then fluff with a fork.

• Heat a large sauté pan over medium-high heat. Drain lamb and pat dry, reserving marinade. Add to skillet and cook for 2 to 3 minutes, stirring once in a while, until pieces are seared but medium-rare. Pour in marinade; bring to a boil. Simmer for 2 minutes. Serve lamb, using a slotted spoon, over rice with yogurt sauce, tomato, lettuce and harissa.

PER SERVING 567 **CAL**; 32 g **FAT** (12 g **SAT**); 25 g **PRO**; 44 g **CARB**; 1 g **FIBER**; 795 mg **SODIUM**; 84 mg **CHOL**

HAND-CUT FRENCH FRIES

Hand-Cut French Fries

MAKES 8 servings **PREP** 30 minutes **COOK** 2 minutes **FRY** 32 minutes

1	teaspoon olive oil
4	cloves garlic, chopped
1	tablespoon chopped fresh thyme
½	cup light mayonnaise
½	cup ketchup
1	teaspoon curry powder
12	cups canola oil
3	pounds russet potatoes, peeled, cut into ¼-inch-thick sticks and placed in cold water
	Salt to taste

• Heat olive oil in a small skillet over medium heat. Stir in garlic and thyme; cook for 1 minute and stir into mayonnaise. Transfer aioli to a small bowl, cover and refrigerate until serving.

• Wipe out skillet and add ketchup and curry. Bring to a simmer and cook for 1 minute. Transfer to a small bowl, cover and refrigerate until using.

• Heat canola oil in a large heavy-bottomed pot to 325°. Rinse potatoes in a bowl filled with cold water until water is clear (which means the starch is gone). Transfer fries to paper-towel-lined baking sheets and pat dry with additional paper towels. In 4 batches, fry potatoes at 325° for 5 minutes. (Make sure oil returns to 325° before adding each batch.) Remove with a slotted spoon or mesh strainer to fresh paper-towel-lined baking sheets.

• Increase oil temp to 375°. Again, in 4 batches, fry for 3 minutes, until golden brown. Remove to baking sheets and sprinkle with salt. Serve hot with aioli and curry ketchup.

PER SERVING 334 **CAL**; 22 g **FAT** (2 g **SAT**); 3 g **PRO**; 34 g **CARB**; 3 g **FIBER**; 175 mg **SODIUM**; 0 mg **CHOL**

BBQ Brisket Grilled Cheese

MAKES 12 sandwiches **PREP** 15 minutes **SLOW COOK** on LOW for 8 hours **COOK** 4 minutes per batch

¾	**cup ketchup**
2	**tablespoons packed light brown sugar**
2	**tablespoons cider vinegar**
2	**tablespoons Worcestershire sauce**
1	**tablespoon brown mustard**
2	**teaspoons sweet paprika**
1	**teaspoon smoked paprika**
½	**teaspoon salt**
¼	**teaspoon cayenne pepper**
1½	**pounds beef brisket**
1	**small red onion, thinly sliced**
3	**cloves garlic, chopped**
24	**slices potato bread**
3	**cups (12 ounces) shredded sharp white cheddar cheese**
12	**tablespoons unsalted butter**

• In a bowl, combine ketchup, brown sugar, vinegar, Worcestershire and mustard. Stir until smooth.

• In another small bowl, combine sweet paprika, smoked paprika, salt and cayenne. Rub onto brisket.

• Pour half the barbecue sauce into bottom of a 4-quart slow cooker. Place brisket on top. Scatter onion and chopped garlic over brisket, and pour remaining sauce over it. Cover and cook on LOW for 8 hours.

• Remove brisket and pour liquid into a fat separator. Allow to cool slightly, about 5 minutes. Chop brisket into ½-inch chunks. Toss with ¾ cup of the sauce, including as much of the onion and garlic as possible.

• Scoop ¼ cup of the brisket onto a slice of bread. Top with ¼ cup of the cheddar. Press down with another slice of bread. Repeat with remaining brisket, cheddar and bread. Heat 3 tablespoons of the butter in a nonstick skillet over medium heat. Cook 3 sandwiches at a time for 2 minutes per side, until cheese is melted and bread is browned and crispy. Repeat 3 more times, until all sandwiches are cooked.

PER SANDWICH 589 **CAL**; 35 g **FAT** (17 g **SAT**); 24 g **PRO**; 46 g **CARB**; 2 g **FIBER**; 814 mg **SODIUM**; 106 mg **CHOL**

BBQ BRISKET GRILLED CHEESE

Banana Split Waffles

MAKES 6 waffles **PREP** 5 minutes
COOK per manufacturer's directions

- ½ **cup heavy cream**
- 2 **tablespoons plus 2 teaspoons sugar**
- 1 **cup all-purpose flour**
- 1 **teaspoon baking powder**
- ½ **teaspoon salt**
- 1 **cup milk**
- 4 **tablespoons unsalted butter, melted**
- 1 **egg, separated, plus 1 egg white**
- ½ **teaspoon vanilla extract**
- 6 **tablespoons chocolate-hazelnut spread**
- 2 **cups sliced bananas**
- 2 **cups sliced strawberries**

• Heat waffle iron. In a bowl, beat heavy cream with 2 teaspoons sugar to stiff peaks. Set aside.

• In a large bowl, whisk together flour, remaining 2 tablespoons sugar, the baking powder and salt. In a separate bowl, stir together milk, butter, egg yolk and vanilla. Pour wet mixture into dry mixture and stir until just combined. Place egg whites in another bowl and beat with a hand mixer on high until fluffy. Fold into batter.

• Ladle batter into waffle iron (about ½ cup per waffle). Cook according to manufacturer's directions. Repeat with remaining batter. (Makes about 6 standard waffles.)

• Top each warm waffle with 1 tablespoon chocolate-hazelnut spread, ⅓ cup sliced bananas, ⅓ cup sliced strawberries and whipped cream.

PER WAFFLE 407 **CAL**; 22 g **FAT** (11 g **SAT**); 8 g **PRO**; 48 g **CARB**; 3 g **FIBER**; 232 mg **SODIUM**; 87 mg **CHOL**

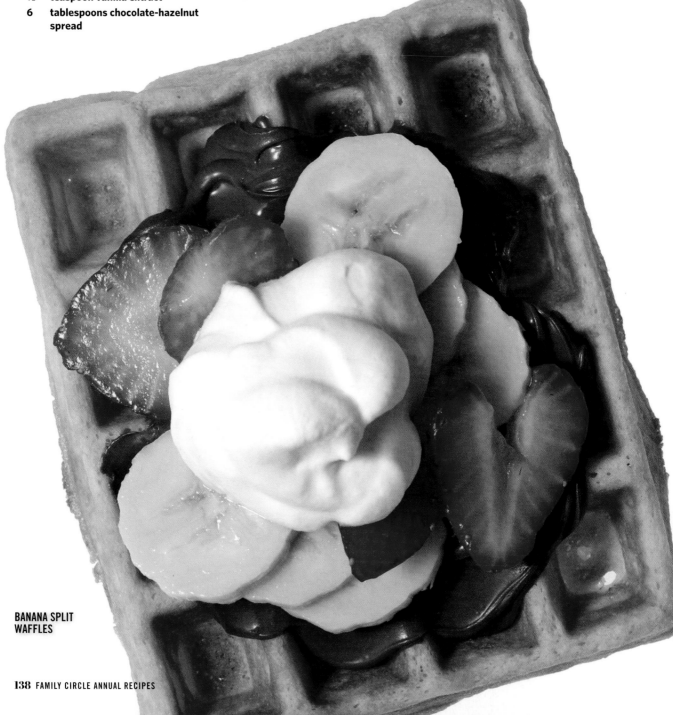

BANANA SPLIT
WAFFLES

Mint Chocolate Latte

MAKES 1 latte **PREP** 5 minutes

- ⅔   **cup milk**
- 2   **tablespoons unsweetened cocoa powder**
- 3   **tablespoons Mint Syrup (recipe follows)**
- 1   **ounce espresso or very strong coffee**
       Whipped cream, chocolate curls and fresh mint (optional)

• In a small lidded pot, whisk together milk, cocoa and mint syrup until hot and slightly foamy. Pour into a mug with espresso. Top with whipped cream, chocolate curls and a mint sprig, if desired.

Mint Syrup In a small lidded pot, combine 1 cup sugar, 1 cup water and 1 cup fresh mint. Bring to a boil. Turn off heat and cover. Steep 1 hour. Strain and place in a resealable container in the refrigerator for up to 2 weeks.

PER LATTE 278 **CAL**; 7 g **FAT** (4 g **SAT**); 7 g **PRO**; 52 g **CARB**; 4 g **FIBER**; 77 mg **SODIUM**; 16 mg **CHOL**

MINT CHOCOLATE LATTE

PB&J ICE
CREAM

PB&J Ice Cream

MAKES 12 servings (about 6 cups)
PREP 10 minutes **COOK** 8 minutes
PROCESS per manufacturer's directions
FREEZE 2 hours

- 4   **egg yolks**
- ½   **cup sugar**
- 2   **cups whole milk**
- 1   **cup heavy cream**
- ⅛   **teaspoon salt**
- ½   **cup extra-crunchy peanut butter**
- ⅓   **cup grape jelly**

• In a bowl, whisk together egg yolks and ¼ cup of the sugar. Heat milk, cream, salt and remaining ¼ cup sugar in a medium pot until simmering. Remove from heat and slowly whisk into egg-sugar mixture to temper. Pour back into pot and set over medium heat. Stir constantly until mixture coats the back of a wooden spoon (170° to 180°), about 4 to 8 minutes. Pour through a strainer into a new bowl. Stir in peanut butter until melted. Cool over an ice bath or in refrigerator.

• Process in an ice cream maker according to manufacturer's directions. Transfer to a lidded, preferably flat, container. In a small bowl, stir jelly well, until very loose. Using the back of a spoon or a long toothpick, swirl jelly into ice cream. Freeze at least 2 hours.

PER HALF CUP 216 **CAL**; 15 g **FAT** (7 g **SAT**); 5 g **PRO**; 17 g **CARB**; 1 g **FIBER**; 94 mg **SODIUM**; 100 mg **CHOL**

TAPAS PLATE, PAGE 146

JUNE

148

153

160

HEALTHY FAMILY DINNERS

From no-cook to one-pot, these recipes help you get dinner on the table fast.

LINGUINE WITH SCALLOPS,
RED PEPPER AND
BROCCOLINI, PAGE 148

PORTOBELLO PIZZA
CHEESEBURGERS,
PAGE 151

HALIBUT, PEARL COUSCOUS
AND HARISSA

Halibut, Pearl Couscous and Harissa

MAKES 4 servings **PREP** 5 minutes
COOK 17 minutes

1	tablespoon canola oil
4	halibut or swordfish steaks (about 5 ounces each)
¾	teaspoon salt
½	teaspoon black pepper
1	cup sliced onion
2	tablespoons chopped garlic
2½	cups vegetable broth
1¼	cups pearl couscous (also called Israeli couscous)
1	package (5 ounces) baby spinach
4	plum tomatoes, roughly chopped
3	tablespoons harissa
2	tablespoons chopped fresh parsley
1	lemon, cut into wedges

• Heat oil in a large skillet over medium-high heat. Season fish with ¼ teaspoon each of the salt and pepper. Add to skillet; cook for 3 minutes per side. Remove to a plate.

• Add onion and garlic; cook for 2 minutes, stirring so that garlic doesn't burn. Add broth and couscous; simmer, covered, for 4 minutes. Stir in spinach, tomatoes, harissa and remaining ½ teaspoon salt and ¼ teaspoon pepper; cook for 2 minutes. Return fish to skillet. Cover and simmer for 3 minutes or until couscous is tender.

• To serve, garnish with parsley and lemon wedges.

PER SERVING 414 **CAL**; 7 g **FAT** (1 g **SAT**); 37 g **PRO**; 49 g **CARB**; 6 g **FIBER**; 724 mg **SODIUM**; 45 mg **CHOL**

SAUSAGE AND BEAN
TORTILLA SOUP

Sausage and Bean Tortilla Soup

MAKES 6 servings **PREP** 5 minutes **COOK** 15 minutes

2	tablespoons canola oil
2	cups frozen chopped onions and peppers, thawed
2	fully cooked jalapeño chicken sausages (such as Aidells spicy mango with jalapeño), sliced
1	can (14.5 ounces) reduced-sodium stewed tomatoes
1	can (14.5 ounces) reduced-sodium chicken broth
1	can (15 ounces) pinto beans, drained and rinsed
1	can (15 ounces) black beans, drained and rinsed
1	cup frozen corn, thawed
1	teaspoon ancho chile powder
1	teaspoon dried oregano
⅛	teaspoon salt
2	ounces baked tortilla chips
¼	cup sliced scallion
1	avocado, diced

• Heat oil in a large pot over medium-high heat. Add onions and peppers; cook for 2 minutes, stirring occasionally. Add sausages; cook for 3 minutes.

• Stir in tomatoes, breaking up with a spoon. Add chicken broth, pinto beans, black beans, corn, chile powder, oregano and salt. Bring to a boil; lower heat and simmer, covered, for 10 minutes.

• To serve, spoon into soup bowls; crush tortilla chips over each serving and top with scallion and avocado.

PER SERVING 382 **CAL**; 13 g **FAT** (2 g **SAT**); 17 g **PRO**; 54 g **CARB**; 14 g **FIBER**; 780 mg **SODIUM**; 17 mg **CHOL**

GRILLED CITRUS CHICKEN RICE BOWL

When the weather is warm and you want something cool and easy for dinner, go for a crisp main-dish salad or a plate of cold cuts, cheeses, fruits, and vinaigrette-dressed chickpeas.

Grilled Citrus Chicken Rice Bowl

MAKES 4 servings PREP 20 minutes MARINATE 2 to 4 hours GRILL 16 minutes

¼	cup orange juice
3	tablespoons olive oil
2	tablespoons lemon juice
1	tablespoon white wine vinegar
1	teaspoon orange zest
1	teaspoon salt
½	teaspoon sugar
¼	teaspoon black pepper
2	scallions, finely chopped
1	pound boneless, skinless chicken breasts
3	cups cooked brown rice
1	cup baby arugula
1	cup carrot matchsticks
½	cup cucumber matchsticks
2	tablespoons chopped mint

• In a medium bowl, whisk together orange juice, olive oil, lemon juice, vinegar, orange zest, ¾ teaspoon of the salt, the sugar, pepper and scallions.

• Place chicken in a resealable plastic bag and add 3 tablespoons of the citrus dressing. Seal bag and shake to coat chicken with dressing. Marinate in refrigerator for 2 to 4 hours.

• Heat a gas or stovetop grill to medium-high or the coals in a charcoal grill to medium-hot. Remove chicken from marinade and discard marinade. Grill chicken for 7 to 8 minutes per side or until internal temperature reaches 160°. Slice chicken thinly on the bias.

• In a large salad bowl, combine rice, arugula, carrot, cucumber and mint. Toss with 4 tablespoons of the citrus dressing and season with remaining ¼ teaspoon salt.

• Serve rice salad with sliced chicken and drizzle with remaining dressing.

PER SERVING 399 CAL; 14 g FAT (2 g SAT); 27 g PRO; 40 g CARB; 4 g FIBER; 519 mg SODIUM; 63 mg CHOL

Tapas Plate

MAKES 4 servings PREP 15 minutes

1	can (15 ounces) chickpeas, drained and rinsed
½	cup sweetened dried cranberries
¼	cup roasted red peppers, coarsely chopped
¼	cup chopped red onion
2	tablespoons olive oil
2	tablespoons fruit-infused balsamic vinegar (such as pomegranate or cherry)
1	tablespoon chopped fresh parsley
4	cups frisée
2	ripe tomatoes, sliced
12	thin slices reduced-fat, reduced-sodium ham (about 4 ounces)
12	thin slices reduced-fat, reduced-sodium Swiss cheese (about 4 ounces)
¼	cup Kalamata olives
1	cup grapes
12	slices crusty French bread (½ inch thick; about 4 ounces total)

• In a medium bowl, combine chickpeas, cranberries, red peppers, onion, olive oil, vinegar and parsley.

• On 4 dinner plates, arrange equal amounts of frisée, tomatoes, ham, cheese, olives and grapes. Spoon an equal amount of chickpea mixture over frisée. Serve with bread.

PER SERVING 444 CAL; 19 g FAT (6 g SAT); 22 g PRO; 47 g CARB; 6 g FIBER; 800 mg SODIUM; 35 mg CHOL

TAPAS PLATE

Linguine with Scallops, Red Pepper and Broccolini

MAKES 4 servings **PREP** 10 minutes **COOK** 10 minutes

8	ounces linguine
1	bunch Broccolini, cut into 1-inch pieces
1	red sweet pepper, seeded and thinly sliced
2	tablespoons olive oil
2	tablespoons unsalted butter
1	pound scallops, tough muscle removed, rinsed
3	tablespoons Wondra flour
¾	teaspoon salt
½	teaspoon black pepper
6	cloves garlic, finely chopped
2	teaspoons cornstarch
½	cup vegetable broth
3	tablespoons chopped fresh parsley
2	tablespoons lemon juice
2	tablespoons grated Parmesan cheese

• Cook pasta according to package directions, about 9 minutes; add Broccolini and red pepper during last 2 minutes of cooking. Reserve ½ cup cooking water. Drain.

• Meanwhile, heat 1 tablespoon each of the oil and butter in a large stainless skillet over medium-high heat. Coat scallops with flour and season with ¼ teaspoon each of the salt and black pepper. Sauté 2 minutes per side; reserve. Add remaining 1 tablespoon oil and butter to skillet and cook garlic for 30 seconds. Combine cornstarch and broth; add to skillet and simmer for 1 minute.

• Add pasta, parsley, lemon juice, remaining ½ teaspoon salt, remaining ¼ teaspoon pepper and scallops. Toss gently to combine and simmer for 1 minute. Add some of the reserved cooking water if needed.

• Spoon into a large serving bowl. Sprinkle with Parmesan.

PER SERVING 500 **CAL**; 15 g **FAT** (5 g **SAT**); 30 g **PRO**; 59 g **CARB**; 4 g **FIBER**; 702 mg **SODIUM**; 55 mg **CHOL**

LINGUINE WITH
SCALLOPS, RED PEPPER
AND BROCCOLINI

PORTOBELLO PIZZA
CHEESEBURGERS

It's amazing what broiling or grilling vegetables with just a little bit of olive oil, salt, and pepper does for flavor. Both the mini sweet peppers and the portobello mushrooms get that simple treatment in this 20-minute recipe that's made for summer nights when you want to get in and out of the kitchen fast.

Portobello Pizza Cheeseburgers

MAKES 6 servings **PREP** 5 minutes **BROIL** 15 minutes

1	pound small sweet peppers (such as Pero Family Farms)
2	tablespoons olive oil
¼	teaspoon salt
¼	teaspoon black pepper
6	medium portobello mushrooms
1	can (14.5 ounces) Italian-seasoned diced tomatoes
1	cup reduced-fat shredded Italian 4-cheese blend
1	loaf (about 12 ounces) crusty Italian bread, sliced in half horizontally and cut into 6 equal pieces

• Heat broiler to high. Set one rack 6 inches from heat source. Place second rack as far from heat source as possible.

• Place peppers on a rimmed baking sheet. Toss with 1 tablespoon of the olive oil and ⅛ teaspoon each of the salt and pepper. Place on lower rack of oven and cook for 15 minutes, turning once halfway through, until peppers are tender and slightly browned.

• Meanwhile, clean mushrooms and remove gills. Brush with remaining 1 tablespoon oil and place on a separate baking sheet, cap side up. Place on top rack and broil for 4 minutes. Turn and season with remaining ⅛ teaspoon each salt and pepper. Broil for an additional 3 minutes. Fill with tomatoes and top each mushroom with 3 tablespoons cheese. Broil for 3 to 4 minutes.

• Sandwich mushrooms between bread slices and serve peppers on the side.

PER SERVING 307 **CAL**; 11 g **FAT** (3 g **SAT**); 13 g **PRO**; 40 g **CARB**; 5 g **FIBER**; 689 mg **SODIUM**; 10 mg **CHOL**

LOCO FOR TACOS

Celebrate the start of summer with an alfresco feast.

Handmade Corn Tortillas

MAKES 1¼ pounds dough, enough for fourteen 5½- to 6-inch tortillas or thirty-five 4-inch tortillas **PREP** 5 minutes **LET STAND** 5 minutes **COOK** about 1 minute, 45 seconds per tortilla

- 2 **cups masa harina (corn tortilla flour)**
- ½ **teaspoon salt**
- 1½ **to 1¾ cups warm water**
- 1 **tortilla press (found at cooking-supply stores or imusausa.com)**
- 2 **6-inch rounds of plastic (cut from a ziplock bag)**

• Combine masa harina, salt and 1½ cups of the water in a large bowl and knead with your hands until a uniform dough forms, 1 to 2 minutes. The dough should be slightly moister than fresh Play-Doh but just stiff enough to form into a ball. If necessary, knead a little more water into the dough. Let stand, covered with plastic wrap, for 5 minutes. The dough will dry out as it sits, so keep it covered with plastic while you work.

• For 5½- to 6-inch tortillas: Pinch off 3 tablespoons dough and form into a 1½-inch ball (about the size of a golf ball). Form more balls as you press and cook them. For 4-inch tortillas: Pinch off 1 tablespoon dough and form a ¾-inch ball. Form more balls as you press and cook them.

• Heat a comal or flat griddle over medium heat until hot, about 2 minutes. Press a ball of dough between plastic rounds in tortilla press to form a tortilla. If uneven, rotate tortilla 180° and press again to desired size. Peel off 1 plastic round, then, holding tortilla over the edge of your palm, carefully peel off the other round so that tortilla is dangling from your palm. Transfer tortilla to griddle by letting the dangling edge touch it and slowly pulling your hand back as you lay the tortilla down on the griddle. This will take a little practice, but it's better than flipping tortillas onto the griddle because they rarely end up lying flat.

• Cook until edges lift just slightly from griddle, about 15 seconds. Turn over (you can lift the edge of the tortilla with a butter knife or spatula to help you, but then grab it with your fingers and flip it over). Cook until a few faint brown spots appear on the underside, about 45 seconds. Turn over again and cook until tortilla inflates slightly (this may not always happen) and small brown spots appear on the second side, another 45 seconds. Transfer tortilla to a cloth-lined tortilla basket to keep warm as you make more tortillas.

GRILLED PORK TACOS

GRILLED GARLIC-MARINATED SKIRT STEAK TACOS

Homemade tortillas should puff when they have been turned over twice, a sign that they are about done and ready to be kept warm in a cloth-lined tortilla basket.

Grilled Pork Tacos

MAKES 9 to 12 tacos **PREP** 15 minutes
MARINATE 1 to 24 hours
GRILL 4 minutes per batch

1	orange
1	lime
3	medium cloves garlic, peeled
1	teaspoon salt
½	teaspoon whole peppercorns
4	½-inch-thick bone-in pork chops (about 1½ pounds) or boneless pork chops, pounded to flatten
	Vegetable oil
	Warm corn tortillas, Cherry Tomato Salsa (page 155), avocado, chopped white onion and fresh cilantro

• Squeeze juice from orange and lime into a blender. Add garlic, salt and peppercorns. Blend until pepper is ground. Pour marinade into a wide container and put pork chops in marinade, turning to season evenly. Cover and chill chops for at least 1 hour or up to 24 hours, turning occasionally.

• Prepare a grill or heat a grill pan. Brush grill rack or pan lightly with oil and cook pork chops (in batches, if necessary) until just cooked through, about 2 minutes per side. Transfer chops to a plate to rest for a few minutes, then thinly slice meat and mix with any juices on plate. Make tacos with tortillas, salsa, avocado, onion and cilantro.

Grilled Garlic-Marinated Skirt Steak Tacos

MAKES 18 to 24 tacos **PREP** 5 minutes
MARINATE 30 minutes to 24 hours
GRILL 6 minutes

3	pounds skirt steak (about 3 long steaks)
3	tablespoons finely chopped garlic
3	tablespoons olive oil
	Coarse salt, to taste
3	tablespoons fresh lime juice
	Warm corn or flour tortillas
	Charred Spring Onions (recipe below)
	Sliced avocado, sliced radishes and fresh cilantro

• If necessary, trim membrane from steaks by pulling it away in one piece. Place steaks in a baking dish, rub with garlic and oil, and marinate, chilled, for at least 30 minutes up to 24 hours.

• Prepare a grill or heat the broiler. Season steaks generously with coarse salt and grill over glowing coals or direct heat on a gas grill about 3 minutes on each side, turning once, for medium-rare. (Alternatively, broil steaks 3 inches from heat about 4 minutes on each side.) Transfer steaks to a platter and drizzle with lime juice. Let stand, loosely covered with foil, for 5 minutes. Cut diagonally across the grain into thin slices. Make tacos with tortillas, Charred Spring Onions, avocado, radishes and cilantro.

Charred Spring Onions

MAKES 20 onions **PREP** 5 minutes
GRILL 7 minutes

• Prepare a grill or heat the broiler. Trim roots and ends from 20 spring onions, leaving about 8 inches of green stalk. In a large bowl, toss onions with 1 tablespoon vegetable oil or mild olive oil and ½ teaspoon salt.

• Grill onions on heated grill, turning them with tongs 3 or 4 times, for 5 to 7 minutes or until softened and lightly charred. If you don't have a grill, broil onions on a broiler pan about 3 inches from heat, turning 2 or 3 times, for 10 to 12 minutes. Transfer onions to a platter and squeeze 2 lime halves over them.

CUCUMBER AND GREENS

Cucumber and Greens

MAKES 6 servings **PREP** 20 minutes

6	cups packed baby romaine
6	cups packed baby arugula
1	cup thinly sliced red sweet pepper strips
1	medium cucumber
¼	cup plain Greek yogurt
¼	cup light mayonnaise
¼	cup milk
3	tablespoons fresh lime juice
2	tablespoons olive oil
½	teaspoon sugar
¼	teaspoon salt
⅛	teaspoon black pepper
	Crumbled goat, farmer or Cotija cheese (optional)

• Combine romaine, arugula and red pepper strips in a large bowl. Trim cucumber, then shave with a vegetable peeler onto paper towels (discard seeds). Blot dry and add to bowl with lettuces.

• In a medium bowl, whisk yogurt, mayonnaise, milk, lime juice, olive oil, sugar, salt and black pepper. Drizzle about half of the dressing over salad and toss to combine. Sprinkle with crumbled cheese, if desired.

CHERRY TOMATO SALSA

TACOS WITH GRILLED
SHRIMP IN ADOBO

Tacos with Grilled Shrimp in Adobo

MAKES 8 to 10 tacos PREP 5 minutes
MARINATE 20 minutes to 2 hours
GRILL 4 minutes per batch

- 1 **pound medium shrimp (30 to 35 count), peeled and deveined**
- ½ **teaspoon salt**
- ⅓ **cup Adobo Marinade (see recipe, right), plus more for drizzling**
  Metal or soaked bamboo skewers
  Warm tortillas, sliced avocado, chopped onion, sliced radishes and fresh cilantro

• Toss shrimp in a large bowl with salt. Add Adobo Marinade and toss to coat.

• Thread shrimp onto skewers and refrigerate on a tray, covered with plastic wrap, for at least 20 minutes or up to 2 hours. (You can chill them before threading onto skewers if you prefer.)

• Prepare a grill or heat a grill pan. Grill shrimp until just cooked through, about 2 minutes per side.

• Remove shrimp from skewers and make tacos with the accompaniments, using 3 to 4 shrimp per taco. Drizzle with additional marinade before serving.

Adobo Marinade

MAKES 1½ cups PREP 5 minutes
COOK 10 minutes SOAK 20 minutes

• Heat a flat griddle or a large heavy skillet. Toast 5 large garlic cloves, unpeeled, turning once or twice until they are somewhat softened (they'll give slightly when squeezed) and browned in patches, about 8 minutes. Peel.

• In same griddle or skillet, toast 4 large ancho chiles (2 ounces total), cut open and seeded, in batches, turning and pressing with tongs until they are fragrant, pliable and have turned a brighter red, about 1 minute. Transfer chiles to a bowl of cold water and soak to soften, about 20 minutes. Drain.

• Toast ½ teaspoon cumin seeds, 5 whole peppercorns and 1 whole clove in a small skillet over medium heat, stirring, until fragrant, about 1 minute.

• Combine spices, drained chiles, toasted garlic, 1 clove raw garlic, ½ cup water, 1 teaspoon cider vinegar, ¼ teaspoon dried Mexican oregano, ½ teaspoon salt and ½ teaspoon sugar in a blender. Blend until smooth, about 2 minutes, adding more water, 1 tablespoon at a time, only if necessary to help mixture blend properly.

Cherry Tomato Salsa

MAKES 3 cups PREP 15 minutes

- 1½ **pints assorted cherry tomatoes, quartered**
- ⅓ **cup finely chopped red onion**
- 1 **jalapeño, seeds removed, finely chopped**
- 2 **cloves garlic, minced**
- 1 **tablespoon chopped fresh cilantro**
- 1 **tablespoon lime juice**
- ¼ **teaspoon salt**
- ⅛ **teaspoon black pepper**

• In a medium bowl, combine tomatoes, red onion, jalapeño, garlic, cilantro and lime juice. Season with salt and pepper and stir to combine.

Strawberry Agua Fresca

MAKES 5 cups   PREP 10 minutes

- **2** **to 3 cups cut-up strawberries**
- **2** **cups water; more as desired**
- **1** **to 2 cups ice**
- **1** **to 2 tablespoons fresh mint leaves**
- **Sugar (optional)**
- **Juice of 1 lime (optional)**

• Put strawberries, water, ice and mint in a blender and blend until smooth (you don't want chips of ice). Taste and add sugar or lime juice as desired and blend again. If seeds will bother you, strain through a sieve. Serve in a pitcher with additional ice. Thin with more water for a very light drink, if desired.

Jalapeño Margaritas

MAKES 6 servings   PREP 15 minutes
COOK 2 minutes

- **⅓** **cup sugar**
- **¾** **cup fresh lime juice (from 4 limes)**
- **3** **tablespoons fresh lemon juice (from 1 lemon)**
- **1** **large jalapeño, seeds and white ribs removed, sliced**
- **1½** **cups silver tequila (100% agave)**
- **⅓** **cup triple sec (orange liqueur)**
- **Lime wedges**
- **White or green decorating sugar, for garnish**
- **Ice**

• Combine sugar and ⅓ cup water in a small saucepan. Cook over high heat until simmering; stir until sugar is completely dissolved, about 2 minutes. Cool completely.

• Combine cooled sugar syrup (should be ⅓ cup), lime juice, lemon juice and jalapeño in a blender. Blend on highest speed until pureed, about 1 minute. Pour into a pitcher.

• Add tequila and triple sec to pitcher. Refrigerate until serving. To serve, run a lime wedge around rims of 6 glasses. Dip glass rims in white or green decorating sugar and fill glasses with ice. Pour margaritas over ice and serve.

Tres Leches Cake

MAKES 16 servings   PREP 15 minutes
BAKE at 350° for 27 minutes
REFRIGERATE overnight

CAKE

- **1½** **cups all-purpose flour**
- **2** **teaspoons baking powder**
- **5** **eggs, separated**
- **¾** **cup plus 2 tablespoons sugar**
- **1** **teaspoon vanilla extract**

SOAKING LIQUID

- **1** **can (13.5 ounces) coconut milk**
- **1** **can (14 ounces) sweetened condensed milk**
- **½** **cup fresh milk**

FROSTING

- **1** **cup heavy cream**
- **2** **tablespoons sugar**

• Heat oven to 350°. Coat a 13 x 9 x 2-inch baking pan with nonstick cooking spray. Line bottom of pan with wax paper; coat paper.

• **Cake.** In a medium bowl, whisk together flour and baking powder. In a large bowl, beat egg whites until soft peaks form. Slowly add ¼ cup of the sugar; beat until stiff peaks form.

• In a separate large bowl, beat egg yolks with remaining ½ cup plus 2 tablespoons sugar and the vanilla until thick, about 3 minutes. Fold in egg whites, then flour mixture. Pour batter into pan and spread to edges. Bake at 350° for 27 minutes or until top springs back when pressed. Invert onto a wire rack and cool completely.

• **Soaking Liquid.** In a medium bowl, whisk together coconut milk, condensed milk and fresh milk. Remove wax paper from cake and, with a wooden skewer, poke holes all over cake, 1 inch apart. Return cake to pan (upside down).

• Slowly pour half of the soaking liquid over top, letting it seep into holes. Repeat (there will be some liquid sitting on top of the cake). Cover with plastic wrap and refrigerate overnight.

• **Frosting.** Whip heavy cream and sugar on medium-high speed until medium-stiff peaks form. Spread over cake.

SMALL WONDERS

These little sliders pack big flavor!

Mini Bacon Cheeseburgers

MAKES 8 sliders **PREP** 15 minutes
COOK 4 minutes

1	**pound ground beef chuck**
1	**tablespoon Worcestershire sauce**
1	**teaspoon garlic flakes**
1	**teaspoon onion flakes**
1	**tablespoon vegetable oil**
8	**slices (¼-inch-thick) sharp cheddar cheese**
8	**slider buns (sesame seeded, if available)**
4	**slices cooked bacon, each cut into 4 pieces crossways**

• In a medium bowl, combine beef, Worcestershire sauce, garlic flakes and onion flakes. Form into 8 patties, about 2½ inches in diameter.

• Heat oil in a large nonstick skillet over medium-high heat. Add patties and cook for 2 minutes. Turn and add a cheddar slice to each; cook for an additional 2 minutes, until cheddar melts.

• Place slider on bun and top each with 2 pieces of bacon.

PER SLIDER 311 **CAL**; 16 g **FAT** (8 g **SAT**); 22 g **PRO**; 22 g **CARB**; 1 g **FIBER**; 483 mg **SODIUM**; 56 mg **CHOL**

Southwest Turkey Sliders

MAKES 12 sliders **PREP** 15 minutes
REFRIGERATE 30 minutes **COOK** 6 minutes

¼	**cup unseasoned bread crumbs**
3	**tablespoons milk**
1¼	**pounds ground turkey**
1	**egg, lightly beaten**
3	**tablespoons chopped fresh cilantro**
2	**tablespoons chopped pickled jalapeños**
1	**tablespoon salt-free Southwest seasoning**
½	**teaspoon salt**
12	**small slices (½ ounce each) pepper Jack cheese**
12	**dinner-size potato rolls**
6	**teaspoons reduced-fat mayonnaise**
4	**plum tomatoes, thinly sliced**
	Fresh cilantro sprigs, for garnish
	Lime wedges, for squeezing

• In a large bowl, combine bread crumbs and milk. Add turkey, egg, cilantro, jalapeños, seasoning and salt. Mix until combined. Form into twelve 3-inch patties. Place on a wax-paper-lined baking sheet and refrigerate for 30 minutes.

• Heat a gas grill or stovetop grill to medium-high. Lightly grease grill rack or stovetop grill. Grill sliders for 3 minutes. Turn and place cheese on top; grill for an additional 3 minutes.

• Spread ½ teaspoon mayonnaise on bottom of each roll. Layer with a patty, tomato, cilantro, and a squeeze of lime.

PER SLIDER 214 **CAL**; 9 g **FAT** (3 g **SAT**); 14 g **PRO**; 17 g **CARB**; 1 g **FIBER**; 574 mg **SODIUM**; 68 mg **CHOL**

Grilled Shiitake Sliders

MAKES 8 sliders **PREP** 15 minutes
GRILL 4 minutes

32	**shiitake mushrooms, cleaned and stems removed**
2	**tablespoons olive oil**
⅛	**teaspoon salt**
⅛	**teaspoon black pepper**
8	**seeded slider rolls**
8	**tablespoons sun-dried-tomato pesto**
8	**slices (about 1 ounce each) smoked Gouda cheese, at room temperature**
1	**cup roasted red pepper strips**
1	**cup watercress**

• Heat a gas grill or stovetop grill to medium-high. Lightly grease grill racks or grill pan.

• Brush mushrooms with oil and season with salt and black pepper. Grill for 2 minutes per side.

• To serve, spread bottom half of each roll with 1 tablespoon pesto. Layer with mushrooms, Gouda, red pepper strips and watercress. Top with roll top.

PER SLIDER 270 **CAL**; 14 g **FAT** (6 g **SAT**); 12 g **PRO**; 26 g **CARB**; 2 g **FIBER**; 552 mg **SODIUM**; 33 mg **CHOL**

Buffalo Chicken Sliders

MAKES 8 sliders **PREP** 15 minutes
COOK 4 minutes

4	thinly sliced chicken cutlets (about 3 ounces each), cut in half or thirds crossways
2	eggs, lightly beaten
½	cup unseasoned bread crumbs
2	tablespoons vegetable oil
2	large ribs celery, cut into 1-inch matchsticks
1	carrot, cut into 1-inch matchsticks
2	tablespoons chunky blue cheese dressing
8	small brioche buns, split
16	teaspoons Frank's Wing Sauce

• Dip chicken pieces in egg and dredge in bread crumbs.

• Heat oil in a large nonstick skillet over medium-high heat. Add chicken and cook for 2 minutes per side, until lightly browned. Remove to a plate.

• In a small bowl, combine celery, carrot and dressing.

• Place a piece of chicken on bottom half of each bun; add 2 teaspoons wing sauce and ⅛ of the celery mixture to each and top with bun tops.

PER SLIDER 243 **CAL**; 11 g **FAT** (3 g **SAT**); 15 g **PRO**; 23 g **CARB**; 1 g **FIBER**; 402 mg **SODIUM**; 78 mg **CHOL**

Crab Cake Sliders

MAKES 8 sliders **PREP** 15 minutes
REFRIGERATE 1 hour **COOK** 10 minutes

8	ounces crab claw meat (such as Phillips)
⅓	cup panko bread crumbs
3	tablespoons mayonnaise
3	tablespoons finely chopped red sweet pepper
1	scallion, chopped
1	tablespoon teriyaki sauce
⅛	teaspoon ground ginger
2	tablespoons canola oil
8	small potato rolls, split
8	small pieces frisée
8	teaspoons wasabi mayonnaise
8	lime wedges for squeezing (optional)

• In a medium bowl, gently combine crab meat, panko, mayonnaise, red pepper, scallion, teriyaki sauce and ginger. Form into 8 small patties and place on a dish; refrigerate for 1 hour.

• Heat oil in a large nonstick skillet over medium-high heat. Add 4 crab cakes and cook for 4 to 5 minutes, without moving, until well browned. Gently turn and cook for an additional 4 to 5 minutes. Remove to a plate and keep warm. Repeat with remaining crab cakes.

• Place a piece of frisée on bottom of each roll and top with a crab cake. Spread cut side of each top half with 1 teaspoon wasabi mayonnaise and place on top of crab cake. Serve immediately with lime wedges, if desired.

PER SLIDER 290 **CAL**; 11 g **FAT** (2 g **SAT**); 13 g **PRO**; 36 g **CARB**; 1 g **FIBER**; 409 mg **SODIUM**; 26 mg **CHOL**

Mini Lamb Sliders

MAKES 8 sliders **PREP** 15 minutes
COOK 6 minutes

1	pound ground lamb
1	teaspoon dried Greek seasoning (such as McCormick)
¼	teaspoon salt
¼	teaspoon black pepper
2	cups baby spinach
⅓	cup crumbled feta cheese
¼	small red onion, thinly sliced
1	tablespoon olive oil
2	teaspoons red wine vinegar
16	mini pitas, heated

• In a medium bowl, gently combine lamb, Greek seasoning, salt and pepper. Form into 8 patties.

• Heat a large nonstick skillet over medium-high heat. Add patties and cook for 3 minutes per side. Remove to a plate and keep warm.

• In a medium bowl, combine spinach, feta, onion, oil and vinegar; gently toss.

• Place each patty on a pita with some of the spinach salad. Top with another pita and serve immediately.

PER SLIDER 255 **CAL**; 14 g **FAT** (6 g **SAT**); 17 g **PRO**; 13 g **CARB**; 1 g **FIBER**; 303 mg **SODIUM**; 61 mg **CHOL**

Meatball Sliders

MAKES 12 sliders **PREP** 20 minutes
BAKE at 350° for 30 minutes

1	pound ground meatloaf mix (beef, pork and veal)
½	cup unseasoned bread crumbs
1	egg, lightly beaten
1	teaspoon Italian seasoning
⅛	teaspoon salt
⅛	teaspoon black pepper
1½	cups jarred marinara sauce, heated
6	ounces thinly sliced Fontina cheese
12	radicchio leaves
12	fresh basil leaves
12	King's Hawaiian sweet dinner rolls

• Heat oven to 350°. Line a rimmed baking sheet with foil and lightly coat with nonstick cooking spray.

• In a large bowl, combine meatloaf mix, bread crumbs, egg, Italian seasoning, salt and pepper. Form into 12 meatballs and place on prepared baking sheet. Bake at 350° for 30 minutes. Spoon 2 tablespoons sauce over each meatball. Divide Fontina into 12 portions, and fold over and place on top of meatballs. Return to oven for 1 minute, until Fontina starts to melt slightly.

• Place a radicchio leaf, a basil leaf and a meatball on bottom half of each roll. Top with roll tops.

PER SLIDER 388 **CAL**; 16 g **FAT** (9 g **SAT**); 19 g **PRO**; 41 g **CARB**; 3 g **FIBER**; 523 mg **SODIUM**; 90 mg **CHOL**

BBQ Pulled-Chicken Sliders

MAKES 20 sliders **PREP** 15 minutes
SLOW COOK on HIGH for 4 hours

½	cup ketchup
⅓	cup light brown sugar
2	tablespoons reduced-sodium soy sauce
1	tablespoon reduced-sodium Worcestershire sauce
1	teaspoon chili powder
1	teaspoon garlic powder
1	teaspoon paprika
1	bottle (12 ounces) Samuel Adams Boston lager
2	pounds boneless, skinless chicken breasts (about 4 large breasts)
2	packages (12 ounces each) refrigerated buttermilk biscuits, baked according to package directions
60	bread-and-butter pickle slices

• Coat slow cooker bowl with nonstick cooking spray. Add ketchup, brown sugar, soy sauce, Worcestershire, chili powder, garlic powder and paprika. Whisk until smooth; whisk in beer.

• Add chicken, cover and cook on HIGH for 4 hours. Remove chicken to a plate and shred with 2 forks. Return to slow cooker and stir to coat chicken with sauce.

• To serve, spoon about ¼ cup chicken on each biscuit and top with 3 pickles.

PER SLIDER 195 **CAL**; 5 g **FAT** (1 g **SAT**); 11 g **PRO**; 25 g **CARB**; 0 g **FIBER**; 589 mg **SODIUM**; 25 mg **CHOL**

Caprese Sliders

MAKES 8 sliders **PREP** 15 minutes
BAKE at 400° for 12 minutes **GRILL** 3 minutes

1	package (12 ounces) frozen Alexia artisan French rolls
2	medium tomatoes, cut into ½-inch slices
1	tablespoon olive oil
8	teaspoons prepared basil pesto
16	small fresh basil leaves
½	pound fresh mozzarella, cut into ¼-inch slices
16	thin slices ripe avocado

• Heat oven to 400°. Place rolls on a baking sheet and bake for 10 to 12 minutes, following package directions. Allow to cool.

• Heat a stovetop grill to medium-high. Brush tomato slices with oil and grill for 2 minutes. Turn and grill for an additional 1 minute.

• Split rolls horizontally and spread bottom half of each with 1 teaspoon pesto. Layer each with 1 tomato slice, 2 basil leaves, 1 mozzarella slice and 2 avocado slices. Top with roll tops.

PER SLIDER 256 **CAL**; 13 g **FAT** (1 g **SAT**); 9 g **PRO**; 23 g **CARB**; 3 g **FIBER**; 358 mg **SODIUM**; 27 mg **CHOL**

CHERRY TOMATO
BRUSCHETTA, PAGE 185

JULY

171

182

192

GRILL HAPPY

Get fired up with a mix of rubs, marinades and sauces.

CHICKEN AND GRILLED
PINEAPPLE SALSA, PAGE 168

CHILI-LIME SWORDFISH
AND GRILLED CORN,
PAGE 173

Don't throw away leftover rub. It can be mixed into meatloaf, rubbed onto chicken thighs or sprinkled over salmon before baking or roasting

Coffee-Rubbed Steak with Charred Zucchini

MAKES 6 servings **PREP** 15 minutes **GRILL** 14 minutes **MICROWAVE** 90 seconds **LET REST** 5 minutes

2	**tablespoons espresso ground coffee (decaf if desired)**
1	**teaspoon chili powder**
1	**teaspoon garlic powder**
1¼	**teaspoons salt**
1	**teaspoon sugar**
½	**teaspoon smoked paprika**
¼	**teaspoon plus ⅛ teaspoon black pepper**
1½	**pounds boneless sirloin steak (at least 1 inch thick)**
4	**small zucchini, trimmed and quartered lengthwise**
1	**package (10 ounces) button mushrooms, trimmed**
1	**yellow sweet pepper, cut from core into 4 pieces**
2	**tablespoons light balsamic salad dressing**
1	**package (8.5 ounces) heat-and-serve white or brown rice**

• Heat grill to medium-high. In a small bowl, combine espresso, chili powder, garlic powder, ¾ teaspoon of the salt, the sugar, paprika and ¼ teaspoon of the black pepper. Sprinkle 1 tablespoon of the rub over one side of steak and press in with your hands. Turn steak over and repeat. (Reserve remaining rub for another use.)

• Season zucchini with ¼ teaspoon of the remaining salt and remaining ⅛ teaspoon black pepper. Thread mushrooms onto 2 skewers. Brush mushrooms and yellow pepper pieces with balsamic dressing. Grill vegetables for 6 minutes, turning once. Grill steak for 6 to 8 minutes, depending on thickness, turning once.

• Meanwhile, microwave rice for 90 seconds. Remove steak from grill and let rest for 5 minutes. Quarter mushrooms and dice yellow pepper. Toss in a bowl with rice and remaining ¼ teaspoon salt. Slice steak and serve with zucchini and grilled veggie rice.

PER SERVING 408 **CAL**; 11 g **FAT** (3 g **SAT**); 44 g **PRO**; 34 g **CARB**; 3 g **FIBER**; 704 mg **SODIUM**; 71 mg **CHOL**

CHICKEN AND GRILLED PINEAPPLE SALSA

BBQ Burgers

MAKES 4 servings   PREP 15 minutes
GRILL 12 minutes

1¼	pounds 92% lean ground beef
½	cup grated onion
7	tablespoons bottled barbecue sauce
2	tablespoons grated Parmesan cheese
2	teaspoons Dijon mustard
½	teaspoon garlic powder
4	slices sourdough bread (about 1½ ounces each)
1	tablespoon extra-virgin olive oil
4	small leaves Boston lettuce
4	tablespoons French's fried onions
	Mixed green salad with fat-free dressing (optional)

• Heat grill to medium-high. In a large bowl, combine ground beef, onion, 3 tablespoons of the barbecue sauce, the Parmesan, mustard and garlic powder. Gently mix until combined, then shape into 4 patties about the size of the sourdough slices.

• Brush sourdough on both sides with olive oil. Grill for 2 minutes per side, turning once. Transfer to a platter and top with Boston lettuce leaves.

• Grill burger patties on oiled grill for 4 minutes. Spritz burgers with nonstick cooking spray and flip over. Grill for an additional 4 minutes, or to desired doneness. Transfer to lettuce-topped bread and spoon 1 tablespoon barbecue sauce onto each burger. Top each with 1 tablespoon fried onions and serve with a mixed green salad, if desired.

PER SERVING 483 CAL; 18 g FAT (7 g SAT); 34 g PRO; 47 g CARB; 2 g FIBER; 773 mg SODIUM; 78 mg CHOL

Chicken and Grilled Pineapple Salsa

MAKES 5 servings   PREP 15 minutes
GRILL 24 minutes

2	teaspoons grated fresh lemon peel plus 2 tablespoons fresh lemon juice (from 1 lemon)
2	cloves garlic, minced
1	teaspoon ground coriander
¾	teaspoon salt
½	teaspoon ground cumin
½	teaspoon ground black pepper
⅛	teaspoon ground cayenne pepper
1	package (24 ounces) Perdue Perfect Portions boneless chicken breasts or 5 small chicken breast halves (4 to 5 ounces each)
1	tablespoon olive oil
1	peeled and cored pineapple, cut into 6 wedges
2	avocados, halved, pitted and peeled
½	small red onion, minced
2	tablespoons chopped fresh cilantro
10	corn tortillas, warmed

• Heat grill to medium-high. In a small bowl, combine lemon peel, garlic, coriander, ½ teaspoon of the salt, the cumin, black pepper and cayenne. Rub half onto both sides of chicken. Whisk lemon juice and olive oil into remaining rub and brush onto pineapple and avocados. Grill pineapple for 12 minutes, turning twice so all sides are nicely marked. Meanwhile, grill avocado halves, cut side down, for 3 minutes, until nicely marked. Transfer pineapple and avocado to a cutting board.

• Grill chicken for 10 to 12 minutes, turning once. Meanwhile, dice pineapple and avocados and gently mix together with red onion, cilantro and remaining ¼ teaspoon salt.

• Divide pineapple salsa among 5 plates. Top with a chicken breast half and serve with 2 tortillas per plate.

PER SERVING 472 CAL; 18 g FAT (3 g SAT); 37 g PRO; 45 g CARB; 11 g FIBER; 469 mg SODIUM; 79 mg CHOL

PORK AND PLUM
SKEWERS

Pork and Plum Skewers

MAKES 4 servings **PREP** 15 minutes
COOK 8 minutes **GRILL** 6 minutes

½	teaspoon ground cinnamon
½	teaspoon ground cumin
1	teaspoon ground ginger
½	teaspoon black pepper
¼	cup plum preserves
¼	cup cider vinegar
¾	teaspoon plus ⅛ teaspoon salt
2	tablespoons olive oil
2	pounds boneless pork loin, trimmed and cut into 1½-inch pieces
½	of a red onion, cut into 1½-inch pieces
3	red plums, pitted, each cut into 6 wedges
1	cup Israeli pearl couscous
2	cups packed baby spinach, shredded
¼	cup crumbled feta cheese
¼	cup toasted sliced almonds

• In a small bowl, whisk together cinnamon, cumin, ginger, pepper, preserves, vinegar and ½ teaspoon of the salt. While whisking, add oil in a thin stream. Set aside 3 tablespoons of the sauce for couscous.

• Thread 6 metal skewers with pork, onion and plum wedges: Use 5 or 6 pieces of pork per skewer, alternating with 3 plum wedges and as much red onion as desired.

• Heat grill to medium-high. While grill is heating, cook couscous in lightly salted boiling water for 8 minutes. Drain and rinse with cool water. Toss with spinach, feta, almonds, ¼ teaspoon of the remaining salt and reserved 3 tablespoons sauce. Set aside.

• Brush skewers with some of the sauce. Place on oiled grill, sauce side down. Brush with remaining sauce. Grill for 3 minutes, then flip over. Grill for 3 minutes more, until pork is no longer pink. Season with remaining ⅛ teaspoon salt and serve with couscous salad.

PER SERVING 439 **CAL**; 16 g **FAT** (4 g **SAT**); 38 g **PRO**; 34 g **CARB**; 3 g **FIBER**; 492 mg **SODIUM**; 89 mg **CHOL**

GRILLED RATATOUILLE

Grilled Ratatouille

MAKES 4 servings **PREP** 35 minutes **MARINATE** 30 minutes **GRILL** 14 minutes

1	eggplant (about 1 pound), trimmed and cut lengthwise into ½-inch-thick pieces
2	medium zucchini, trimmed and cut lengthwise into ½-inch-thick pieces
1	red sweet pepper, cut from core into 4 pieces
1	orange sweet pepper, cut from core into 4 pieces
⅓	cup balsamic vinegar
2	teaspoons honey
1	teaspoon grainy mustard
½	teaspoon plus ⅛ teaspoon salt
¼	teaspoon black pepper
¼	cup extra-virgin olive oil
2	large cloves garlic, minced
1	cup cherry tomatoes
1	can (19 ounces) chickpeas, drained and rinsed
¼	cup fresh parsley, chopped
¼	cup grated ricotta salata cheese

• Place eggplant, zucchini and sweet peppers in a large resealable plastic bag. In a medium bowl, whisk together vinegar, honey, mustard, ½ teaspoon of the salt and the black pepper. While whisking, add oil in a thin stream. Stir garlic into marinade and set aside ¼ cup. Add remaining marinade to bag with vegetables. Marinate for 30 minutes.

• Thread cherry tomatoes onto 1 or 2 skewers. Oil grill grate and heat grill to medium-high. Grill marinated vegetables for 8 to 10 minutes, turning once. You may need to do this in a few batches, depending on the size of your grill. Grill tomato skewers for 4 minutes, turning once.

• Transfer eggplant, zucchini and peppers to a cutting board. Transfer tomatoes to a serving bowl with chickpeas. Dice eggplant, zucchini and peppers. Add to bowl with reserved marinade, parsley and remaining ⅛ teaspoon salt. Top with ricotta salata just before serving.

PER SERVING 400 **CAL**; 12 g **FAT** (2 g **SAT**); 14 g **PRO**; 62 g **CARB**; 14 g **FIBER**; 779 mg **SODIUM**; 4 mg **CHOL**

When you use acidic ingredients such as lime juice or vinegar, limit marinating time to 20 minutes. Otherwise, the fish, chicken or beef can get mushy.

Chili-Lime Swordfish and Grilled Corn

MAKES 4 servings **PREP** 15 minutes **MARINATE** 20 minutes **GRILL** 10 minutes **COOK** 3 minutes

FISH

1	cup coconut water
1	jalapeño, thinly sliced
2	cloves garlic, thinly sliced
1	lime (to yield 1 teaspoon zest and 2 tablespoons juice)
2	teaspoon chili powder
½	teaspoon salt
¼	teaspoon black pepper
4	5-ounce swordfish, mahi mahi or halibut fillets, thawed if frozen
12	ounces (about 3 cups) spicy sweet potato fries

CORN

4	ears corn, shucked
1½	tablespoons butter, melted
1	teaspoon lime zest
1	teaspoon lime juice
	Pinch of salt

• In a medium bowl, combine coconut water, jalapeño, garlic, lime zest and juice, chili powder, salt and pepper. Place fish in a resealable plastic bag. Add marinade and refrigerate for 20 minutes.

• Meanwhile, bake sweet potato fries per package directions. Heat grill to medium. Add corn and grill for 10 minutes, turning occasionally.

• After corn has cooked for 4 minutes, add fish to grill, reserving marinade. Grill for 6 minutes, turning once. Remove to a platter. Pour marinade into a small saucepan and bring to a boil. Boil for 3 minutes and spoon over fish.

• In a small bowl, blend butter, lime zest, lime juice and salt. Brush over corn. Serve fish and corn with sweet potato fries.

PER SERVING 451 **CAL**; 17 g **FAT** (4 g **SAT**); 32 g **PRO**; 49 g **CARB**; 6 g **FIBER**; 807 mg **SODIUM**; 63 mg **CHOL**

DOWN-HOME DELICIOUS

Celebrate Independence Day with a Low Country-inspired feast.

LOW COUNTRY
SHRIMP BOIL, PAGE 179

SOUTH CAROLINA
PULLED PORK WITH
MUSTARD BARBECUE
SAUCE, PAGE 181

COLLARD GREENS

CHEESE GRITS

There is a type of restaurant in the South known as a "meat and three"—a cafeteria-style spot where you pick your meat (fried chicken, ham, meatloaf, etc.) and three sides from a dizzying array. Southern-style sides are so tasty and satisfying, you could make a meal on them alone—minus the meat.

Collard Greens

MAKES 8 servings PREP 20 minutes COOK 58 minutes

- ½ **pound smoked slab bacon (or thick-cut bacon), diced**
- 1 **onion, diced**
- 3 **cloves garlic, smashed**
- 2¾ **to 3 pounds collard greens, stems removed, cut into 2-inch pieces**
- 2 **cups chicken stock**
- ⅛ **teaspoon salt**

• Heat a large stockpot over medium heat. Add bacon; cook for 8 minutes, stirring occasionally. Add onion and garlic; sauté for 5 minutes. Stir in greens, chicken stock and 2 cups water; bring to a boil. Cover and reduce heat to medium-low; cook for 20 minutes. Uncover and cook for 25 minutes. Stir in salt.

• Using tongs, remove greens to a serving bowl, allowing excess liquid to drip off.

PER SERVING 104 **CAL**; 4 g **FAT** (1 g **SAT**); 7 g **PRO**; 10 g **CARB**; 4 g **FIBER**; 385 mg **SODIUM**; 10 mg **CHOL**

Cheese Grits

MAKES 8 servings PREP 5 minutes COOK 14 minutes

- 1 **cup Quaker Oats grits (not instant)**
- 8 **ounces shredded cheddar cheese**
- 2 **tablespoons unsalted butter**
- 1 **teaspoon salt**
  Freshly cracked black pepper

• In a large pot, bring 4½ cups water to a boil. Gradually whisk grits into water. Reduce heat to medium-low, cover and cook for 12 to 14 minutes, until thickened. Stir in cheese and butter until melted. Stir in salt and pepper.

PER SERVING 212 **CAL**; 12 g **FAT** (7 g **SAT**); 9 g **PRO**; 18 g **CARB**; 0 g **FIBER**; 759 mg **SODIUM**; 38 mg **CHOL**

LOW COUNTRY
SHRIMP BOIL

Low Country Shrimp Boil

MAKES 8 servings **PREP** 5 minutes
COOK 17 minutes

3	**pounds small red potatoes**
1½	**pounds kielbasa, sliced into 2-inch pieces**
¼	**cup seafood seasoning (such as J.O. Spice Company or Old Bay), plus more for sprinkling (optional)**
4	**ears corn, husks and silks removed, halved**
3	**pounds shrimp, shells on**

• Place potatoes and kielbasa in bottom of a large stockpot. Fill with 5 quarts cold water. If desired, stir in seasoning. Cover and bring to a boil; cook for 5 minutes. Remove lid and carefully add corn; cook for 10 minutes. Stir in shrimp and cook for 2 minutes, until pink and just cooked. Drain. Sprinkle with additional seasoning, if desired.

PER SERVING 520 **CAL**; 20 g **FAT** (6 g **SAT**); 47 g **PRO**; 39 g **CARB**; 4 g **FIBER**; 1,120 mg **SODIUM**; 297 mg **CHOL**

Deviled Crab Dip

MAKES 24 (¼-cup) servings **PREP** 15 minutes **BAKE** at 375° for 30 minutes **BROIL** 2 minutes

1	**cup light mayonnaise**
2	**eggs**
¼	**cup fresh lemon juice**
¼	**cup milk**
1	**tablespoon seafood seasoning (such as J.O. Spice Company or Old Bay)**
1	**teaspoon dry mustard**
1	**pound crab claw meat**
1	**red sweet pepper, diced**
½	**cup diced onion**
2	**ribs celery, diced**
1	**cup plus 2 tablespoons plain bread crumbs**
2	**tablespoons olive oil**

• Heat oven to 375°. In a large bowl, whisk together mayonnaise, eggs, lemon juice, milk, seafood seasoning and dry mustard. Carefully fold in crab, pepper, onion, celery and 1 cup of the bread crumbs.

• Transfer mixture to a shallow 1½-quart oven-safe baking dish. Sprinkle remaining 2 tablespoons bread crumbs on top and drizzle with oil. Bake at 375° for 30 minutes. Broil on HIGH for 2 minutes or until browned. Serve with crackers.

PER SERVING 96 **CAL**; 5 g **FAT** (1 g **SAT**); 6 g **PRO**; 6 g **CARB**; 0 g **FIBER**; 282 mg **SODIUM**; 43 mg **CHOL**

SOUTH CAROLINA
PULLED PORK
WITH MUSTARD
BARBECUE SAUCE

South Carolina Pulled Pork with Mustard Barbecue Sauce

MAKES 24 (⅓-cup) servings **PREP** 30 minutes **STAND** 30 minutes **SLOW ROAST** at 300° for 7 hours **COOK** 18 minutes

PULLED PORK

1	**bone-in pork shoulder (about 7 pounds)**
1	**teaspoon salt**
½	**teaspoon black pepper**
	Small hamburger buns (optional)

MUSTARD BARBECUE SAUCE

1	**tablespoon unsalted butter**
½	**yellow onion, grated**
2	**cloves garlic, grated**
1	**cup yellow mustard**
1	**tablespoon dry mustard**
¾	**cup cider vinegar**
¾	**cup packed light brown sugar**
1	**teaspoon Tabasco**

• **Pulled Pork.** Heat oven to 300°. Let pork sit at room temperature for 30 minutes before cooking; season with salt and pepper. Wrap tightly in aluminum foil, then place on a rimmed baking sheet fitted with a rack. Slow roast at 300° for 7 hours, until pork reaches 200° in the thickest part and pulls apart easily with a fork.

• **Mustard Barbecue Sauce.** During the last 20 minutes of roasting, heat butter in a small pot over medium-low heat. Add onion and garlic. Cook for 3 minutes. Whisk in yellow mustard, dry mustard, vinegar, brown sugar and Tabasco. Reduce heat to medium-low and simmer for 15 minutes.

• Allow pork to cool slightly, then shred with 2 forks. Discard fat, skin and bone. Toss with barbecue sauce. Serve pork alongside buns, if desired.

PER SERVING 288 **CAL**; 18 g **FAT** (6 g **SAT**); 23 g **PRO**; 8 g **CARB**; 0 g **FIBER**; 270 mg **SODIUM**; 89 mg **CHOL**

SOUTHERN SWEET TEA

Banana Pudding

MAKES 8 servings **PREP** 10 minutes
COOK 5 minutes **REFRIGERATE** at least 3 hours
or overnight

½	cup plus 1 tablespoon sugar
3	tablespoons cornstarch
3	cups 2% or whole milk
6	egg yolks, beaten
1	teaspoon vanilla extract
3	tablespoons unsalted butter
8	9-ounce glass canning jars with lids
48	vanilla wafer cookies
4	bananas, sliced
1	cup heavy cream, chilled

• Blend ½ cup of the sugar and the cornstarch in a medium pot. Stir in milk. Bring to a simmer, stirring often. Whisk 1 cup of the mixture into beaten egg yolks. Stir egg mixture back into pot. Cook for 4 to 5 minutes, until it reaches 160°, thickens and begins to bubble. Remove from heat; stir in vanilla and butter. Cool completely.

• In the bottom of each jar, place 3 vanilla wafers. Cover with a layer of bananas. Spoon a scant ¼ cup of the pudding on top of each. Repeat layering. Secure lids; refrigerate at least 3 hours or overnight.

• Just before serving, combine heavy cream and remaining 1 tablespoon sugar in a bowl. Using a hand mixer, whisk until stiff peaks form. Spoon over each dessert.

PER SERVING 523 **CAL**; 25 g **FAT** (13 g **SAT**); 7 g **PRO**; 76 g **CARB**; 2 g **FIBER**; 126 mg **SODIUM**; 218 mg **CHOL**

For an adult take on this classic Southern refreshment, combine 4 ounces Southern Sweet Tea with 2 ounces vodka and ½ ounce fresh lemon juice. Serve in a tall glass over ice.

Southern Sweet Tea

MAKES 12 servings **PREP** 5 minutes
STEEP 30 minutes

10	black tea bags (such as Lipton)
¾	cup sugar
1	lemon, sliced, plus more slices for garnish (optional)

• Secure tea bags around the handle of a small lidded pot filled with 4 cups water. Bring to a boil. Turn off heat, stir in sugar and cover. Let steep for 30 minutes. Cool completely.

• Pour cooled tea into a pitcher with 4 cups cold water. Add lemon slices and enough ice to fill pitcher. Serve over ice in tall glasses. Garnish with more lemon slices, if desired.

PER SERVING 31 **CAL**; 0 g **FAT** (0 g **SAT**); 0 g **PRO**; 9 g **CARB**; 0 g **FIBER**; 0 mg **SODIUM**; 0 mg **CHOL**

BANANA PUDDING

TOMATO SEASON

This juicy fruit peaks in midsummer. Celebrate with these Italian-style bites.

CHERRY TOMATO
BRUSCHETTA

Cherry Tomato Bruschetta

MAKES 16 bruschettas **PREP** 20 minutes **GRILL** 3 minutes

1	**loaf (10 ounces) Italian bread, trimmed and cut into 16 pieces (each about ½ inch thick)**
3	**tablespoons extra-virgin olive oil**
1	**cup ricotta cheese**
¼	**cup fresh basil leaves, chopped, plus small leaves for garnish**
½	**teaspoon lemon zest**
½	**teaspoon salt**
½	**teaspoon freshly ground black pepper**
2	**cloves garlic, halved lengthwise**
1½	**pounds heirloom cherry tomatoes, sliced**
1	**tablespoon lemon juice**

• Heat grill or grill pan to medium-high. Brush bread slices on one side with 1 tablespoon of the oil. Grill, oiled side down, for 1½ minutes. Brush with 1 tablespoon oil and flip slices over. Grill another 1½ minutes or until toasted and lightly marked. Transfer to a platter.

• In a medium bowl, stir together ricotta, 1 tablespoon of the chopped basil, the lemon zest and ¼ teaspoon each of the salt and pepper.

• Rub cut side of a garlic clove half on 4 of the bread slices. Repeat with remaining garlic clove halves and remaining grilled bread.

• Gently toss cherry tomato slices with remaining 1 tablespoon oil, remaining chopped basil, remaining ¼ teaspoon each salt and pepper, and the lemon juice.

• Spread 1 tablespoon of the ricotta mixture on each grilled bread slice. Top with a spoonful of the tomato mixture and garnish with basil leaves.

PER BRUSCHETTA 106 **CAL**; 5 g **FAT** (2 g **SAT**); 4 g **PRO**; 11 g **CARB**; 1 g **FIBER**; 191 mg **SODIUM**; 8 mg **CHOL**

LETTUCE EAT

You'll be bowled over by these surprising and satisfying salads.

ARUGULA, BLUEBERRY
AND CORN SALAD

KALE CAESAR SALAD

Arugula, Blueberry and Corn Salad

MAKES 4 side salads **PREP** 10 minutes
GRILL 15 minutes

	Nonstick cooking spray
4	**ears corn on the cob, shucked**
2	**tablespoons balsamic vinegar**
2	**tablespoons extra-virgin olive oil**
1	**teaspoon Dijon mustard**
½	**teaspoon salt**
1	**package (5 ounces) arugula**
6	**ounces blueberries**
½	**small red onion, thinly sliced**
1	**log (4 ounces) blueberry, cranberry or plain goat cheese, sliced into 8 rounds**
	Freshly cracked black pepper

• Coat a grill or grill pan with nonstick cooking spray or brush lightly with oil. Heat grill or grill pan to medium. Grill corn for 15 minutes, turning several times, until lightly charred. Cool slightly, then slice kernels off cobs.

• Whisk together vinegar, olive oil, mustard and ¼ teaspoon of the salt. Toss with corn, arugula, blueberries, onion and remaining ¼ teaspoon salt. Place 2 goat cheese rounds on each serving and garnish with cracked pepper.

PER SALAD 245 **CAL**; 14 g **FAT** (5 g **SAT**); 9 g **PRO**; 27 g **CARB**; 4 g **FIBER**; 438 mg **SODIUM**; 13 mg **CHOL**

Kale Caesar Salad

MAKES 4 side salads **PREP** 10 minutes **COOK** 2 minutes

2	**pasteurized egg yolks**
2	**tablespoons lemon juice**
1	**clove garlic, grated**
1	**teaspoon anchovy paste**
½	**teaspoon Dijon mustard**
3	**tablespoons extra-virgin olive oil**
3	**tablespoons vegetable oil**
¼	**teaspoon plus ⅛ teaspoon salt**
2	**tablespoons capers**
½	**cup plain bread crumbs**
1	**package (5 ounces) chopped kale**
	Freshly cracked black pepper
2	**ounces (½ cup) shaved Parmesan cheese**

• In a bowl, whisk together egg yolks, lemon juice, garlic, anchovy paste, mustard, olive oil, 2 tablespoons of the vegetable oil and ¼ teaspoon of the salt until well combined. Stir in capers and set aside.

• In a sauté pan, heat remaining 1 tablespoon vegetable oil over medium heat. Add bread crumbs and stir for 2 minutes, until golden brown. Cool.

• Toss kale with dressing, remaining ⅛ teaspoon salt and the pepper. Gently fold in bread crumbs and Parmesan.

PER SALAD 328 **CAL**; 27 g **FAT** (6 g **SAT**); 9 g **PRO**; 16 g **CARB**; 1 g **FIBER**; 884 mg **SODIUM**; 112 mg **CHOL**

Spanish cured chorizo is similar to Italian pepperoni. It's a dried and cured sausage that does not need to be cooked before eating—just sliced thinly or cut in small dice.

Chipotle Potato Salad

MAKES 6 side salads **PREP** 15 minutes
COOK 12 minutes

2	pounds baby red potatoes (1 to 2 inches wide)
3	ounces cured chorizo, diced
¾	cup light mayonnaise
¼	cup sour cream
3	chipotles in adobo, seeded and chopped, plus 2 teaspoons adobo sauce
1	tablespoon cider vinegar
¼	teaspoon salt
1	cup fresh cilantro, chopped
6	scallions, sliced

• Place potatoes in a pot and cover with 1 inch cold water. Bring to a boil. Reduce to a simmer, cover and cook for 12 minutes, until fork-tender. Drain and cool slightly. Cut into bite-size pieces.

• Meanwhile, heat a sauté pan over medium heat. Add chorizo. Cook for 5 minutes, until slightly crispy. Set aside.

• In a large bowl, whisk together mayonnaise, sour cream, chipotles and adobo sauce, vinegar and salt. Fold in potatoes, chorizo, cilantro and scallions.

PER SALAD 306 CAL; 18 g FAT (5 g SAT); 7 g PRO; 29 g CARB; 4 g FIBER; 676 mg SODIUM; 30 mg CHOL

Chicken, Fennel and Orange Salad

MAKES 4 main-dish salads **PREP** 15 minutes **MARINATE** 1 hour **GRILL** 12 minutes

¼	cup extra-virgin olive oil
2	tablespoons fresh orange juice
2	tablespoons white wine vinegar
1	teaspoon honey
¾	teaspoon salt
¼	teaspoon black pepper
1	pound boneless, skinless chicken breasts
1	small head fennel, cored and thinly sliced
4	medium oranges, peeled and thinly sliced into rounds
1	can (15 ounces) cannellini beans, drained and rinsed
4	cups arugula
½	cup pitted Kalamata olives, roughly chopped

• In a bowl, whisk together oil, orange juice, vinegar, honey, ½ teaspoon of the salt and ⅛ teaspoon of the pepper. Pour half the dressing (about ¼ cup) into a large resealable plastic bag; add chicken breasts. Marinate in the refrigerator for 1 hour. Set aside remaining dressing.

• Heat a grill or grill pan to medium. Pat chicken dry and discard marinade. Grill for 6 minutes per side (12 minutes total) or until 165°. Cool chicken slightly, then chop into 1-inch pieces.

• Toss chicken with fennel, oranges, beans, arugula, olives, reserved dressing, remaining ¼ teaspoon salt and remaining ⅛ teaspoon pepper.

PER SALAD 462 CAL; 19 g FAT (3 g SAT); 33 g PRO; 40 g CARB; 9 g FIBER; 907 mg SODIUM; 66 mg CHOL

CHIPOTLE POTATO SALAD

CITRUSY SALMON SALAD

Citrusy Salmon Salad

MAKES 4 main-dish salads PREP 15 minutes
COOK 6 minutes

- 1¼ **pounds skin-on salmon fillets**
- ¾ **teaspoon salt**
- ⅛ **teaspoon black pepper**
- 3 **tablespoons extra-virgin olive oil**
- 2 **tablespoons lemon juice plus 2 teaspoons zest**
- 1 **teaspoon Dijon mustard**
- 10 **ounces frozen peas, thawed**
- 6 **cups watercress**
- 1 **package (5 ounces) mesclun**
- ½ **cup roasted and salted sunflower seeds**

• Pat salmon dry and season with ¼ teaspoon of the salt and the pepper. Heat 1 tablespoon of the oil in a sauté pan over medium-high heat. Place fillets skin side up in pan; cook for 3 minutes. Flip and cook for 3 minutes more for medium. Cool slightly on a plate, then cover with plastic wrap and refrigerate until cold.

• In a large bowl, whisk remaining 2 tablespoons oil, the lemon juice and zest, mustard and remaining ½ teaspoon salt. Remove salmon from fridge and flake into large pieces with a fork, discarding skin. Gently toss salmon in bowl with peas, watercress, mesclun and sunflower seeds.

PER SALAD 428 CAL; 24 g FAT (3 g SAT); 39 g PRO; 16 g CARB; 6 g FIBER; 714 mg SODIUM; 81 mg CHOL

THAI BEEF SALAD

Thai Beef Salad

MAKES 4 main-dish salads PREP 25 minutes COOK 10 minutes LET REST 10 minutes

- 3 **tablespoons lime juice**
- 2 **tablespoons fish sauce**
- 2 **tablespoons canola oil**
- 1 **tablespoon minced garlic**
- 1½ **teaspoons sugar**
- ½ **teaspoon red pepper flakes**
- 1¼ **pounds skirt steak**
- ¼ **teaspoon salt**
- 1 **cup fresh cilantro**
- 1 **cup fresh mint**
- 6 **cups roughly chopped romaine**
- 2 **plum tomatoes, sliced**
- 1 **large red sweet pepper, sliced**
- 1 **cucumber, sliced**
- ⅓ **cup thinly sliced shallots**

• In a bowl, whisk together lime juice, fish sauce, oil, garlic, sugar and red pepper flakes. Set aside.

• Heat a grill or grill pan to medium-high. Spray or brush lightly with oil. Season steak on both sides with salt. Cook on medium-high for 3 to 5 minutes per side, until medium-rare. Let rest 10 minutes to cool, then slice thinly against the grain. (Alternately, steak can be cooked ahead of time, refrigerated, then sliced.)

• Roughly chop cilantro and mint, then gently toss with sliced steak, dressing, romaine, tomatoes, sweet pepper, cucumber and shallots.

PER SALAD 364 CAL; 19 g FAT (5 g SAT); 34 g PRO; 15 g CARB; 5 g FIBER; 954 mg SODIUM; 81 mg CHOL

Persian Lentil and Rice Salad

MAKES 8 side salads **PREP** 15 minutes **COOK** 15 minutes

1	cup uncooked jasmine rice
8	ounces (1¼ cups) red lentils
3	tablespoons extra-virgin olive oil
3	tablespoons pomegranate molasses (see Note)
1¼	teaspoons salt
3	cups packed baby spinach, chopped
1	cup fresh mint, chopped
1	cup dried cherries
1	cup walnuts, toasted and chopped
½	cup crumbled feta cheese

• Cook rice per package directions. Cool 15 minutes in lidded pot. Fluff, then transfer to a rimmed baking sheet. Cool in refrigerator.

• Meanwhile, bring a separate pot of water to a boil. Add lentils. Return to a boil; cook for 6 minutes. Drain and rinse under cold water until cool.

• In a large bowl, whisk together oil, pomegranate molasses and salt. Stir into cooled rice and lentils. Gently fold in spinach, mint, cherries, walnuts and feta. Serve at room temperature or chilled.

Note: Can't find pomegranate molasses? Whisk together 1 tablespoon honey with 2 tablespoons pure pomegranate juice.

PER SALAD 358 CAL; 15 g FAT (3 g SAT); 12 g PRO; 44 g CARB; 8 g FIBER; 489 mg SODIUM; 8 mg CHOL

Shrimp Pesto Pasta Salad

MAKES 6 main-dish salads **PREP** 20 minutes **COOK** 7 minutes

3	cups packed fresh basil
½	cup shelled unsalted pistachios
1	clove garlic, halved
1	tablespoon lemon juice
½	cup extra-virgin olive oil
¼	cup grated Parmesan cheese, plus more for serving
¾	teaspoon salt
⅛	teaspoon black pepper
1	pound dry cavatappi
1	pound raw peeled and deveined shrimp
1	pound asparagus, trimmed and cut into 1-inch pieces

• Combine basil, pistachios, garlic and lemon juice in a food processor. While running, drizzle in olive oil until well combined. Remove to a large bowl. Stir in Parmesan, salt and pepper. Set aside.

• Bring a large pot of lightly salted water to a boil. Add cavatappi; return to a boil and cook for 5 minutes. Add shrimp and asparagus to pot; return to a boil and cook for 2 more minutes. Reserve ¾ cup pasta water. Drain and rinse pasta, shrimp and asparagus under cold water. Stir pasta water into pesto. Fold pasta, shrimp and asparagus into pesto. Serve at room temperature or chilled, sprinkled with Parmesan, if desired.

PER SALAD 577 CAL; 26 g FAT (4 g SAT); 27 g PRO; 61 g CARB; 5 g FIBER; 482 mg SODIUM; 115 mg CHOL

SHRIMP PESTO PASTA SALAD

Summer Spelt Salad

MAKES 6 side salads **SOAK** overnight
PREP 15 minutes **COOK** 40 minutes
COOL 30 minutes

1½	cups spelt, soaked overnight
3	tablespoons extra-virgin olive oil
3	tablespoons tarragon vinegar
1	tablespoon honey
1¼	teaspoons salt
¼	teaspoon black pepper
2	cups heirloom or regular cherry tomatoes, halved
8	radishes, thinly sliced
2	tablespoons tarragon
1	cup sprouts

• Drain spelt. Add to a pot with 6 cups water. Bring to a boil. Cover and reduce to a simmer; cook for 40 minutes. (Cooking will take longer if grains are not soaked.) Drain and transfer to a large bowl.

• In a small bowl, whisk together oil, vinegar, honey, salt and pepper. Pour half over warm spelt. Cool for 30 minutes. Stir in tomatoes, radishes, tarragon and remaining dressing. Top with sprouts. Serve immediately or chilled.

PER SALAD 233 **CAL**; 8 g **FAT** (1 g **SAT**); 7 g **PRO**; 37 g **CARB**; 5 g **FIBER**; 393 mg **SODIUM**; 0 mg **CHOL**

GRILLED FRUIT SALAD

Grilled Fruit Salad

MAKES 12 servings **PREP** 30 minutes **GRILL** 18 minutes

2	cups mango, cut into 2-inch pieces
2	cups pineapple, cut into 2-inch pieces
2	cups watermelon, cut into 2-inch pieces
2	cups strawberries, trimmed
2	bananas, peeled
1	lime, halved
⅓	cup pepitas
⅛	teaspoon salt
⅛	teaspoon cayenne pepper

• Heat a grill or grill pan to medium. Skewer mango, pineapple and watermelon pieces and strawberries (about 12 skewers). Grill half the skewers for 3 minutes. Turn and grill for 3 minutes more. Repeat with second batch of skewers. Grill bananas for 3 minutes; turn and grill another 3 minutes. Grill lime halves cut side down for 3 minutes (add to grill when bananas are turned).

• Slice bananas and place in a bowl with fruit (removed from skewers). Juice lime and pour over fruit. Gently toss with pepitas, salt and cayenne. Serve warm.

PER SERVING 83 **CAL**; 2 g **FAT** (0 g **SAT**); 2 g **PRO**; 17 g **CARB**; 2 g **FIBER**; 27 mg **SODIUM**; 0 mg **CHOL**

BLUEBERRY-THYME PIE,
PAGE 227

AUGUST

202

212

223

OVENS OFF

Keep it cool with six no-cook meals!

SINGAPORE SHRIMP
NOODLES, PAGE 201

CHICKEN AND GOAT CHEESE
CREPES, PAGE 202

GREENS AND GRAIN SALAD

Boost the protein in any salad with canned salmon. It's an easy, economical alternative to fresh salmon with all the health benefits, including heart-healthy omega-3 fatty acids.

SINGAPORE SHRIMP NOODLES

Greens and Grain Salad

MAKES 4 servings PREP 15 minutes
MICROWAVE 3 minutes

- **1** container (6 ounces) plain fat-free yogurt (not Greek)
- **2** tablespoons white wine vinegar
- **⅓** cup chopped fresh dill
- **1** teaspoon sugar
- **½** teaspoon salt
- **¼** teaspoon black pepper
- **1** cup frozen fully cooked wheat berries
- **1** cup cooked lentils
- **1** package (8.8 ounces) refrigerated cooked beets, diced
- **8** cups chopped butter lettuce
- **8** cups baby spinach
- **½** cup chopped unsalted pistachios
- **1** can (6 ounces) canned salmon, drained (optional)

• In a large bowl, stir together yogurt, vinegar, fresh dill, sugar, salt and pepper. Set aside.

• Heat wheat berries in a microwave-safe bowl for 2 minutes; stir and heat 1 minute more, until thawed.

• Toss wheat berries, lentils, beets, lettuce, spinach and pistachios in bowl with dressing. Fold in salmon, if desired.

PER SERVING 424 **CAL**; 10 g **FAT** (1 g **SAT**); 33 g **PRO**; 64 g **CARB**; 15 g **FIBER**; 765 mg **SODIUM**; 20 mg **CHOL**

Singapore Shrimp Noodles

MAKES 4 servings PREP 15 minutes SOAK 10 minutes MICROWAVE 2 minutes

- **1** package (7 ounces) vermicelli rice noodles
- **3** tablespoons vegetable oil
- **3** tablespoons low-sodium soy sauce
- **2** tablespoons rice vinegar
- **2** tablespoons curry powder
- **2** teaspoons sesame oil
- **1** 1-inch piece ginger, peeled and grated
- **1** clove garlic, grated
- **1** pound frozen cooked, peeled and deveined shrimp, thawed
- **1** red sweet pepper, thinly sliced
- **1** bunch scallions, sliced
- **1** cup bean sprouts
- **1** jalapeño, thinly sliced
- **¼** cup fresh cilantro, chopped

• In a large bowl, cover rice noodles with 2 inches very hot water. Soak for 10 minutes. Microwave for 2 minutes. Let cool slightly, then carefully remove noodles to a cutting board, reserving ¼ cup of the soaking liquid. Cut noodles into thirds.

• In the same bowl, whisk together reserved liquid, vegetable oil, soy sauce, vinegar, curry powder, sesame oil, ginger and garlic. Return noodles to bowl, and toss with shrimp, red pepper, scallions, bean sprouts, jalapeño and cilantro.

PER SERVING 427 **CAL**; 15 g **FAT** (2 g **SAT**); 29 g **PRO**; 44 g **CARB**; 4 g **FIBER**; 717 mg **SODIUM**; 221 mg **CHOL**

CHICKEN AND GOAT CHEESE CREPES

Quinoa with Summer Vegetables and Sausage

MAKES 4 servings **PREP** 15 minutes
MICROWAVE 8 minutes

2	tablespoons extra-virgin olive oil
2	tablespoons white balsamic vinegar
1	tablespoon Dijon mustard
¼	teaspoon salt
¼	teaspoon black pepper
16	ounces (about 3 cups) cooked plain quinoa
1	package (12 ounces) Al Fresco roasted garlic chicken sausage
2	cups frozen fire-roasted corn
2	cups grape tomatoes, halved
1	cup roasted red peppers, sliced
1	tablespoon chopped fresh thyme

• In a large bowl, whisk together oil, vinegar, mustard, salt and black pepper. Set aside.

• Heat quinoa in microwave 3 to 4 minutes, or per package directions. Place sausage on a plate; microwave 2 minutes. Allow sausage to rest while heating corn in a microwave-safe bowl with 1 tablespoon water for 2 minutes. Slice sausage into coins.

• Toss quinoa, sausage, corn, tomatoes, roasted red peppers and thyme in bowl with dressing. Serve.

PER SERVING 459 **CAL**; 17 g **FAT** (3 g **SAT**); 23 g **PRO**; 54 g **CARB**; 6 g **FIBER**; 782 mg **SODIUM**; 65 mg **CHOL**

Chicken and Goat Cheese Crepes

MAKES 4 servings (2½ crepes per serving) **PREP** 15 minutes

5	cups packed arugula
1	cup fresh basil leaves
1	teaspoon extra-virgin olive oil
1	teaspoon fresh lemon juice
	Pinch salt
	Freshly cracked black pepper
1	container (5.3 ounces) Chavrie sweet basil goat cheese
1	package (5 ounces) Melissa's ready-to-use crepes
2½	cups shredded rotisserie chicken

• In a bowl, gently toss arugula, basil, oil, lemon juice, salt and pepper.

• Spread 1 tablespoon of the goat cheese on each crepe. Add ¼ cup of the shredded chicken, then top with ½ cup of the greens. Fold or roll and serve.

PER SERVING 390 **CAL**; 16 g **FAT** (6 g **SAT**); 33 g **PRO**; 24 g **CARB**; 1 g **FIBER**; 427 mg **SODIUM**; 118 mg **CHOL**

QUINOA WITH SUMMER
VEGETABLES AND SAUSAGE

BLT-STUFFED TOMATOES

What better way to enhance the perfect summer tomato than by stuffing it with a savory mixture of wild rice, Canadian bacon, walnuts and herbs in a creamy mayo-yogurt sauce?

BLT-Stuffed Tomatoes

MAKES 4 servings **PREP** 15 minutes **MICROWAVE** 3 minutes

4	large beefsteak tomatoes (14 ounces each)
1	package (10 ounces) frozen fully cooked wild rice (such as Stahlbush Island Farms), or 1¾ cups cooked wild rice
4	ounces Canadian bacon, diced
⅓	cup finely chopped walnuts
3	tablespoons light mayonnaise
3	tablespoons nonfat yogurt
¼	cup chopped fresh parsley
¼	teaspoon freshly cracked black pepper
¼	teaspoon plus a pinch salt
8	cups chopped romaine
1	tablespoon extra-virgin olive oil
1	tablespoon white wine vinegar
4	ounces French bread

• Cut the top fifth off tomatoes and scoop out flesh. Discard or save for another use.

• In a microwave-safe bowl, heat wild rice for 2 minutes. Stir in Canadian bacon and cook 1 minute more. Stir in walnuts, mayonnaise, yogurt, parsley, pepper and ¼ teaspoon of the salt. Scoop rice mixture evenly into tomatoes; replace the tops.

• Toss romaine with oil, vinegar and a pinch of salt. Serve tomatoes alongside salad and bread.

PER SERVING 411 **CAL**; 16 g **FAT** (3 g **SAT**); 18 g **PRO**; 53 g **CARB**; 10 g **FIBER**; 746 mg **SODIUM**; 18 mg **CHOL**

"Tartine" is French for a slice of buttered bread—but in practice, it is more than that. A tartine is essentially a simple open-face sandwich. Mix and match these fresh, light slices and add a cup of chilled Cucumber-Avocado Soup for a summer supper that satisfies.

Cucumber-Avocado Soup

MAKES 4 servings **PREP** 10 minutes

1	pound cucumbers, peeled
1	avocado, pitted and peeled
2	scallions, roughly chopped
3	tablespoons lime juice
½	cup fresh cilantro
½	teaspoon plus ⅛ teaspoon salt
⅛	teaspoon cayenne pepper

• In a food processor, combine all ingredients with ½ cup cold water. Process until smooth.

PER SERVING 100 CAL; 8 g FAT (1 g SAT); 2 g PRO; 8 g CARB; 4 g FIBER; 371 mg SODIUM; 0 mg CHOL

Radish-Crème Fraîche Tartine

MAKES 1 tartine **PREP** 5 minutes

1	tablespoon crème fraîche
1	slice black rye bread (such as Rubschlager)
1	thinly sliced radish
1	tablespoon sprouts
	Sea salt and freshly cracked black pepper

• Spread crème fraîche on bread. Layer on radish slices and scatter sprouts over tartine. Season with salt and pepper. Cut in half.

PER SERVING 143 CAL; 6 g FAT (6 g SAT); 4 g PRO; 22 g CARB; 4 g FIBER; 178 mg SODIUM; 20 mg CHOL

Egg Tartine

MAKES 1 tartine **PREP** 5 minutes

1	peeled hard-cooked egg (such as Eggland's Best), thinly sliced
1	slice black rye bread (such as Rubschlager)
2	teaspoons capers
2	teaspoons fresh dill, chopped
	Olive oil, salt and freshly cracked black pepper

• Layer egg slices on bread. Top with capers and chopped dill. Drizzle with olive oil and season with salt and pepper. Cut in half.

PER SERVING 209 CAL; 10 g FAT (2 g SAT); 9 g PRO; 22 g CARB; 4 g FIBER; 402 mg SODIUM; 212 mg CHOL

Red Pepper-Hummus Tartine

MAKES 1 tartine **PREP** 5 minutes

4	teaspoons plain hummus
1	slice black rye bread (such as Rubschlager)
2	tablespoons chopped roasted red pepper
1	teaspoon tahini
	Harissa and fresh parsley

• Spread hummus on bread. Scatter roasted red pepper on top, then drizzle with tahini. Garnish with harissa and parsley. Cut in half.

PER SERVING 163 CAL; 5 g FAT (1 g SAT); 6 g PRO; 27 g CARB; 6 g FIBER; 354 mg SODIUM; 0 mg CHOL

TARTINE AND CUCUMBER-
AVOCADO SOUP

RIPE FOR THE PICKING

Ten takes on fruit-filled summer sweets.

RAINBOW FRUIT
SKEWERS, PAGE 211

**STONE-FRUIT COBBLER,
PAGE 212**

STRAWBERRY FROZEN
ZABAGLIONE

Strawberry Frozen Zabaglione

MAKES 12 servings **PREP** 25 minutes
COOK 15 minutes **FREEZE** 2 hours, then overnight

1	**quart (1 pound) hulled and sliced strawberries**
1	**cup sugar**
4	**egg yolks**
2	**eggs**
¾	**cup Moscato**
	Red food coloring
1	**cup heavy cream**
	Halved strawberries, for garnish (optional)
	Additional whipped cream (optional)

• Coat a 9 x 5 x 2-inch loaf pan with nonstick cooking spray. Line pan with plastic wrap, smoothing any wrinkles.

• Blend strawberries in a blender until smooth. Pour into a small bowl and stir in ¼ cup of the sugar. Set aside.

• On top of a double boiler over simmering water, whisk together egg yolks, eggs and remaining ¾ cup sugar. Whisk in Moscato. Continue to whisk until mixture reaches 160° and mounds on top of itself when whisk is lifted, about 15 minutes.

• Remove top of double boiler and place in an ice-water bath. Whisk egg mixture until cool. Stir in strawberry puree. Place half the mixture in a separate bowl and tint with a few drops of red food coloring.

• Beat cream in a bowl until soft peaks form. Fold half the whipped cream into red portion and half into untinted portion in the other bowl.

• Spread red mixture into prepared pan; freeze for 2 hours. Spoon untinted mixture on top of frozen layer. Cover and freeze overnight.

• To unmold and serve, briefly dip loaf pan into warm water. Invert onto serving plate and shake gently. Remove pan and plastic wrap. Garnish with whipped cream and halved strawberries, if desired.

PER SERVING 197 **CAL**; 13 g **FAT** (8 g **SAT**); 3 g **PRO**; 16 g **CARB**; 1 g **FIBER**; 27 mg **SODIUM**; 144 mg **CHOL**

RAINBOW FRUIT SKEWERS

Rainbow Fruit Skewers

MAKES 12 skewers **PREP** 20 minutes

12	**10-inch wood skewers**		12	**large green grapes**
12	**mint leaves**			**Greek vanilla yogurt (optional)**
6	**strawberries, tops removed (if desired), halved lengthwise**			
12	**1-inch pieces watermelon**			
12	**1-inch pieces mango**			
12	**1-inch pieces pineapple**			
12	**1-inch pieces honeydew melon**			
12	**½-inch-thick half-moons kiwi**			

• On each skewer, thread one mint leaf; one strawberry half; one piece each watermelon, mango, pineapple, honeydew and kiwi; and one grape. Serve with yogurt, if desired.

PER SKEWER 47 **CAL**; 0 g **FAT** (0 g **SAT**); 1 g **PRO**; 12 g **CARB**; 1 g **FIBER**; 6 mg **SODIUM**; 0 mg **CHOL**

STONE-FRUIT COBBLER

Peach Melba Ice Cream Cake

MAKES 16 servings **PREP** 20 minutes
COOK 10 minutes **FREEZE** overnight
LET STAND 10 minutes

1	package (10 ounces) shortbread cookies, finely crushed
¼	cup unsalted butter, melted
2	packages (6 ounces each) raspberries (3 cups)
3	tablespoons sugar
2	teaspoons cornstarch
3	containers (14 ounces each) vanilla ice cream, softened slightly
4	fresh peaches, peeled and cut into ¼-inch slices
3	tablespoons toasted sliced almonds

• Place crushed cookies in a large bowl; stir in butter until thoroughly combined. Press mixture into the bottom and partially up the side of a 9-inch springform pan. Refrigerate until ready to fill.

• Place raspberries, 2 tablespoons of the sugar and the cornstarch in a small saucepan. Over medium heat, bring to a gentle simmer; cook 10 minutes, stirring occasionally. Strain and let cool.

• Stir ⅓ cup of the raspberry puree into softened ice cream and swirl. Spoon into springform pan and level off with a small spatula. Freeze overnight.

• Remove cake from freezer and let stand at room temperature for 10 minutes. Toss peaches with remaining 1 tablespoon sugar; fan over top. Wrap a warm damp towel around side of pan. Run a spatula around edge of cake; carefully remove side of pan.

• Garnish with toasted almonds and serve with remaining raspberry puree.

PER SERVING 376 **CAL**; 23 g **FAT** (12 g **SAT**); 6 g **PRO**; 38 g **CARB**; 2 g **FIBER**; 136 mg **SODIUM**; 89 mg **CHOL**

Stone-Fruit Cobbler

MAKES 8 servings **PREP** 25 minutes **BAKE** at 400° for 25 minutes

2½	pounds peaches, plums and nectarines, peeled and cut into chunks (about 5 cups)
1	cup plus 3 tablespoons sugar
2	tablespoons tapioca
¾	teaspoon ground ginger
½	teaspoon ground cinnamon
¼	teaspoon ground nutmeg
¼	teaspoon salt
1	cup Bisquick
2	tablespoons unsalted butter, melted
⅓	cup milk
	Vanilla ice cream (optional)

• Heat oven to 400°. Coat a 6-cup shallow baking dish with nonstick cooking spray.

• In a large bowl, combine fruit, 1 cup of the sugar, the tapioca, ginger, cinnamon, nutmeg and salt. Spoon into prepared dish.

• In a medium bowl, whisk together Bisquick, 2 tablespoons of the sugar, the butter and milk. Stir until thick batter forms. Dollop heaping tablespoonfuls over fruit. Sprinkle remaining 1 tablespoons sugar over top. Bake at 400° for 25 minutes, until fruit is bubbly and topping has browned. Serve warm with vanilla ice cream, if desired.

PER SERVING 220 **CAL**; 6 g **FAT** (3 g **SAT**); 3 g **PRO**; 45 g **CARB**; 2 g **FIBER**; 266 mg **SODIUM**; 9 mg **CHOL**

**PEACH MELBA ICE
CREAM CAKE**

Mixed-Berry Tiramisu Cake

MAKES 10 servings **PREP** 25 minutes
MICROWAVE 1 minute **REFRIGERATE** overnight

1	**quart (1 pound) strawberries, hulled and sliced**
1	**cup sugar**
½	**cup liquid egg substitute**
1	**package (8 ounces) mascarpone cheese**
1	**teaspoon vanilla extract**
1	**cup heavy cream**
2	**packages (3 ounces each) soft ladyfingers**
1	**package (6 ounces) raspberries, plus more for garnish**
1	**package (6 ounces) blueberries, plus more for garnish**
4	**tablespoons cocoa powder**

• Place strawberries and ½ cup of the sugar in a medium bowl. Cover with plastic wrap and microwave on high for 1 minute. Stir and let cool.

• In a large bowl, beat liquid egg substitute and remaining ½ cup sugar until foamy. Add mascarpone and vanilla; beat until smooth. In a separate bowl, whip cream until soft peaks form. Fold cream into mascarpone mixture.

• Arrange half the ladyfingers in the bottom of a 9-inch square glass baking dish. Combine strawberries, raspberries and blueberries; spoon half the mixture over ladyfingers, followed by half the mascarpone mixture. Sift 1½ tablespoons of the cocoa powder over the top. Repeat layering.

• Cover and refrigerate overnight. To serve, sift remaining 1 tablespoon cocoa powder over top and garnish with additional berries.

PER SERVING 365 **CAL**; 21 g **FAT** (11 g **SAT**); 6 g **PRO**; 42 g **CARB**; 3 g **FIBER**; 167 mg **SODIUM**; 97 mg **CHOL**

GRILLED FIGS WITH RUM-INFUSED RICOTTA

Grilled Figs with Rum-Infused Ricotta

MAKES 4 servings **PREP** 10 minutes **GRILL** 4 minutes

⅓	**cup plus 2 tablespoons honey**
2	**tablespoons unsalted butter**
1	**cup ricotta**
1	**tablespoon rum, or 1 teaspoon rum extract**
12	**fresh figs, halved lengthwise**

• Heat a gas grill to medium-high or heat a stovetop grill pan over medium-high heat.

• In a small saucepan, bring ⅓ cup of the honey to a gentle simmer and stir in butter until melted. Set aside.

• In a bowl, combine ricotta, rum and remaining 2 tablespoons honey. Set aside.

• Lightly grease grates of grill. Dip figs in honey-butter mixture and grill, cut side down, for 2 minutes. Turn and grill an additional 1 to 2 minutes or until softened and nice grill marks form.

• Serve with rum-infused ricotta.

PER SERVING 378 **CAL**; 11 g **FAT** (7 g **SAT**); 8 g **PRO**; 65 g **CARB**; 4 g **FIBER**; 81 mg **SODIUM**; 34 mg **CHOL**

HONEYDEW-KIWI ICE

Plum and Blackberry Tart

MAKES 6 servings   **PREP** 15 minutes
BAKE at 400° for 17 minutes

1	sheet puff pastry (from a 17.5-ounce package)
¼	cup agave nectar
2	teaspoons fresh thyme or lemon thyme leaves
2	red plums, thinly sliced
2	black plums, thinly sliced
12	blackberries, halved
3	ounces goat cheese
3	tablespoons milk

• Heat oven to 400°. Lightly coat a baking sheet with nonstick cooking spray.

• Unfold pastry sheet on prepared baking sheet. Cut a 1-inch-wide strip from each long side. Brush a 1-inch-wide strip along the two long sides with water. Lay a cut strip along each side to form a border. Brush bottom of tart with 2 tablespoons of the agave nectar and sprinkle thyme over the bottom. Using a fork, prick pastry all over, about 1 inch apart.

• Bake at 400° for 16 to 17 minutes or until nicely browned. Transfer baking sheet to a wire rack; let cool. Gently press down center of tart if puffed.

• Fan plums and blackberries in a decorative pattern over tart. Drizzle remaining 2 tablespoons agave nectar over top. Whip goat cheese and milk together and dollop over top. Return to oven for a few minutes to gently heat fruit and goat cheese. Serve warm or at room temperature.

PER SERVING 142 **CAL**; 5 g **FAT** (3 g **SAT**); 4 g **PRO**; 21 g **CARB**; 2 g **FIBER**; 89 mg **SODIUM**; 7 mg **CHOL**

Honeydew-Kiwi Ice

MAKES 6 servings   **PREP** 15 minutes   **FREEZE** 3 hours

2	cups cubed honeydew melon
1	cup cubed kiwi
¼	cup light corn syrup
¼	cup honey
2	tablespoons sugar
1	tablespoon lemon juice
	Sliced kiwi for garnish (optional)
	Fresh mint for garnish (optional)

• Blend honeydew, kiwi, ½ cup water, corn syrup, honey, sugar and lemon juice in a food processor until smooth. Pour into a 13 x 9 x 2- inch baking dish.

• Freeze for 3 hours or until firm. Cut into pieces and place in food processor. Whirl until smooth.

• To serve, scoop into dishes and garnish with sliced kiwi and mint, if desired.

PER SERVING 131 **CAL**; 0 g **FAT**; 1 g **PRO**; 35 g **CARB**; 1 g **FIBER**; 20 mg **SODIUM**; 0 mg **CHOL**

PLUM AND
BLACKBERRY TART

**TROPICAL FRUIT
WAFFLE CONES**

BLUEBERRY-CHERRY
BUCKLE

Tropical Fruit Waffle Cones

MAKES 6 servings **PREP** 15 minutes
MICROWAVE about 2 minutes

4	ounces bittersweet chocolate, chopped
6	waffle cones (such as Keebler)
1	cup diced mango
1	cup diced pineapple
1	cup diced papaya
1	pint coconut gelato (such as Talenti Caribbean Coconut)
½	cup toasted coconut

• Place chocolate in a medium bowl. Microwave on high for 1 minute and stir. Continue to microwave in 30-second intervals, stirring after each, until smooth.

• With a pastry brush, cover the inside and rims of waffle cones with melted chocolate. Allow chocolate to dry.

• In a medium bowl, combine mango, pineapple and papaya. Fill each cone with ⅓ cup gelato and ½ cup fruit. Sprinkle toasted coconut over each and serve.

PER SERVING 343 **CAL**; 11 g **FAT** (6 g **SAT**); 5 g **PRO**; 51 g **CARB**; 4 g **FIBER**; 44 mg **SODIUM**; 0 mg **CHOL**

Blueberry-Cherry Buckle

MAKES 12 servings **PREP** 25 minutes **BAKE** at 350° for 55 minutes **COOL** 15 minutes

TOPPING

½	cup all-purpose flour
¼	cup packed light brown sugar
¼	cup granulated sugar
½	teaspoon ground cinnamon
4	tablespoons cold unsalted butter, cut into pieces

BATTER

2	cups all-purpose flour
2	teaspoons baking powder
¼	teaspoon salt
½	cup unsalted butter, softened
½	cup granulated sugar
1	egg
1	teaspoon vanilla extract
½	cup milk
1	cup blueberries
1	cup dark cherries, pitted
	Crème fraîche (optional)

• Heat oven to 350°. Butter and flour a 10-inch tube pan with a removable bottom.

• **Topping.** In a small bowl, combine flour, sugars and cinnamon. Cut in butter until crumbly.

• **Batter.** In a medium bowl, whisk together flour, baking powder and salt.

• In a large bowl, beat butter until smooth. Add sugar; beat until fluffy. Beat in egg and vanilla. On low speed, add flour mixture alternately with milk, beating well after each addition.

• Spread half the batter in prepared pan. Cover with blueberries and cherries. Drop remaining batter on top by tablespoonfuls. Cover with topping.

• Bake at 350° for 50 to 55 minutes, until golden brown. Remove pan to a wire rack. Run a small offset spatula around side. Cool for 15 minutes. Remove side. Run spatula around center and bottom of pan; place two wide spatulas under cake and gently lift cake from pan bottom. Serve with crème fraîche, if desired.

PER SERVING 271 **CAL**; 12 g **FAT** (8 g **SAT**); 4 g **PRO**; 38 g **CARB**; 1 g **FIBER**; 129 mg **SODIUM**; 49 mg **CHOL**

SUMMER FEAST

Gather friends and family for a meal that celebrates the season's peak produce.

ORGANIC BABY
LETTUCES AND QUINOA
SALAD, PAGE 224

CHICKEN CACCIATORE,
PAGE 223

SUMMER MINESTRONE

Summer Minestrone

MAKES 12 servings **PREP** 30 minutes
COOK 16 minutes

2	**tablespoons olive oil**
1	**onion, chopped**
4	**cloves garlic, chopped**
2	**carrots, cut into ¼-inch coins**
1	**large zucchini, cut into ¼-inch half-moons**
1	**summer squash, cut into ¼-inch half-moons**
½	**pound green beans**
2	**ears corn, sliced or kernels cut off cobs**
2	**vegetable bouillon cubes dissolved in 6 cups water**
4	**cups plum tomatoes, seeded and diced**
1	**teaspoon dried Italian seasoning**
1	**teaspoon salt**
½	**teaspoon black pepper**
8	**ounces ditalini pasta**
1	**can (15 ounces) red kidney beans, drained and rinsed**
1	**tablespoon fresh oregano leaves**
1	**package fully cooked Italian seasoned chicken sausage, cut into ¼-inch coins (optional)**
1	**bag (8 ounces) baby spinach**
1	**cup fresh basil leaves**
	Grated Parmesan cheese (optional)

• Heat oil in a large soup pot over medium-high heat. Add onion and garlic; cook 3 minutes, stirring occasionally. Add carrots, zucchini, squash, green beans, corn, broth, tomatoes, Italian seasoning, salt and pepper. Bring to a boil and simmer 3 minutes. Add pasta and cook 8 minutes.

• Stir in kidney beans and oregano. Simmer 2 minutes more, until pasta is tender. If using sausage, add at this time. Gradually stir in spinach until wilted. Add basil.

• Serve with Parmesan, if desired.

PER SERVING 202 **CAL**; 4 g **FAT** (1 g **SAT**); 8 g **PRO**; 37 g **CARB**; 8 g **FIBER**; 383 mg **SODIUM**; 0 mg **CHOL**

Chicken Cacciatore

MAKES 6 servings **PREP** 20 minutes **COOK** 41 minutes

2	**tablespoons olive oil**
1	**whole cut-up chicken (8 pieces; about 5 pounds), skin removed (reserve wings for another use)**
1½	**teaspoons salt**
¼	**teaspoon black pepper**
1	**large onion, diced**
1	**large green bell pepper, seeded and diced**
2	**fresh hot cherry peppers, seeded and sliced**
4	**cloves garlic, sliced**
2	**cups quartered mixed mushrooms, such as button, baby bella and shiitake**
3	**tablespoons tomato paste**
1	**cup chicken broth**
6	**cups diced, seeded plum tomatoes (about 2½ pounds)**
2	**sprigs fresh oregano**
2	**sprigs fresh thyme**
½	**cup fresh basil leaves**
	Polenta (optional)

• Heat 1 tablespoon of the olive oil in a large Dutch oven over medium-high heat. Season chicken with ½ teaspoon of the salt and ⅛ teaspoon of the black pepper. Cook, skinned side down 5 minutes; turn and cook 3 minutes. Remove to a plate.

• Add remaining 1 tablespoon olive oil; stir in onion, peppers and garlic. Cook 5 minutes, stirring occasionally. Add mushrooms and tomato paste; cook 3 minutes. Stir in broth and tomatoes, scraping any browned bits from bottom of pan. Bring to a boil and simmer, with lid ajar, 10 minutes.

• Stir in remaining 1 teaspoon salt, remaining ⅛ teaspoon black pepper, and the oregano and thyme. Place chicken pieces into sauce and add any accumulated juices from plate. Simmer, with lid ajar, 15 minutes. Stir in basil. Serve with polenta, if desired.

PER SERVING 382 **CAL**; 8 g **FAT** (2 g **SAT**); 60 g **PRO**; 16 g **CARB**; 4 g **FIBER**; 1,128 mg **SODIUM**; 140 mg **CHOL**

ORGANIC BABY
LETTUCES AND
QUINOA SALAD

Classic Pizza Margherita

MAKES 6 servings **PREP** 15 minutes
BAKE at 500° for 14 minutes

1	large heirloom tomato, thinly sliced
½	teaspoon salt
1	recipe Pizza Dough (recipe follows), or 1¼ pounds frozen pizza dough, thawed
1	cup jarred marinara sauce
½	pound fresh mozzarella, sliced
2	tablespoons fresh oregano leaves
2	tablespoons shredded Parmesan cheese
1	tablespoon olive oil
½	cup fresh basil leaves

• Heat oven to 500°.

• Place tomato slices on paper towels and sprinkle with salt. After about 10 minutes, blot dry with additional paper towels.

• Coat a 14-inch perforated pizza pan with nonstick cooking spray. On a well-floured surface, roll out dough to a 14-inch circle. Place on prepared pan.

• Spread dough with sauce; fan on tomato and mozzarella slices. Scatter oregano and Parmesan over top. Drizzle with oil.

• Bake at 500° for 13 to 14 minutes or until nicely browned.

• Gently slide pizza onto a cutting board. Cool slightly and scatter basil over pizza before slicing.

Pizza Dough In a measuring cup, combine 1 cup warm (110°) water with 1 package (0.25 ounce) active dry yeast and 1 teaspoon sugar. Let stand 5 minutes, until foamy. In the bowl of a food processor, add 3 cups all-purpose flour and 1 teaspoon salt. With motor running, add yeast mixture and 2 tablespoons olive oil. Process 1 to 2 minutes, until a ball forms. Place in a bowl coated with olive oil and turn to coat both sides. Cover with plastic wrap and allow to rise for 2 hours. Punch down and proceed with recipe.

PER SERVING 384 **CAL**; 17 g **FAT** (6 g **SAT**); 17 g **PRO**; 48 g **CARB**; 3 g **FIBER**; 1,034 mg **SODIUM**; 31 mg **CHOL**

Organic Baby Lettuces and Quinoa Salad

MAKES 6 servings **PREP** 20 minutes

3	tablespoons extra-virgin olive oil
1	tablespoon balsamic vinegar
1	teaspoon Dijon mustard
¼	teaspoon salt
¼	teaspoon black pepper
6	cups mixed baby organic lettuces
1	cup cooked quinoa, cooled
2	cups corn kernels (from 2 ears corn)
1	cup blanched snow peas
2	cups heirloom cherry tomatoes, halved
1	avocado, diced
½	small red onion, thinly sliced
½	cup shaved Parmesan cheese

• Place oil, vinegar, 1 tablespoon water, mustard, salt and pepper in a small lidded jar. Shake until combined.

• In a large salad bowl, combine lettuces, quinoa, corn, snow peas, tomatoes, avocado and onion. Toss with dressing and top with Parmesan. Serve immediately.

PER SERVING 253 **CAL**; 15 g **FAT** (3 g **SAT**); 7 g **PRO**; 26 g **CARB**; 6 g **FIBER**; 312 mg **SODIUM**; 5 mg **CHOL**

CLASSIC PIZZA MARGHERITA

**RUSTIC GRILLED
VEGETABLE TART**

Rustic Grilled Vegetable Tart

MAKES 8 servings PREP 30 minutes
GRILL 10 minutes BAKE at 450° for 10 minutes
and at 350° for 65 minutes COOL 15 minutes

1	large ear of corn, shucked
2	plum tomatoes, halved lengthwise and seeded
2	scallions, trimmed
1	tablespoon vegetable oil
1	refrigerated ready-to-roll piecrust (from a 14.1-ounce package)
¾	cup shredded dill Havarti cheese
⅛	teaspoon salt
3	eggs
1	egg yolk
½	cup heavy cream
1	tablespoon grainy mustard
	Dill for garnish (optional)

• Heat grill to medium-high. Brush corn, tomatoes and scallions with oil and place on grill. Grill corn 8 to 10 minutes, until lightly charred, turning often. Meanwhile, grill tomatoes and scallions about 3 minutes, turning once until lightly charred. Chop tomatoes and scallions; cut kernels from cob.

• Heat oven to 450°. On a well-floured surface, roll crust into a 17 x 7-inch rectangle and fit into a 13½ x 4½-inch rectangular tart pan with removable bottom. Prick bottom and sides of crust with fork. Line with foil; fill with pie weights or dry beans.

• Bake at 450° for 10 minutes. Remove from oven, remove foil and weights, and reduce heat to 350°.

• Toss together Havarti, corn, tomatoes and scallions; season with salt. Scatter over bottom of tart. Whisk together eggs, egg yolk, cream and mustard. Pour over corn and tomato mixture.

• Place tart pan on a baking sheet. Bake at 350° for 55 to 65 minutes or until a knife inserted near center comes out clean. Remove to a wire rack and cool 15 minutes before removing side of pan.

PER SERVING 286 CAL; 20 g FAT (10 g SAT); 7 g PRO; 19 g CARB; 1 g FIBER; 280 mg SODIUM; 140 mg CHOL

BLUEBERRY-THYME PIE

Blueberry-Thyme Pie

MAKES 12 servings PREP 15 minutes BAKE at 400° for 15 minutes and at 350° for 60 minutes

2	refrigerated ready-to-roll piecrusts
5	cups blueberries
¾	cup plus 1 tablespoon sugar
1	tablespoon fresh thyme leaves
⅓	cup quick-cooking tapioca
1	teaspoon lemon zest
2	tablespoons lemon juice
1	egg white, lightly beaten
	Whipped cream (optional)

• Heat oven to 400°. Fit one piecrust into a 9-inch deep-dish pie plate.

• In a large bowl, toss together blueberries, ¾ cup of the sugar, the thyme, tapioca, lemon zest and juice.

• Cut remaining crust into 1-inch-wide strips with a pastry or pizza cutter.

• Spoon blueberry mixture into pie plate. Weave a lattice top, alternating strips of crust. Crimp edges to seal. Brush crust with egg white and sprinkle with remaining 1 tablespoon sugar.

• Bake pie at 400° for 15 minutes. Reduce heat to 350° and continue baking for 55 to 60 minutes or until center is bubbly and crust is golden. Tent sides with foil after 40 minutes so sides do not get too brown.

• Remove to a wire rack and cool completely. Serve with freshly whipped sweetened cream, if desired.

PER SERVING 248 CAL; 10 g FAT (4 g SAT); 2 g PRO; 41 g CARB; 2 g FIBER; 139 mg SODIUM; 7 mg CHOL

JARFULS OF SWEETS

These summery desserts combine fun and flavor in a pretty presentation.

Peanut Butter S'mores

MAKES 8 servings **PREP** 15 minutes
BAKE at 325° for 30 minutes
MICROWAVE 30 seconds
BROIL 1 minute

9	graham cracker boards, finely crushed
3	tablespoons melted butter
1	teaspoon sugar
⅛	teaspoon salt
8	4.4- or 6.75-ounce glass jars
2	cups marshmallow creme
1	box (18 ounces) Ghirardelli double chocolate brownie mix
1	large egg
⅓	cup oil
4	tablespoons creamy peanut butter
2⅔	cups miniature marshmallows

• Heat oven to 325°. In a small bowl, stir together graham cracker crumbs, melted butter, sugar and salt. Spoon 3 tablespoons crumb mixture into each jar. Press mixture with a small spice jar to flatten into bottom.

• Spoon ¼ cup marshmallow creme into each jar and set jars aside. (Marshmallow creme should spread to edge of jar; spread level with the back of a greased spoon, if necessary.) Meanwhile, prepare brownie mix per package instructions, using egg, oil and ¼ cup water. Divide batter among jars, using a heaping ¼ cup per jar. Bake at 325° for 30 minutes. (Marshmallow may puff up in center of jar.)

• Heat peanut butter in microwave for 30 seconds. Spoon ½ tablespoon peanut butter into each jar. Top with a little of the remaining graham cracker mixture and ⅓ cup miniature marshmallows. Increase oven heat to broil. Broil s'mores 4 inches from heat for 30 seconds to 1 minute, until lightly browned. Cool slightly before serving.

PER SERVING 677 **CAL**; 29 g **FAT** (8 g **SAT**); 6 g **PRO**; 102 g **CARB**; 3 g **FIBER**; 471 mg **SODIUM**; 38 mg **CHOL**

Strawberry Shortcakes

MAKES 6 servings **PREP** 15 minutes
BAKE at 350° per package directions
COOL 10 minutes

1	box (1 pound) pound cake mix
⅔	cup orange juice or water
2	eggs
¼	cup unsalted butter, softened
1	teaspoon orange peel
4	cups sliced strawberries
6	tablespoons strawberry jam
6	9.8-ounce glass jars
2	cups frozen whipped topping, thawed

• Heat oven to 350°. Combine cake mix, orange juice, eggs, butter and orange peel in a large bowl. Beat on low for 30 seconds, until blended, and then on high for 2 minutes. Pour into a greased and floured 9 x 5-inch loaf pan. Bake at 350° per package directions. Cool in pan for 10 minutes, then turn out onto a wire rack and cool completely. Alternately, you can use store-bought pound cake, if desired.

• Combine sliced strawberries, jam and 2 tablespoons water in a medium bowl. Stir until berry slices are well coated with jam.

• Cut pound cake into 12 slices, each about ¾ inch thick. Use a 2½-inch round cookie cutter to cut out 6 cake rounds. Use a 2¾-inch round cutter to cut out 6 slightly larger rounds. Save scraps for snacking. Press one small cake round into bottom of each jar. Top each with ⅓ cup strawberries and sauce and a few tablespoons of the whipped topping. Top with larger cake rounds, another ⅓ cup strawberries and sauce and remaining whipped topping.

PER SERVING 567 **CAL**; 23 g **FAT** (12 g **SAT**); 3 g **PRO**; 84 g **CARB**; 3 g **FIBER**; 405 mg **SODIUM**; 20 mg **CHOL**

Blueberry-Peach Parfaits

MAKES 4 servings **PREP** 15 minutes

1	box (3.8 ounces) vanilla, lemon or banana-flavor instant pudding mix
2	cups milk
8	shortbread cookies
4	7.4-ounce glass jars
1⅓	cups fresh or frozen peach slices
½	cup blueberries

• Combine pudding mix and milk in a bowl. Beat with a hand mixer for 2 minutes, or until soft set.

• Crumble one shortbread cookie into the bottom of one jar. Top with ¼ cup pudding, some peach slices and some blueberries.

• Repeat layering with a second crumbled cookie, 2 tablespoons pudding and more fruit. Top with 2 tablespoons pudding and garnish with more fruit. Repeat with three remaining jars. Refrigerate until serving.

PER SERVING 339 **CAL**; 11 g **FAT** (5 g **SAT**); 7 g **PRO**; 53 g **CARB**; 2 g **FIBER**; 526 mg **SODIUM**; 22 mg **CHOL**

PORK TENDERLOIN
SALAD, PAGE 244

SEPTEMBER

237

244

233

PICK OF THE SEASON

The best of summer produce takes center stage in this gorgeous fresh pasta.

Summertime Linguine

MAKES 6 servings **PREP** 15 minutes **COOK** 14 minutes

4	ears yellow corn, shucked
½	pound haricots verts, halved if desired
1	pound linguine or fettuccine
¼	cup extra-virgin olive oil
6	plum tomatoes (about 14 ounces), cored and cut into 1-inch pieces
1	orange sweet pepper, sliced
2	cloves garlic, sliced
3	scallions, sliced
2	tablespoons fresh lemon juice
2	tablespoons chopped parsley
¾	teaspoon salt
¼	teaspoon cracked black pepper Grated Parmesan cheese to taste (optional)

• Bring a large pot of lightly salted water to a boil. Add corn and haricots verts; cook for 2 minutes. Remove with a slotted spoon to a large bowl.

• Return water to a boil and add linguine. Cook for 12 minutes or per package directions. Drain, reserving ½ cup of the pasta water.

• Meanwhile, heat 3 tablespoons of the olive oil in a large skillet over medium heat. Cut corn kernels from cobs and set aside. Add tomatoes, sweet pepper, garlic and scallions to skillet. Cook, stirring, for 3 minutes.

• In a large bowl, toss pasta with remaining 1 tablespoon olive oil. Add tomato mixture, corn, haricots verts, lemon juice, parsley, salt and black pepper. Gently toss and add some of the reserved pasta water if mixture is too dry. Stir in Parmesan to taste. Serve warm.

PER SERVING 466 **CAL**; 13 g **FAT** (2 g **SAT**); 16 g **PRO**; 77 g **CARB**; 6 g **FIBER**; 354 mg **SODIUM**; 3 mg **CHOL**

HOW DOES YOUR GARDEN GRILL?

With a medley of sizzling farm-fresh vegetables, all in a row.

ASSORTED VEGETABLE PLATTER, PAGE 238

TANDOORI GRILLED
VEGETABLES WITH
MINT RAITA, PAGE 241

SPICY THAI
VEGETABLES

Spicy Thai Vegetables

MAKES 6 servings **PREP** 25 minutes **MARINATE** 15 minutes **GRILL** 13 minutes

3	tablespoons reduced-sodium soy sauce
2	tablespoons canola oil
2	tablespoons lime juice
1	tablespoon fish sauce
1	tablespoon chopped fresh ginger
1	tablespoon chopped lemongrass
2	teaspoons sugar
1	red Thai chile or small serrano chile, seeded and chopped
6	baby bok choy (about 1½ pounds), sliced in half lengthwise, stem end left intact
1	large bunch scallions, trimmed
6	red Thai chiles (optional)
2	cups red, orange and yellow grape tomatoes
4	ounces sugar snap peas
	Lime wedges for squeezing
	Hot chili oil (optional)
	Thai basil (optional)

● In a mini chopper, combine soy sauce, canola oil, lime juice, fish sauce, ginger, lemongrass, sugar and chopped Thai chile or serrano. Whirl to blend. Place in a dish with bok choy, scallions and whole Thai chiles, if using. Marinate 15 minutes.

● Heat a gas grill to medium-high or the coals in a charcoal grill to medium-hot. Lightly grease grates.

● Remove vegetables from marinade and reserve remaining liquid. Grill bok choy for about 4 minutes per side, and scallions and chiles (if using) for 2 to 3 minutes per side. Remove to a platter.

● Place a grilling grid on grill and heat for a few minutes. Grill tomatoes and sugar snap peas on grid for about 5 minutes, turning frequently. Remove to platter with other vegetables; drizzle with reserved marinade. Serve with lime wedges for squeezing and, if desired, hot chili oil. Garnish with Thai basil, if desired.

PER SERVING 96 **CAL**; 5 g **FAT** (0 g **SAT**); 5 g **PRO**; 10 g **CARB**; 3 g **FIBER**; 607 mg **SODIUM**; 0 mg **CHOL**

ASSORTED VEGETABLE PLATTER

Pepper and Cremini Mushroom Skewers

MAKES 6 servings **PREP** 20 minutes
GRILL 20 minutes

2	tablespoons champagne vinegar
1	teaspoon Dijon mustard
⅛	teaspoon plus ¼ teaspoon salt
¼	teaspoon black pepper
6	tablespoons olive oil
2	teaspoons chopped fresh oregano
1	teaspoon chopped fresh thyme
6	metal skewers
1	pound small sweet peppers (such as Pero Farms)
8	ounces cremini mushrooms, woody stems removed and large ones cut in half
1	red onion, peeled and cut into thin wedges
	Oregano and thyme sprigs for garnish

• In a small bowl, whisk together vinegar, mustard, ⅛ teaspoon of the salt and ⅛ teaspoon of the black pepper. Gradually drizzle in oil, whisking constantly until mixture emulsifies; add chopped oregano and thyme. Set aside.

• Thread skewers, using about 4 peppers, alternating with 4 pieces of onion and 4 mushrooms, for each. Brush generously with dressing.

• Heat a gas grill to medium-high or the coals in a charcoal grill to medium-hot. Lightly grease grates. Grill skewers for about 5 minutes, turn and brush with additional dressing. Grill for 5 minutes more or until vegetables are crisp-tender.

• Remove to a serving platter and season with remaining ¼ teaspoon salt and ⅛ teaspoon pepper. Garnish with oregano and thyme sprigs.

PER SERVING 158 **CAL**; 14 g **FAT** (2 g **SAT**); 2 g **PRO**; 8 g **CARB**; 3 g **FIBER**; 172 mg **SODIUM**; 0 mg **CHOL**

Assorted Vegetable Platter

MAKES 6 servings **PREP** 30 minutes **GRILL** 10 minutes

3	tablespoons pomegranate balsamic vinegar
3	tablespoons honey
½	teaspoon salt
¼	teaspoon black pepper
6	tablespoons canola oil
1	tablespoon chopped fresh sage
1	tablespoon chopped fresh parsley
1	teaspoon chopped fresh rosemary
1	pound asparagus, trimmed
1	medium eggplant (about 1 pound), cut into ½-inch slices
1	large summer squash (about 8 ounces), cut into ½-inch slices
1	red sweet pepper, seeded and cut into ½-inch strips
8	ounces baby carrots, halved lengthwise
2	large shallots (about 6 ounces), peeled and cut into 8 pieces

• In a small bowl, whisk together vinegar, honey, ¼ teaspoon of the salt and the black pepper. Gradually whisk in oil; add sage, parsley and rosemary. Set aside.

• Heat a gas grill to medium-high or the coals in a charcoal grill to medium-hot. Lightly grease grates.

• Brush vegetables with dressing. Grill for about 5 minutes per side, until crisp-tender. Brush with additional dressing and turn as needed to prevent burning. Cook in batches if necessary. (You may want to use a grilling grid for thinner vegetables.)

• To serve, arrange on a platter and drizzle with remaining dressing. Season with remaining ¼ teaspoon salt.

PER SERVING 239 **CAL**; 14 g **FAT** (1 g **SAT**); 5 g **PRO**; 28 g **CARB**; 6 g **FIBER**; 228 mg **SODIUM**; 0 mg **CHOL**

PEPPER AND CREMINI
MUSHROOM SKEWERS

SWEET-AND-SOUR
CABBAGE

We were happily surprised by how delicious this delicate cabbage is when grilled.

TANDOORI GRILLED VEGETABLES WITH MINT RAITA

Sweet-and-Sour Cabbage

MAKES 4 servings PREP 10 minutes
GRILL 14 minutes

½	cup peach preserves
⅓	cup apple cider vinegar
2	tablespoons sugar
2	tablespoons canola oil
2	tablespoons unsalted butter, melted
½	teaspoon salt
¼	teaspoon black pepper
1	small napa cabbage (about 1½ pounds)

• In a medium bowl, whisk together peach preserves, vinegar, sugar, oil, butter, salt and pepper. Set aside.

• Heat a gas grill to medium-high or the coals in a charcoal grill to medium-hot.

• Trim outer leaves of cabbage, keeping stem end intact. Slice lengthwise into 4 equal pieces.

• Lightly grease grates. Generously brush cabbage with peach sauce. Close lid and grill for 5 to 7 minutes on uncut side. Turn and grill on cut side for 5 to 7 minutes, turning if necessary to avoid burning. Brush with additional sauce as needed.

• Serve warm with any remaining sauce on the side.

PER SERVING 265 CAL; 13 g FAT (4 g SAT); 2 g PRO; 35 g CARB; 2 g FIBER; 315 mg SODIUM; 15 mg CHOL

Tandoori Grilled Vegetables with Mint Raita

MAKES 8 servings PREP 30 minutes COOK 2 minutes REFRIGERATE 30 minutes GRILL 6 minutes

1	cup plain Greek yogurt
2	tablespoons lemon juice
2	tablespoons chopped fresh ginger
1	tablespoon canola oil
1	clove garlic, chopped
1	teaspoon salt
1	teaspoon garam masala
1	teaspoon turmeric
1	teaspoon paprika
¼	teaspoon cayenne pepper
1	small head broccoli, cut into large florets (about 5 cups)
½	head cauliflower, cut into large florets (about 4 cups)
2	medium firm-ripe tomatoes, each cut into 8 wedges
1	large yellow onion, cut into 16 wedges
8	wood skewers (soaked in cold water for at least 1 hour)
	Mint Raita (recipe follows)
	Grilled naan bread (optional)

• In a large bowl, combine yogurt, lemon juice, ginger, oil, garlic, salt, garam masala, turmeric, paprika and cayenne. Whisk until smooth. Set aside.

• Bring a large pot of lightly salted water to a boil. Add broccoli and cauliflower; simmer for 2 minutes. Drain and run under cold water. Pat dry.

• Add broccoli, cauliflower, tomatoes and onion to yogurt mixture; stir gently to coat. Cover and refrigerate for 30 minutes.

• Heat a gas grill to medium-high or the coals in a charcoal grill to medium-hot. Lightly grease grates. Alternately thread broccoli, cauliflower, tomato wedges and onion onto wood skewers. Grill 2 to 3 minutes per side, until lightly charred. Remove to a serving platter.

• Serve with Mint Raita and, if desired, grilled naan.

Mint Raita In a small bowl, combine 1 cup plain Greek yogurt; ¼ of a seedless cucumber, peeled and shredded; 3 tablespoons chopped fresh mint; 1 teaspoon lemon juice and ⅛ teaspoon salt. Cover and refrigerate until serving.

PER SERVING 93 CAL; 3 g FAT (1 g SAT); 7 g PRO; 12 g CARB; 4 g FIBER; 406 mg SODIUM; 2 mg CHOL

HEALTHY FAMILY DINNERS

Prep ahead + easy recipes = 5 super suppers.

**TOMATO SOUP AND GRILLED
CHEESE PANINI, PAGE 244**

SAUSAGE AND PEPPER BAKE, PAGE 249

TOMATO SOUP AND GRILLED CHEESE PANINI

Tomato Soup and Grilled Cheese Panini

MAKES 5 servings   PREP 20 minutes   REFRIGERATE overnight
SLOW COOK on HIGH for 6 hours or on LOW for 8 hours   COOK 3 minutes per batch

3	pounds plum tomatoes
2	cloves garlic
1	can (14.5 ounces) reduced-sodium vegetable broth
¼	cup fresh basil leaves, plus 15 large leaves for sandwiches
¼	teaspoon salt
¼	teaspoon black pepper
10	slices whole-grain bread
1	tablespoon jarred basil pesto
8	ounces fresh mozzarella
1	large tomato

• The night before cooking, core, halve and seed tomatoes. Thinly slice garlic and combine in a resealable bag with tomatoes. Refrigerate overnight.

• In the morning, combine tomatoes and garlic with broth and the ¼ cup basil leaves in a 4½-quart slow cooker. Season with salt and pepper, cover and cook on HIGH for 6 hours or on LOW for 8 hours.

• Once soup is almost done, heat panini press. Place 5 slices of the bread on a work surface. Spread ½ teaspoon pesto on each slice. Cut mozzarella and the large tomato into 10 thin slices each. Place 2 slices of the mozzarella on bread. Add 3 basil leaves to each sandwich and top each with 2 slices tomato. Top with 5 remaining bread slices and coat both sides of sandwiches with nonstick cooking spray. Cook sandwiches in panini press for 3 minutes (2 or 3 sandwiches per batch), until browned and cheese is melted.

• While sandwiches cook, ladle half the tomato mixture into a blender. Blend until smooth. Add remaining tomato mixture to blender if there is space (or do in batches); blend until smooth (or you can use an immersion blender instead). Divide among 5 bowls (about 1⅓ cups per serving). Serve with a sandwich.

PER SERVING 408 CAL; 17 g FAT (8 g SAT); 19 g PRO; 42 g CARB; 9 g FIBER; 795 mg SODIUM; 47 mg CHOL

Pork Tenderloin Salad

MAKES 4 servings   PREP 20 minutes
ROAST at 425° for 35 minutes
REFRIGERATE overnight

1	bag (24 ounces) baby red potatoes, quartered
2	tablespoons olive oil
½	teaspoon salt
¼	teaspoon black pepper
1	canned chipotle in adobo, chopped, plus 2 teaspoons adobo
1	tablespoon light mayonnaise
2½	teaspoons Dijon mustard
2	teaspoons fresh oregano, chopped
1	pork tenderloin (1¼ pounds)
3	tablespoons red wine vinegar
1	teaspoon honey
1	package (5 ounces) salad greens
1	pear, cored and diced

• The night before, heat oven to 425°. Toss potatoes with 1 tablespoon of the oil, ¼ teaspoon of the salt and ⅛ teaspoon of the pepper. Spread onto a rimmed baking sheet. In a small bowl, blend chipotle, 1 teaspoon of the adobo, the mayonnaise, 2 teaspoons of the mustard, 1 teaspoon of the oregano, ⅛ teaspoon of the salt and remaining ⅛ teaspoon pepper. Brush onto pork tenderloin on a rimmed baking sheet.

• Roast potatoes at 425° for 35 minutes, stirring occasionally. Roast pork at 425° for 30 minutes, or until it registers 140° on an instant-read thermometer. Remove from oven and cover pork with foil. Cool both pork and potatoes, and refrigerate overnight.

• Meanwhile, whisk together vinegar, remaining 1 tablespoon oil, ⅛ teaspoon salt, 1 teaspoon adobo, 1 teaspoon oregano and the honey. Wrap and store at room temperature overnight.

• At dinnertime, in a large bowl, toss together roasted potatoes, salad greens, diced pear and dressing. Divide among 4 bowls. Thinly slice pork and fan on top.

PER SERVING 427 CAL; 13 g FAT (3 g SAT); 34 g PRO; 43 g CARB; 5 g FIBER; 802 mg SODIUM; 93 mg CHOL

**PORK TENDERLOIN
SALAD**

Bacon Cheeseburger Quiche

MAKES 6 servings **PREP** 20 minutes **MICROWAVE** 5 minutes **COOL** overnight
COOK 8 minutes **BAKE** at 350° for 25 minutes, plus 1 hour 10 minutes

5	slices Applegate Farms Good Morning bacon
1	refrigerated piecrust (rolled out to 12 inches)
½	pound ground sirloin (90% lean)
½	cup diced red onion
2	teaspoons Worcestershire sauce
3	cups baby spinach, chopped
1	medium tomato, seeded and diced
¼	teaspoon salt
¼	teaspoon black pepper
2	large eggs
4	large egg whites
¾	cup skim milk
3	tablespoons ketchup
2	tablespoons yellow mustard
¾	cup shredded 2% cheddar cheese
	Salad (optional)

• The night before, layer bacon between paper towels on a plate and microwave for 3 to 5 minutes, until crisp. Set aside. Heat oven to 350°. Fit crust into a 9-inch deep-dish pie plate and line crust with foil, pressing down. Bake at 350° for 10 minutes. Remove foil and bake 15 minutes more, until crust holds its shape but small bubbles form. Cool on a wire rack, then cover and store at room temperature overnight.

• Meanwhile, heat a large nonstick skillet over medium-high heat. Crumble in ground sirloin and add onion and Worcestershire sauce. Cook for 5 minutes. Stir in spinach, crumbled bacon and tomato. Cook for 3 minutes and add salt and pepper. Spoon into a lidded container, cover and refrigerate.

• The next day, heat oven to 350°. Break filling apart and spoon into piecrust. In a bowl, whisk together eggs, egg whites, milk, ketchup and mustard. Sprinkle cheese over filling in piecrust. Pour in egg mixture and transfer to oven. Bake at 350° for 1 hour 10 minutes, until a toothpick inserted in center comes out clean. Cover edge with foil if it's browning too quickly. Cool 10 minutes before slicing. Serve with salad alongside, if desired.

PER SERVING 348 **CAL**; 18 g **FAT** (8 g **SAT**); 21 g **PRO**; 26 g **CARB**; 1 g **FIBER**; 741 mg **SODIUM**; 119 mg **CHOL**

BACON
CHEESEBURGER
QUICHE

Squash and Farro Salad

MAKES 6 servings **PREP** 25 minutes
ROAST at 450° for 20 minutes
REFRIGERATE overnight **COOK** 16 minutes
MICROWAVE 2 minutes

- 1½ **pounds diced fresh butternut squash (from a peeled and seeded 2½-pound squash)**
- 4 **tablespoons olive oil**
- 1 **teaspoon salt**
- ½ **teaspoon black pepper**
- 1 **small rotisserie chicken**
- 1½ **cups parboiled farro**
- ½ **cup sweetened dried cranberries**
- ½ **teaspoon ground cumin**
- ½ **teaspoon ground ginger**
- ½ **teaspoon ground cinnamon**
- ¼ **cup cider vinegar**
- 2 **teaspoons Dijon mustard**
- 1 **teaspoon honey**
- 2 **cups mixed baby kale, shredded**
- ½ **cup crumbled goat cheese**
- ⅓ **cup toasted walnuts, chopped**

• Heat oven to 450°. Toss diced squash with 2 tablespoons of the oil and ¼ teaspoon each of the salt and pepper, and spread onto a large rimmed baking sheet. Roast at 450° for 20 minutes, stirring halfway through; cool.

• Meanwhile, remove and discard skin from chicken. Shred meat into pieces, discarding bones (you'll need 3 cups shredded chicken). Refrigerate roasted squash and chicken overnight.

• The next evening, combine farro, ½ teaspoon of the salt and 4½ cups water in a large pot. Bring to a boil. Boil for 10 minutes, then stir in dried cranberries. Boil for an additional 5 minutes; drain and rinse.

• In a small skillet, combine remaining ¼ teaspoon each salt and pepper, the cumin, ginger and cinnamon. Toast over medium heat for 1 minute.

• In a small bowl, whisk together vinegar, mustard, honey and remaining 2 tablespoons oil. Slowly whisk into skillet with seasonings. Remove from heat. Reheat squash and chicken in microwave for 2 minutes.

• Combine farro, squash, chicken and kale in a large serving bowl. Drizzle with dressing, toss, and sprinkle with goat cheese and walnuts; serve immediately.

PER SERVING 479 **CAL**; 18 g **FAT** (3 g **SAT**); 24 g **PRO**; 59 g **CARB**; 9 g **FIBER**; 673 mg **SODIUM**; 38 mg **CHOL**

SAUSAGE AND PEPPER BAKE

Sausage and Pepper Bake

MAKES 6 servings **PREP** 25 minutes **REFRIGERATE** overnight
BAKE at 375° for 30 minutes and at 350° for 30 minutes

- 2 **packages (10 ounces each) microwave-ready frozen brown rice**
- 2 **tablespoons chopped fresh parsley**
- 1 **teaspoon chopped fresh rosemary**
- 1 **teaspoon chopped fresh oregano**
- 1 **bag (8 ounces) 2% Italian cheese blend**
- 1 **red sweet pepper, sliced**
- 1 **green bell pepper, sliced**
- 1 **package (8 ounces) sliced mushrooms**
- 2 **plum tomatoes, cored and diced**
- 1 **package (12 ounces) fully cooked sweet pepper and Asiago chicken sausage, cut into coins**
- 2 **tablespoons balsamic vinegar**
- 1 **tablespoon olive oil**
- ¼ **teaspoon salt**
- ¼ **teaspoon black pepper**
- 2 **tablespoons grated Parmesan cheese**

• Toss frozen rice with herbs and spread into bottom of a 3-quart baking dish. Top with 1 cup of the Italian cheese blend.

• Combine sweet pepper, bell pepper, mushrooms, tomatoes and sausage in a large bowl. Whisk together vinegar, oil, salt and black pepper in a small bowl. Toss with sausage mixture. Add to baking dish on top of rice. Cover and refrigerate overnight.

• The next evening, remove casserole from refrigerator. Heat oven to 375°. Remove plastic from casserole; sprinkle dish with remaining Italian cheese blend and the Parmesan. Bake at 375° for 30 minutes. Reduce heat to 350°. Cover with foil and bake 30 minutes more. Serve warm.

PER SERVING 362 **CAL**; 16 g **FAT** (6 g **SAT**); 24 g **PRO**; 9 g **CARB**; 3 g **FIBER**; 762 mg **SODIUM**; 68 mg **CHOL**

DEVILISH CHOCOLATE
FROSTED CUPCAKES,
PAGE 265

GHOULISHLY GOOD
COOKIES, PAGE 266

OCTOBER

255

270

274

APPLES TO APPLES!

Sweet and savory dishes starring America's favorite fruit.

SALTED CARAMEL
APPLE CAKE,
PAGE 259

APPLE HAZELNUT
BLONDIES,
PAGE 256

APPLE FRITTERS WITH
CALVADOS GLAZE

Apple Fritters with Calvados Glaze

MAKES 12 fritters **PREP** 15 minutes
FRY 6 minutes per batch

2	cups all-purpose flour
⅓	cup granulated sugar
1	tablespoon baking powder
½	teaspoon salt
¾	teaspoon cinnamon
¼	teaspoon nutmeg
2	Granny Smith apples, peeled, cored and cut into ¼-inch dice
¾	cup apple cider
2	eggs, lightly beaten
3	tablespoons butter, melted
1	teaspoon vanilla extract
6	cups vegetable oil
2	cups confectioners' sugar
2	tablespoons apple cider
2	tablespoons Calvados

• In a large bowl, whisk together flour, sugar, baking powder, salt, cinnamon and nutmeg. Fold in diced apples. Stir in cider, eggs, butter and vanilla until combined.

• Heat oil in a large, heavy-bottomed Dutch oven to 375°.

• Form 4 fritters, using a ⅓-cup ice cream scoop, and drop into oil. Fry 3 minutes; turn and fry an additional 3 minutes. With a slotted spoon, remove to a cooling rack placed over a baking sheet. Repeat until all fritters are fried.

• Combine confectioners' sugar, cider and Calvados. While fritters are slightly warm, spread a heaping tablespoon of the glaze over each fritter. Serve slightly warm or at room temperature.

PER SERVING 342 **CAL**; 18 g **FAT** (4 g **SAT**); 3 g **PRO**; 43 g **CARB**; 1 g **FIBER**; 213 mg **SODIUM**; 43 mg **CHOL**

SPINACH AND PINK LADY APPLE SALAD

Spinach and Pink Lady Apple Salad

MAKES 6 servings **PREP** 15 minutes

½	cup apple cider
½	teaspoon ground ginger
½	teaspoon dry mustard
1	tablespoon finely chopped shallot
¼	cup canola oil
2	bags (6 ounces each) baby spinach
2	Pink Lady apples, cored, halved and sliced
½	red onion, thinly sliced
¼	teaspoon salt
½	pound cooked bacon, crumbled

• In a small bowl, whisk together apple cider, ginger, mustard and shallot. Gradually whisk in oil.

• In a large bowl, combine spinach, apples and onion. Toss with dressing and season with salt. Fold in crumbled bacon and serve.

PER SERVING 214 **CAL**; 15 g **FAT** (2 g **SAT**); 6 g **PRO**; 16 g **CARB**; 4 g **FIBER**; 478 mg **SODIUM**; 14 mg **CHOL**

APPLE HAZELNUT BLONDIES

Apple Hazelnut Blondies

MAKES 12 blondies PREP 20 minutes BAKE at 350° for 10 minutes (nuts) and 30 minutes (blondies)

BLONDIES

1	cup hazelnuts
¾	cup granulated sugar
¾	cup packed light brown sugar
½	cup (1 stick) butter, melted
2	eggs, lightly beaten
1	teaspoon vanilla extract
2	cups all-purpose flour
2	teaspoons baking powder
¼	teaspoon salt
2	Fuji apples, peeled, cored and chopped (about 2 cups)

MAPLE ICING

1	package (8 ounces) cream cheese, softened
1	cup confectioners' sugar
2	tablespoons maple syrup
¾	teaspoon vanilla extract

• **Blondies.** Heat oven to 350°. Coat a 12-cavity brownie pan (such as Wilton Brownie Bar Pan) with nonstick cooking spray.

• Place nuts on a rimmed baking sheet. Bake at 350° for 10 minutes. Cool slightly and rub nuts with fingers to remove skin. Chop nuts and reserve.

• Meanwhile, in a large bowl, combine sugars, butter, eggs and vanilla. Whisk together flour, baking powder and salt; stir into sugar-and-butter mixture until dry ingredients are just moistened. Fold in chopped apples and ¾ cup of the chopped nuts.

• Spoon batter into prepared brownie pan, about ⅓ cup into each cavity. Bake at 350° for 30 minutes or until a toothpick inserted into center comes out clean. Cool on a wire rack for 30 minutes; turn out onto rack to cool completely.

• **Maple Icing.** In a large bowl, beat cream cheese until smooth. Gradually beat in sugar; add maple syrup and vanilla and beat until smooth.

• Frost each blondie with a generous 2 tablespoons of icing. Sprinkle with remaining ¼ cup chopped hazelnuts.

PER SERVING 423 CAL; 21 g FAT (10 g SAT); 6 g PRO; 56 g CARB; 2 g FIBER; 190 mg SODIUM; 76 mg CHOL

Turkey Medallions in Curried Apple-Shallot Sauce

MAKES 4 servings PREP 20 minutes
COOK 18 minutes

1¼	pounds thin, boneless, skinless turkey breasts, cut in half crosswise
¼	cup all-purpose flour
¼	teaspoon salt
¼	teaspoon black pepper
¾	teaspoon dried thyme
¾	teaspoon dried marjoram
2	tablespoons extra-virgin olive oil
1	tablespoon unsalted butter
2	Braeburn apples, peeled, cored and chopped
2	large shallots, peeled and chopped
3	cloves garlic, chopped
1	cup chicken broth
½	cup white wine
¼	cup heavy cream
1	tablespoon Dijon mustard
1½	teaspoons curry powder
	Steamed green beans (optional side dish)

• Dredge turkey in flour; season with salt, pepper and ½ teaspoon each of the thyme and marjoram.

• In a large skillet, heat 1 tablespoon of the oil and the butter over medium-high heat. Add turkey; cook in batches for 3 minutes, turning once, or until cooked through. Remove to a plate, cover and keep warm.

• Add remaining 1 tablespoon oil to skillet. Stir in apples, shallots and garlic; sauté for 2 minutes, stirring occasionally. Add broth, wine, cream, mustard, curry and remaining ¼ teaspoon each thyme and marjoram. Simmer over medium-low heat 10 minutes, stirring occasionally. Serve turkey with sauce and, if desired, steamed green beans.

PER SERVING 424 CAL; 16 g FAT (6 g SAT); 39 g PRO; 28 g CARB; 2 g FIBER; 602 mg SODIUM; 84 mg CHOL

HARVEST
PORK ROAST

Harvest Pork Roast

MAKES 10 servings **PREP** 20 minutes
MARINATE at least 3 hours or overnight
BAKE at 400° for 15 minutes and at 350° for
45 minutes **BROIL** 8 minutes

PORK

1	can (6 ounces) apple juice concentrate, thawed
3	tablespoons maple syrup
2	tablespoons cider vinegar
2	tablespoons olive oil
2	teaspoons Worcestershire sauce
1	teaspoon salt
½	teaspoon cinnamon
¼	teaspoon black pepper
1	boneless pork roast (about 3 pounds)
1	tablespoon cornstarch

APPLES

4	tablespoons butter, melted
4	tablespoons maple syrup
¼	teaspoon cinnamon
4	Granny Smith apples, peeled, cored and cut into ½-inch-thick slices

• **Pork.** In a large resealable plastic bag, combine apple juice concentrate, maple syrup, cider vinegar, olive oil, Worcestershire sauce, salt, cinnamon and black pepper. Add pork roast and marinate at least 3 hours or overnight, turning occasionally.

• Heat oven to 400°. Remove pork from plastic bag and reserve marinade. Roast at 400° for 15 minutes. Reduce oven temperature to 350° and roast 40 to 45 minutes more, until internal temperature reaches 140°. Place on a serving platter and tent with foil. Allow to rest for 10 minutes.

• **Apples.** Meanwhile, heat broiler to high. In a bowl, combine butter, maple syrup and cinnamon. Place apple slices on a large broiler pan and brush with butter mixture. Broil about 4 minutes per side, turning once, until tender, brushing occasionally with butter mixture.

• Place marinade in a small saucepan and bring to a simmer. Combine cornstarch with 1 tablespoon water; stir into saucepan and simmer for 1 minute.

• To serve, slice pork and serve with apples and sauce.

PER SERVING 363 **CAL**; 17 g **FAT** (7 g **SAT**); 27 g **PRO**; 26 g **CARB**; 1 g **FIBER**; 312 mg **SODIUM**; 87 mg **CHOL**

SALTED CARAMEL APPLE CAKE

Salted Caramel Apple Cake

MAKES 12 servings **PREP** 25 minutes **COOK** 15 minutes **BAKE** at 350° for 50 minutes **COOL** 15 minutes

6	tablespoons cold butter
1½	cups packed light brown sugar
1	teaspoon sea salt
4	Gala apples (about 2 pounds), cored and peeled, each cut into 8 wedges
1½	cups all-purpose flour
1	tablespoon pumpkin pie spice
2	teaspoons baking powder
¼	teaspoon salt
½	cup (1 stick) butter, softened
2	eggs
1	teaspoon vanilla extract
½	cup half-and-half
	Whipped cream (optional)

• Heat oven to 350°. Butter the bottom of a 10-inch round cake pan with 4 tablespoons of the butter. Sprinkle with ½ cup of the brown sugar and the sea salt.

• Heat remaining 2 tablespoons cold butter in a large skillet over medium heat. Add apples; sauté 13 to 15 minutes, until tender. Cool.

• In a large bowl, whisk flour, pumpkin pie spice, baking powder and salt. In a second large bowl, beat softened butter and remaining 1 cup brown sugar until smooth. Beat in eggs, one at a time, then vanilla. On low speed, beat flour mixture into butter mixture, alternating with half-and-half. Scrape down sides of bowl; beat for 1 minute.

• Fan apples over bottom of prepared pan. Spread batter over apples. Bake at 350° for 45 to 50 minutes, until a toothpick inserted in center comes out clean. Cool for 15 minutes.

• Run a small knife around edge of pan. Place a serving plate on top of pan and turn plate and pan over together. Carefully remove pan. If any apples remain in pan, place on cake.

• Serve warm or at room temperature with whipped cream, if desired.

PER SERVING 326 **CAL**; 15 g **FAT** (9 g **SAT**); 3 g **PRO**; 45 g **CARB**; 1 g **FIBER**; 305 mg **SODIUM**; 75 mg **CHOL**

IN THE SPIRIT

Celebrate Halloween with an assortment of spooky treats.

BATTY BITES,
PAGE 268

WHOO, WHOO MADE THE PUNCH

Throw a spellbinding bash with a ghoulish brew of orange punch and an array of sinfully good eats.

Creepy Caramel Popcorn Balls

MAKES 16 popcorn balls   PREP 5 minutes
COOK 8 minutes   COOL 4 minutes

1	bag (3.2 ounces) microwave popcorn (about 6 cups)
½	cup (1 stick) butter
¾	cup firmly packed brown sugar
⅓	cup light corn syrup
1	cup M&M's or candy-coated sunflower seeds

• Microwave popcorn according to package directions. Line a rimmed baking pan with nonstick foil. Spread popcorn onto foil-lined pan.

• Melt butter in a small saucepan over medium heat. Add sugar and corn syrup. Increase heat to high and bring to a boil, stirring constantly. Boil until sugar dissolves, about 2 minutes. Cool for 4 minutes.

• Pour sugar mixture over popcorn on baking pan. Coat a spatula with nonstick cooking spray. Push hot mixture into center of baking pan, folding over to combine. Coat your hands with nonstick cooking spray and sprinkle popcorn mixture with M&M's. Using your hands, quickly combine ingredients and shape into firmly packed 2-inch balls. Cool completely. Wrap each ball in plastic wrap or keep covered until ready to serve.

PER SERVING 196 CAL; 10 g FAT (6 g SAT); 1 g PRO; 26 g CARB; 1 g FIBER; 61 mg SODIUM; 17 mg CHOL

Whoo, Whoo Made the Punch

MAKES 12 servings   PREP 5 minutes

1	quart orange sherbet
1	container (12 ounces) frozen orange juice concentrate
1	bottle (1 liter) cold ginger ale
1	bottle (1 liter) seltzer
2	small navel oranges, sliced Gummy worms (optional)

• Line a baking pan with foil. Place scoops of sherbet on baking pan and freeze until ready to serve.

• To serve, combine orange juice concentrate, ginger ale and seltzer in a punch bowl. Top with scoops of the sherbet and orange slices. Drape gummy worms over rim of punch bowl, if desired.

PER SERVING 147 CAL; 1 g FAT (1 g SAT); 1 g PRO; 33 g CARB; 2 g FIBER; 34 mg SODIUM; 0 mg CHOL

CREEPY CARAMEL
POPCORN BALLS

Treat the ghouls and goblins at your haunted house to an array of spooky sweets that includes rich chocolate cupcakes topped with a swirl of airy homemade frosting that's as light as a ghost!

Devilish Chocolate Frosted Cupcakes

MAKES 12 cupcakes **PREP** 10 minutes **BAKE** at 350° for 24 minutes

½	**cup boiling water**
½	**cup unsweetened cocoa powder**
1¼	**cups all-purpose flour**
½	**teaspoon baking soda**
½	**teaspoon baking powder**
½	**teaspoon salt**
½	**cup (1 stick) unsalted butter, softened**
¾	**cup sugar**
2	**large eggs**
1	**teaspoon vanilla extract**
⅓	**cup buttermilk**
1	**batch Fluffy Frosting (recipe at right)**
	Sprinkles (optional)

• Heat oven to 350°. Line a 12-cupcake baking pan with cupcake liners. Blend boiling water and cocoa in a small bowl; cool for 5 minutes. In a medium bowl, combine flour, baking soda, baking powder and salt.

• In a large bowl, on high speed, beat butter and sugar until light and fluffy. Add eggs and vanilla and beat well. Reduce speed to low and alternately beat in flour mixture and buttermilk until just blended. Add cocoa mixture and mix well. Divide batter among prepared cupcake liners.

• Bake at 350° for 22 to 24 minutes, until a toothpick inserted in center comes out clean. Cool completely in pan on a wire rack. Pipe on Fluffy Frosting and top with sprinkles, if desired.

PER CUPCAKE 462 **CAL**; 26 g **FAT** (16 g **SAT**); 4 g **PRO**; 55 g **CARB**; 1 g **FIBER**; 190 mg **SODIUM**; 103 mg **CHOL**

Fluffy Frosting

MAKES 2½ cups **PREP** 5 minutes

3	**cups confectioners' sugar**
1	**cup (2 sticks) unsalted butter, softened**
1	**tablespoon vanilla extract (see Note)**
4	**tablespoons heavy cream**
	Orange gel food coloring

• On high speed, beat together sugar and butter until fluffy, about 3 minutes. Add vanilla and cream. Continue beating until well combined, 1 minute.

• Transfer half the frosting to a decorating bag fitted with a large star tip. Tint remaining frosting with gel food coloring until desired color. Transfer orange frosting to another decorating bag fitted with a large star tip. Pipe frosting onto cupcakes.

Note: To keep the frosting pure white, use clear vanilla extract.

Tempt revelers with spooky chocolate cookies,
irresistibly decorated.

Ghoulishly Good Cookies

MAKES 32 cookies **PREP** 20 minutes **MICROWAVE** 1 minute **CHILL** 1 hour **BAKE** at 350° for 12 minutes **COOL** 2 minutes

COOKIES

1	**ounce unsweetened chocolate**
¾	**cup (1½ sticks) unsalted butter, softened**
1¼	**cups granulated sugar**
1	**large egg, at room temperature**
2	**teaspoons corn syrup**
1	**teaspoon vanilla extract**
3¾	**cups all-purpose flour**
½	**cup unsweetened cocoa powder**
½	**teaspoon salt**

ROYAL ICING

4	**cups confectioners' sugar**
2	**tablespoons meringue powder (powdered egg whites)**
	Black gel food coloring

• **Cookies.** Place chocolate in a small microwave-safe bowl. Microwave on medium for 1 minute, stirring once halfway through. Stir until smooth and melted. Let cool for 5 minutes.

• Meanwhile, combine butter and granulated sugar in a mixer bowl; beat until light and fluffy, about 3 minutes. Add egg, corn syrup and vanilla; beat until well combined. Scrape down sides of bowl. With mixer on low, add flour, cocoa powder and salt; beat until combined. Stir in melted chocolate and mix until well blended.

• Divide dough into 2 disks, wrap and refrigerate for 1 hour or up to 2 days.

• Heat oven to 350°. Line baking sheets with parchment paper. Roll dough between 2 sheets of wax paper to ¼-inch thickness. Cut dough into 3-inch circles, using a cookie cutter. Place on prepared baking sheets, 1 inch apart, and bake at 350° until edges are just lightly browned, about 10 to 12 minutes. Cool on baking sheet for 2 minutes. Transfer cookies to a wire rack and cool completely. Repeat with any remaining dough.

• **Royal Icing.** Place confectioners' sugar and meringue powder in a bowl with mixer fitted with a whisk; beat on low to combine. Beat in ¼ cup water; increase speed to high and beat until stiff peaks form, about 3 minutes. Add an additional 2 tablespoons water and beat until light and fluffy.

• To decorate, place 1 cup of the icing in a bowl and tint with black food coloring. Transfer to a decorating bag fitted with a #4 writing tip.

• Dilute remaining white icing with 1 teaspoon water at a time until it has the consistency of thick heavy cream. Decorate cookies as desired, following photograph at right.

PER COOKIE 194 **CAL**; 5 g **FAT** (3 g **SAT**); 2 g **PRO**; 35 g **CARB**; 1 g **FIBER**; 45 mg **SODIUM**; 18 mg **CHOL**

GHOULISHLY GOOD
COOKIES

DARE TO DIP

FRIGHTFUL
FLATBREADS

Dare to Dip

MAKES 2½ cups **PREP** 10 minutes
MICROWAVE 3 minutes

1	**bag (12 ounces) frozen shelled edamame (2¼ cups)**
½	**cup firmly packed fresh parsley leaves**
1	**clove garlic**
¼	**cup tahini**
¼	**cup fresh lemon juice**
1	**teaspoon salt**
½	**teaspoon ground cumin**
3	**tablespoons extra-virgin olive oil Assorted cut-up vegetables and crackers, for dipping**

• Place edamame in a microwave-safe bowl, cover and microwave on high for 3 minutes.

• Transfer hot edamame to a food processor fitted with a blade. Add parsley and garlic. Process until pureed. Add tahini, lemon juice, salt and cumin. Pulse until smooth. With motor running, drizzle in ⅓ cup water and the oil until well combined.

• Serve with assorted cut-up vegetables and crackers.

PER ¼ CUP 124 **CAL**; 9 g **FAT** (1 g **SAT**); 5 g **PRO**; 6 g **CARB**; 2 g **FIBER**; 242 mg **SODIUM**; 0 mg **CHOL**

Frightful Flatbreads

MAKES 12 servings **PREP** 5 minutes
BAKE at 425° for 9 minutes

6	**naan flatbreads (4.4 ounces) or pocketless pitas**
⅔	**cup pesto**
3	**medium tomatoes, thinly sliced**
6	**pieces string cheese (1 ounce each)**
9	**large pitted black olives**

• Heat oven to 425°. Place flatbreads on two baking sheets and top with pesto. Divide tomato slices among flatbreads. Slice cheese into thin strips; place on top in the shape of a spider web.

• Bake flatbreads at 425° for 7 to 9 minutes, until cheese melts and flatbreads crisp up. Cut 3 olives in half lengthwise. Use for bodies of spiders. Cut one end of 6 olives for spider heads. Halve remaining olives lengthwise and cut into strips for the spider legs. Assemble spiders on top of cheese webs. Cut flatbreads in half just before serving.

PER SERVING 288 **CAL**; 15 g **FAT** (4 g **SAT**); 11 g **PRO**; 24 g **CARB**; 5 g **FIBER**; 676 mg **SODIUM**; 17 mg **CHOL**

Grilled-Cheese Pumpkin Cutouts

MAKES 12 sandwiches **PREP** 5 minutes
COOK 25 minutes

24	**slices firm white bread**
½	**cup (8 tablespoons) light spreadable butter**
24	**slices sharp cheddar cheese**

• Cut out small eye and mouth shapes from 12 slices of bread. Spread butter on one side of each bread slice.

• Heat a nonstick pan over medium heat. Place one uncut slice, butter side down, in pan. Top with 2 slices cheese. Place one slice with cutouts, butter side down, in pan. Cook until bread is golden brown and cheese melts. Assemble sandwich; keep warm. Repeat with remaining bread and cheese to make 12 sandwiches.

PER SERVING 433 **CAL**; 21 g **FAT** (11 g **SAT**); 16 g **PRO**; 44 g **CARB**; 2 g **FIBER**; 923 mg **SODIUM**; 53 mg **CHOL**

Batty Bites

MAKES 12 sandwiches **PREP** 10 minutes

12	**whole wheat bread slices**
½	**pound sliced smoked turkey**
3	**tablespoons Catalina dressing**

• Cut 2 bat shapes from each slice of bread using a cookie cutter. Stack 2 pieces of turkey and make bat-shape cutouts. Repeat using all the turkey. Divide double-stacked turkey among half the bread shapes. Spread 1 teaspoon dressing on turkey and top with remaining bread cutouts.

PER SERVING 106 **CAL**; 3 g **FAT** (1 g **SAT**); 7 g **PRO**; 14 g **CARB**; 2 g **FIBER**; 337 mg **SODIUM**; 9 mg **CHOL**

GRILLED-CHEESE
PUMPKIN CUTOUTS

SLOW COOKER SUPPERS

Anticipate deliciousness with these fabulous soups—they're worth the wait.

CHICKEN AND
RICE SOUP

Chicken and Rice Soup

MAKES 6 servings **PREP** 25 minutes **SLOW COOK** on LOW for 6 hours

1	cup peeled and sliced carrots
1	cup sliced celery
1	cup diced onion
2	sprigs fresh thyme
4	whole cloves
1	teaspoon whole black peppercorns
1	whole chicken, quartered
4	cups unsalted chicken stock
½	cup fresh dill, chopped
1½	teaspoons salt
1	package (8.8 ounces) Uncle Ben's whole grain brown Ready Rice
	Freshly cracked pepper

• Place carrots, celery, onion, thyme, cloves and peppercorns in a slow cooker. Arrange chicken, including back and wings, on top. Pour in chicken stock and 1 cup water. Cook on LOW for 6 hours.

• Remove chicken from slow cooker. Shred, discarding bones and skin. Return meat to slow cooker and stir in dill, salt and rice. Serve with freshly cracked pepper.

PER SERVING 372 CAL; 7 g FAT (2 g SAT); 55 g PRO; 17 g CARB; 2 g FIBER; 820 mg SODIUM; 135 mg CHOL

MUSHROOM, SAUSAGE AND WHOLE GRAIN SOUP

Asian Beef Noodle Soup

MAKES 6 servings **PREP** 15 minutes
SLOW COOK on HIGH for 6 hours or LOW for 8 hours

1½	**pounds beef chuck or brisket, cut into 1-inch cubes**
½	**medium yellow onion, thinly sliced**
1	**piece ginger (2 inches), peeled and sliced**
4	**cloves garlic, sliced**
1	**bird's-eye or serrano chile, stemmed and sliced lengthwise**
2	**tablespoons rice vinegar**
2	**tablespoons molasses**
¼	**cup low-sodium soy sauce**
7	**cups unsalted beef stock**
1	**package (9.5 ounces) udon noodles**
6	**cups chopped bok choy**
1	**cup sliced scallions, plus more for garnish**
1	**cup fresh cilantro, chopped, plus more for garnish**

• Stir beef, onion, ginger, garlic, chile, vinegar, molasses and 2 tablespoons of the soy sauce into slow cooker. Pour in beef stock. Cook on HIGH for 6 hours or LOW for 8 hours.

• During the last 15 minutes of cooking, bring a large pot of lightly salted water to a boil. Add udon; cook 2 minutes. Add bok choy and cook 2 minutes more. Strain. Add noodles, bok choy, scallions, cilantro and remaining 2 tablespoons soy sauce to soup. Stir and serve. Garnish with additional scallions and cilantro.

PER SERVING 368 **CAL**; 6 g **FAT** (2 g **SAT**); 34 g **PRO**; 41 g **CARB**; 4 g **FIBER**; 698 mg **SODIUM**; 48 mg **CHOL**

Mushroom, Sausage and Whole Grain Soup

MAKES 6 servings **PREP** 15 minutes **COOK** 7 minutes **SLOW COOK** on HIGH for 5 hours

1	**pound sweet Italian sausage, casings removed**
2	**tablespoons white wine vinegar**
1¼	**cups Bob's Red Mill whole grain medley**
2	**cups diced sweet onion**
1	**pound sliced wild mushrooms**
2	**ribs celery, sliced**
3	**cloves garlic, chopped**
1	**tablespoon chopped fresh thyme**
6	**cups unsalted chicken stock**
¾	**teaspoon salt**
¼	**teaspoon black pepper**
	Fresh parsley, for garnish

• Heat a large sauté pan over medium-high heat. Add sausage, breaking apart with a spoon. Cook for 7 minutes, stirring occasionally, until browned. Add vinegar, scraping up browned bits from bottom of pan.

• Transfer sausage to a slow cooker. Stir in grains, onion, mushrooms, celery, garlic and thyme. Pour chicken stock on top, making sure all grains are submerged. Cook on HIGH for 5 hours. Stir in salt and pepper. Garnish with fresh parsley.

PER SERVING 370 **CAL**; 12 g **FAT** (4 g **SAT**); 21 g **PRO**; 43 g **CARB**; 7 g **FIBER**; 904 mg **SODIUM**; 22 mg **CHOL**

ASIAN BEEF NOODLE SOUP

CASSEROLES 2.0

The 1950s dinner staple gets a modern makeover.

**INDIAN MADRAS PIE,
PAGE 275**

BAKED SAUSAGE, SQUASH AND
NOODLES, PAGE 276

Louisiana Shrimp

MAKES 5 servings **PREP** 15 minutes **COOK** 14 minutes **BAKE** at 350° for 45 minutes **LET STAND** 5 minutes

2	tablespoons vegetable oil
1	medium onion, chopped
1	large green bell pepper, diced
2	ribs celery, diced
2	cloves garlic, minced
1½	cups red quinoa
2	teaspoons salt-free Cajun seasoning
1	teaspoon salt
1	cup low-sodium chicken broth
1	pound peeled and deveined shrimp
2	links smoked chicken Andouille sausage, cut into half-moons
3	plum tomatoes, seeded and diced
2	tablespoons chopped fresh parsley

• Heat oven to 350°. Heat oil in a large saucepan over medium heat. Add onion, pepper and celery. Cook, stirring, for 10 minutes. Add garlic; cook 1 minute more. Stir in quinoa, 1½ teaspoons of the Cajun seasoning and ¾ teaspoon of the salt; cook for 1 minute.

• Stir in broth and 1¾ cups water. Bring to a boil over high heat; boil for 2 minutes. Remove from heat and carefully ladle into a 2-quart baking dish. Cover tightly with foil and bake at 350° for 25 minutes.

• In a large bowl, toss together shrimp, sausage, tomatoes, parsley, remaining ½ teaspoon Cajun seasoning and remaining ¼ teaspoon salt. Carefully remove baking dish from oven and uncover. Spoon shrimp mixture over the top, re-cover and return to oven. Bake at 350° for an additional 20 minutes. Let stand for 5 minutes before serving.

PER SERVING 421 **CAL**; 13 g **FAT** (2 g **SAT**); 33 g **PRO**; 43 g **CARB**; 5 g **FIBER**; 789 mg **SODIUM**; 164 mg **CHOL**

LOUISIANA SHRIMP

Indian Madras Pie

MAKES 6 servings **PREP** 20 minutes
COOK 13 minutes **BAKE** at 350° for 20 minutes

2½	**pounds baking potatoes, peeled and cut into 2-inch pieces**
2	**tablespoons vegetable oil**
1	**package (20.8 ounces) ground turkey**
1½	**cups baby carrots, sliced**
3	**medium parsnips, peeled and sliced**
2	**teaspoons ground ginger**
1½	**teaspoons salt**
1	**teaspoon ground cumin**
1	**teaspoon ground coriander**
½	**teaspoon ground cinnamon**
½	**teaspoon ground turmeric**
⅛	**teaspoon cayenne pepper**
1	**cup frozen peas, thawed**
⅔	**cup milk**
2	**tablespoons unsalted butter**
	Pinch cayenne pepper (optional)

• Heat oven to 350°. Place potatoes in a large pot and cover with cold water. Bring to a boil over high heat; cook, boiling, for 12 minutes. Drain and return to pot.

• Meanwhile, heat oil in a large, lidded 3- to 4-quart flameproof dish over medium-high heat. Crumble in turkey and cook, breaking apart with a wooden spoon, for 4 minutes. Stir in carrots, parsnips, ginger, ¾ teaspoon of the salt, the cumin, coriander, cinnamon, turmeric, cayenne and ½ cup water. Cover and cook over medium heat, stirring once or twice, 7 minutes, adding more water if necessary. Uncover and stir in peas. Cook 2 minutes, then remove from heat.

• Mash potatoes in pot with milk, butter and remaining ¾ teaspoon salt. Spread potatoes over turkey mixture and sprinkle with cayenne, if desired. Bake, uncovered, at 350° for 20 minutes.

PER SERVING 435 **CAL**; 18 g **FAT** (5 g **SAT**); 24 g **PRO**; 46 g **CARB**; 6 g **FIBER**; 722 mg **SODIUM**; 90 mg **CHOL**

TAMALE PIE

Tamale Pie

MAKES 6 servings **PREP** 15 minutes **COOK** 16 minutes **BAKE** at 375° for 25 minutes **BROIL** 2 minutes

2	**tablespoons olive oil**
1	**pound zucchini, diced**
1	**red sweet pepper, cored and diced**
1	**medium onion, diced**
2	**tablespoons chili powder**
½	**teaspoon ground cumin**
¼	**teaspoon salt**
¼	**teaspoon black pepper**
2	**cans (15.5 ounces each) dark red kidney beans, drained and rinsed**
1	**can (14.5 ounces) fire-roasted diced tomatoes**
1	**can (8 ounces) no-salt-added tomato sauce**
1	**cup corn kernels, thawed if frozen**
1	**tube (1 pound) prepared plain or chile-cilantro polenta, cut into ¼-inch slices**
	Queso fresco, for garnish (optional)

• Heat oven to 375°. Coat an oval baking dish with nonstick cooking spray. Heat oil in a large nonstick skillet over medium heat. Add zucchini, sweet pepper and onion; cook 7 to 10 minutes.

• Sprinkle with chili powder, cumin, salt and black pepper; cook for 1 minute.

• Stir in beans, tomatoes, tomato sauce and corn. Reduce heat to medium and simmer 5 minutes. Transfer to prepared baking dish.

• Top with sliced polenta. Bake at 375° for 20 to 25 minutes, until chili is bubbly.

• Increase oven heat to broil; broil 2 minutes, until polenta browns slightly. Garnish with crumbled queso fresco, if desired.

PER SERVING 310 **CAL**; 6 g **FAT** (1 g **SAT**); 12 g **PRO**; 54 g **CARB**; 14 g **FIBER**; 800 mg **SODIUM**; 0 mg **CHOL**

BAKED SAUSAGE, SQUASH AND NOODLES

Baked Sausage, Squash and Noodles

MAKES 6 servings **PREP** 30 minutes **COOK** 13 minutes **BAKE** at 350° for 25 minutes

2	tablespoons plus 1 teaspoon unsalted butter
2	tablespoons all-purpose flour
2	cups 1% milk, warmed
½	teaspoon salt
½	teaspoon black pepper
6	ounces goat cheese
2	tablespoons fresh sage, chopped
¾	pound cubed butternut squash
1	bag (12 ounces) whole-grain wide noodles
2	tablespoons Italian seasoned dry bread crumbs
4	links turkey or chicken sausage, casings removed (about 12 ounces)

• Heat oven to 350°. Coat a 13 x 9 x 2-inch baking dish with nonstick cooking spray. Bring a large pot of lightly salted water to a boil.

• In a medium saucepan, melt 2 tablespoon of the butter over medium heat. Whisk in flour and cook for 1 minute. Whisk in milk, salt and pepper and bring to a simmer. Simmer for 2 minutes, whisking constantly. Remove from heat and stir in goat cheese and sage. Set aside.

• Add squash to boiling water and cook 4 to 5 minutes. Stir in noodles, return to a boil and cook 5 minutes more. Drain. Meanwhile, melt remaining 1 teaspoon butter in a 10-inch nonstick skillet over medium-high heat. Add bread crumbs and brown 30 seconds. Transfer to a bowl. Crumble sausage into same skillet. Cook 4 minutes, breaking apart with a wooden spoon.

• Transfer noodles and squash to a large bowl. Stir in sausage and cheese sauce. Fold together until well combined. Pour into prepared dish, spreading level. Top with toasted bread crumbs. Bake at 350° for 20 to 25 minutes.

PER SERVING 483 **CAL**; 18 g **FAT** (9 g **SAT**); 29 g **PRO**; 58 g **CARB**; 8 g **FIBER**; 781 mg **SODIUM**; 65 mg **CHOL**

Greek Baked Eggs and Wheat Berries

MAKES 6 servings **PREP** 10 minutes
COOK 12 minutes **BAKE** at 375° for 35 minutes

1½	cups parcooked wheat berries
2	tablespoons unsalted butter
3	tablespoons all-purpose flour
1½	cups 2% milk, warmed
¾	teaspoon salt
¼	teaspoon black pepper
1	package (5 ounces) baby kale, chopped
2	teaspoons fresh oregano, chopped
1	package (9 ounces) frozen artichoke hearts, thawed
2	tablespoons lemon juice
6	ounces feta cheese, crumbled (about 1¼ cups)
6	large eggs
	Cracked black pepper (optional)

• Heat oven to 375°. Coat a 13 x 9 x 2-inch baking dish with nonstick cooking spray.

• In a medium saucepan, bring 3¾ cups water and the wheat berries to a boil. Cover, reduce heat and simmer 12 minutes. Drain.

• Meanwhile, melt butter in another medium saucepan over medium heat. Whisk in flour; cook for 1 minute. Whisk in milk, ¼ teaspoon of the salt and the pepper. Bring to a boil. Stir in kale and cook 2 minutes. Remove from heat and stir in oregano.

• In a large bowl, combine cooked wheat berries, artichoke hearts, white sauce and remaining ½ teaspoon salt. Fold in lemon juice and all but 1 tablespoon of the feta. Spread into prepared dish.

• Bake at 375° for 10 minutes. Remove from oven and use the bottom of a greased small measuring cup to make 6 indents in wheat berry mixture. Crack eggs into indents. Return to oven and bake at 375° an additional 25 minutes. Sprinkle with reserved feta and, if desired, cracked black pepper.

PER SERVING 409 **CAL**; 16 g **FAT** (8 g **SAT**); 22 g **PRO**; 46 g **CARB**; 8 g **FIBER**; 771 mg **SODIUM**; 236 mg **CHOL**

GREEK BAKED EGGS AND
WHEAT BERRIES

BOURBON SWEET
POTATO PIE, PAGE 284

NOVEMBER

293

297

299

BEAT-THE-CLOCK THANKSGIVING

Time is on your side with these three holiday menu options.

6-Hour Menu

Perked-up classics for the perfect holiday meal.

Herb-Butter-Roasted Turkey
• Roasted Cauliflower and Broccoli with
Spicy Yogurt Sauce • Brussels Sprouts with
Cherries and Pistachios • Cranberry-
Pomegranate Relish • Prosciutto-Sage
Mashed Potatoes • Sausage, Pear and Pecan
Stuffing • Bourbon Sweet Potato Pie

Time Line

6 HOURS BEFORE: Make pie
5 HOURS BEFORE: Bake stuffing; make relish
4 HOURS BEFORE: Roast Brussels sprouts,
cauliflower and broccoli
3 HOURS BEFORE: Roast turkey and make gravy;
finish vegetable dishes; cook mashed potatoes

When you have ample time to prepare for Thanksgiving dinner, this traditional spread of a whole oven-roasted turkey and all the fixings—plus homemade sweet potato pie—is worth the effort.

Herb-Butter–Roasted Turkey

MAKES 12 servings **PREP** 25 minutes **ROAST** at 425° for 2½ hours
LET REST 15 minutes **COOK** 7 minutes

1	turkey (10–12 pounds), thawed if frozen
½	cup (1 stick) unsalted butter, at room temperature
¼	cup fresh parsley, chopped
1	tablespoon fresh thyme, chopped
1	tablespoon fresh rosemary, chopped
1	teaspoon fresh sage, chopped
1¼	teaspoons salt
1	lemon, quartered
1	small yellow onion, quartered
¼	teaspoon plus ⅛ teaspoon black pepper
2	tablespoons all-purpose flour
2	cups unsalted turkey or chicken stock

• Allow turkey to sit at room temperature for 30 minutes before placing in oven. Remove giblets and neck (add neck to roasting pan, if desired); pat dry with paper towels. Heat oven to 425°.

• In a bowl, mix butter, parsley, thyme, rosemary, sage and ¼ teaspoon of the salt until well combined.

• Place lemon and onion inside turkey. Tie legs and place on a rack in a roasting pan, tucking wings underneath turkey. Season with remaining 1 teaspoon salt and ¼ teaspoon of the pepper. Spread 4 tablespoons of the herb butter on the turkey (refrigerate remaining butter; 1 more tablespoon will be used to make gravy and the rest can be for another use). Roast on bottom rack at 425° for 2 to 2½ hours or until temperature in thigh reaches 165°. (Cover legs with foil if darkening too quickly, but resist opening the oven too often.) Transfer turkey to a cutting board and allow to rest for 15 minutes before carving.

• While turkey is resting, make gravy. Place roasting pan over two burners on medium heat. Add 1 tablespoon of the herb butter. When melted, whisk in flour. Cook for 2 minutes. Pour in stock and bring to a boil. Reduce to a simmer and cook for 3 to 5 minutes, until thickened. Season with remaining ⅛ teaspoon pepper. Serve alongside turkey.

PER SERVING 636 CAL; 37 g FAT (23 g SAT); 72 g PRO; 2 g CARB; 0 g FIBER; 352 mg SODIUM; 289 mg CHOL

Cranberry-Pomegranate Relish

MAKES 8 servings **PREP** 5 minutes

1	bag (12 ounces) fresh cranberries
1	cup pomegranate arils
⅔	to ¾ cup sugar
1	tablespoon lemon juice
	Fresh mint (optional garnish)

• In a food processor, pulse cranberries, pomegranate arils, ⅔ cup of the sugar and the lemon juice until combined and a relish-like consistency. Add more sugar, as needed, for desired level of sweetness. If desired, garnish with mint.

PER SERVING 79 CAL; 0 g FAT (0 g SAT); 0 g PRO; 22 g CARB; 3 g FIBER; 1 mg SODIUM; 0 mg CHOL

SAUSAGE, PEAR AND
PECAN STUFFING

Sausage, Pear and Pecan Stuffing

MAKES 8 servings **PREP** 20 minutes
BAKE at 400° for 33 minutes **COOK** 12 minutes

1	loaf (about 12 ounces) challah, cut into ½-inch cubes
½	pound sweet Italian sausage, casings removed
2	pears (Bosc or Anjou), peeled, cored and diced
1	small yellow onion, diced
2	cloves garlic, minced
1½	cups unsalted turkey or chicken stock
1	cup chopped pecans
1	tablespoon chopped fresh thyme
1	tablespoon chopped fresh sage
¾	teaspoon salt
¼	teaspoon black pepper

• Heat oven to 400°. Distribute challah cubes in one layer over two rimmed baking sheets. Bake for 8 minutes, until lightly browned. Transfer to a large bowl.

• Meanwhile, heat a skillet over medium-high heat. Add sausage, breaking apart with a spoon. Cook for 5 to 7 minutes, until browned. Reduce heat to medium. Stir in pears, onion and garlic; cook for 5 minutes. Stir in stock, scraping bottom of pan to release browned bits. Mix in pecans, thyme, sage, salt and pepper. Pour mixture into bowl with challah; stir until well combined. Transfer to a 13 x 9 x 2-inch casserole dish, pressing down a bit with a spatula. Cover dish with aluminum foil and bake at 400° for 20 minutes. Uncover and bake another 5 minutes.

PER SERVING 316 **CAL**; 18 g **FAT** (3 g **SAT**); 10 g **PRO**; 33 g **CARB**; 3 g **FIBER**; 616 mg **SODIUM**; 53 mg **CHOL**

ROASTED CAULIFLOWER AND BROCCOLI WITH SPICY YOGURT SAUCE

Roasted Cauliflower and Broccoli with Spicy Yogurt Sauce

MAKES 8 servings **PREP** 15 minutes **ROAST** at 400° for 25 minutes **COOK** 2 minutes

8	cups cauliflower florets
8	cups broccoli florets
¼	cup olive oil
½	teaspoon plus ⅛ teaspoon salt
⅛	teaspoon black pepper
2	cloves garlic, sliced
½	teaspoon hot paprika
½	teaspoon smoked paprika
⅓	cup plain yogurt

• Heat oven to 400°. In a large bowl, toss cauliflower and broccoli with 3 tablespoons of the olive oil, ½ teaspoon of the salt and the pepper. Distribute in one layer over two rimmed baking sheets. Roast at 400° for 15 minutes. Stir and roast 10 minutes more. If roasting at the same time as the Brussels sprouts (page 284), swap racks.

• Meanwhile, heat remaining 1 tablespoon olive oil in a sauté pan over medium heat. Stir in garlic and both paprikas; cook for 2 minutes. Scrape into yogurt and season with remaining ⅛ teaspoon salt. Drizzle veggies with spicy yogurt sauce.

PER SERVING 116 **CAL**; 7 g **FAT** (1 g **SAT**); 4 g **PRO**; 11 g **CARB**; 4 g **FIBER**; 240 mg **SODIUM**; 1 mg **CHOL**

PROSCIUTTO-SAGE MASHED POTATOES

BRUSSELS SPROUTS WITH CHERRIES AND PISTACHIOS

Brussels Sprouts with Cherries and Pistachios

MAKES 8 servings **PREP** 15 minutes
ROAST at 400° for 25 minutes

2	pounds Brussels sprouts, quartered
2	tablespoons olive oil
½	teaspoon salt
⅛	teaspoon black pepper
2	tablespoons cherry or regular balsamic vinegar
1	teaspoon Dijon mustard
⅓	cup chopped pistachios
½	cup dried sweet cherries
	Freshly cracked black pepper (optional)

• Heat oven to 400°. On a rimmed baking sheet, toss Brussels sprouts with 1 tablespoon of the oil, ¼ teaspoon of the salt and the ⅛ teaspoon pepper. Roast at 400° for 15 minutes. Mix and roast 10 minutes more. If roasting at the same time as the cauliflower and broccoli (page 283), swap racks.

• In a large bowl, whisk vinegar, remaining 1 tablespoon oil, the mustard and remaining ¼ teaspoon salt. Stir in roasted Brussels sprouts, pistachios and cherries. Season with freshly cracked black pepper, if desired.

PER SERVING 136 CAL; 6 g FAT (1 g SAT); 5 g PRO; 18 g CARB; 5 g FIBER; 188 mg SODIUM; 0 mg CHOL

Prosciutto-Sage Mashed Potatoes

MAKES 8 servings **PREP** 15 minutes
COOK 10 minutes

1	cup milk
1	tablespoon chopped fresh sage
4	ounces prosciutto, diced
3	pounds baking potatoes, peeled and diced into 2-inch cubes
3	tablespoons unsalted butter
½	cup mascarpone cheese
1	teaspoon salt

• Bring milk and sage to a simmer over medium-low heat in a small, lidded pot. Remove from heat and keep covered. Add prosciutto to a small saucepan over medium heat; cook for 5 minutes, until crispy. Set aside.

• Meanwhile, add potatoes to a large pot. Cover with cold water by 1 inch. Bring to a boil and cook for 10 minutes, until fork-tender. Drain potatoes and return to pot. Pour in milk-sage mixture, butter and mascarpone. Mash potatoes until everything is well combined. Stir in salt and prosciutto.

PER SERVING 344 CAL; 20 g FAT (11 g SAT); 10 g PRO; 33 g CARB; 3 g FIBER; 672 mg SODIUM; 58 mg CHOL

Bourbon Sweet Potato Pie

MAKES 8 servings **PREP** 15 minutes
MICROWAVE 6 minutes **BAKE** at 400° for 15 minutes and at 350° for 45 minutes
BROIL 2 minutes

1	refrigerated piecrust (from a 15-ounce package)
1	pound sweet potatoes (about 2 large)
2	eggs
4	tablespoons unsalted butter, melted
⅔	cup packed dark brown sugar
¾	cup heavy cream
¼	cup plus 1 tablespoon bourbon
½	teaspoon cinnamon
½	teaspoon vanilla extract
¼	teaspoon nutmeg
4	teaspoons powdered egg whites
¼	cup granulated sugar

• Heat oven to 400°. Roll out piecrust and fit into a 9-inch pie plate. Crimp edges. Place a piece of parchment on crust and fill with pie weights or dried beans. Bake at 400° for 15 minutes. Remove parchment and weights or beans. Reduce heat to 350°.

• Meanwhile, pierce sweet potatoes a few times with a fork and place on a plate. Microwave for 3 minutes. Turn over and cook another 2 to 3 minutes. Let cool slightly, then carefully slice and scoop flesh out into a large bowl. Beat sweet potatoes, whole eggs, butter, brown sugar, heavy cream, ¼ cup of the bourbon, the cinnamon, vanilla and nutmeg until smooth. Transfer to crust and smooth top. Bake at 350° for 40 to 45 minutes, until firm.

• In a mixing bowl, combine powdered egg whites and 3 tablespoons warm water. Stir gently until dissolved. Beat in remaining 1 tablespoon bourbon until frothy. Gradually add granulated sugar and beat with an electric mixer until stiff peaks form, 5 to 7 minutes. Spoon onto warm pie, making sure meringue reaches edge of crust. Broil on HIGH for 1 to 2 minutes, until lightly browned, watching carefully.

PER SERVING 417 CAL; 22 g FAT (12 g SAT); 5 g PRO; 46 g CARB; 1 g FIBER; 160 mg SODIUM; 103 mg CHOL

BOURBON SWEET POTATO PIE

4-Hour Menu

A fried turkey means the oven is free for sides and desserts.

**Roasted Garlic and Sage Fried Turkey
• Honeyed Sweet Potatoes • Sautéed Green Beans with Parmesan • Creamy Corn and Bacon Casserole • Quick Cranberry Chutney • Smoky Southern Cornbread Dressing • Spiced Olive Oil Cake**

Time Line

4 HOURS BEFORE: Bake cake
3 HOURS BEFORE: Make chutney; prep sweet potatoes; assemble dressing
2 HOURS BEFORE: Heat oil in fryer; trim green beans; assemble corn casserole; inject turkey with seasonings
DURING LAST HOUR: Fry turkey; bake dressing and corn casserole; cook green beans and sweet potatoes; frost cake

Turkey-fryer devotees claim a bird that emerges from the hot oil is the juiciest you'll ever taste. Two side benefits to frying your turkey: The oven is free to prepare other dishes, and the cook time for a whole bird is significantly less than for an oven-roasted one.

Roasted Garlic and Sage Fried Turkey

MAKES 8 servings **PREP** 30 minutes **MICROWAVE** 6 minutes **FRY** 3 to 4 minutes per pound

	Peanut or canola oil
1	turkey fryer
1	head garlic
1	teaspoon olive oil
½	cup low-sodium chicken or turkey broth
1	tablespoon fresh sage
1	teaspoon fresh thyme leaves
¾	teaspoon salt
½	teaspoon black pepper
1	turkey (about 11 pounds), thawed if frozen
1	injector

• Follow directions on your turkey fryer as to how much oil you will need (we used a scant 2 gallons). Pour oil into fryer and heat per manufacturer's directions.

• Cut off top of head of garlic, so cloves are showing. Place in a small glass bowl and add 3 tablespoons water. Drizzle top of garlic with olive oil. Cover with plastic wrap and microwave at 50% power for 6 minutes, checking halfway through. Remove to a cutting board and let cool slightly. Squeeze cloves from papery skin and transfer to a mini chopper along with broth, sage, thyme and ¼ teaspoon each of the salt and pepper. Whirl until smooth and herbs are very finely chopped.

• Place turkey in a disposable foil pan and remove neck and giblets. Discard or save for another use. Pat turkey dry (inside and out) with paper towels. Pour some of the roasted garlic mixture into the injector and inject into breast meat, thighs and drumsticks of turkey (you should be able to use all the liquid).

• Place turkey in fryer basket and carefully lower into hot oil per manufacturer's directions. Cover and fry turkey 3 to 4 minutes per pound, until meat registers 165° (it's fine if top of turkey is not immersed). Let oil drain from turkey for 10 minutes. Carefully remove turkey from fryer basket and transfer to a serving platter.

PER SERVING 588 **CAL**; 20 g **FAT** (6 g **SAT**); 95 g **PRO**; 1 g **CARB**; 0 g **FIBER**; 446 mg **SODIUM**; 398 mg **CHOL**

Quick Cranberry Chutney

MAKES 8 servings **PREP** 5 minutes
COOK 10 minutes **COOL** 1 hour

1	bag (12 ounces) fresh or frozen cranberries
¾	cup orange juice
¾	cup sugar
¾	cup golden raisins
¼	teaspoon ground cardamom (optional)
½	teaspoon ground ginger
	Pinch salt

• Combine cranberries, juice, sugar, raisins, cardamom and ginger in a saucepan. Bring to a boil over high heat. Reduce heat to medium and simmer 10 minutes, stirring, until cranberries have burst and sauce thickens.

• Remove pan from heat and stir in salt. Transfer chutney to a serving bowl and cool for at least 1 hour.

PER SERVING 103 **CAL**; 0 g **FAT** (0 g **SAT**); 0 g **PRO**; 26 g **CARB**; 2 g **FIBER**; 37 mg **SODIUM**; 0 mg **CHOL**

SMOKY SOUTHERN CORNBREAD DRESSING

SAUTÉED GREEN BEANS WITH PARMESAN

1⅔	cups chicken or turkey stock
2	teaspoons fresh sage
½	teaspoon salt
⅛	teaspoon cayenne pepper
3	large eggs, lightly beaten

• Heat oven to 375°. Spread cornbread onto a large baking sheet. Toast at 375° for 17 minutes, until lightly browned.

• Meanwhile, cook bacon in a large skillet over medium-high heat for 5 to 6 minutes, until crisp. Remove to a plate with a slotted spoon. Reduce heat to medium, and add onion and celery to skillet. Cook, stirring, for 6 minutes. Stir in 1⅓ cups of the stock, the sage, salt and cayenne, and bring to a simmer.

• Combine toasted cornbread and bacon in a large bowl. Carefully pour contents of skillet into bowl and gently stir to blend. Fold in eggs. Transfer to a 2-quart baking dish. Bake at 375° for 25 minutes. Drizzle remaining ⅓ cup stock over dressing and bake an additional 10 minutes.

PER SERVING 250 CAL; 9 g FAT (3 g SAT); 7 g PRO; 36 g CARB; 2 g FIBER; 919 mg SODIUM; 92 mg CHOL

Honeyed Sweet Potatoes

MAKES 8 servings PREP 10 minutes
COOK 10 minutes

3	pounds sweet potatoes, peeled and cut into 1½-inch pieces
3	tablespoons unsalted butter
¼	cup honey
¼	teaspoon ground cinnamon
⅛	teaspoon cayenne pepper
¾	teaspoon salt
¼	teaspoon black pepper
½	cup toasted pecans

• Bring a large pot of lightly salted water to a boil (or use water from cooking green beans, at left). Add sweet potatoes, return to a boil and cook for 8 minutes. Drain.

• Melt butter in a large nonstick skillet over medium heat. Add honey, cinnamon and cayenne. Stir in sweet potatoes and season with salt and black pepper. Cook, stirring to coat, for 2 minutes. Remove to a platter or bowl and top with toasted pecans.

PER SERVING 222 CAL; 9 g FAT (3 g SAT); 3 g PRO; 33 g CARB; 4 g FIBER; 255 mg SODIUM; 11 mg CHOL

Sautéed Green Beans with Parmesan

MAKES 8 servings PREP 10 minutes
COOK 9 minutes

1½	pounds green beans, trimmed
2	tablespoons unsalted butter
1	package (8 ounces) sliced baby bella mushrooms
1	teaspoon fresh thyme, chopped
½	teaspoon fresh oregano, chopped
½	teaspoon salt
	Freshly ground black pepper
¼	cup shaved Parmesan cheese

• Bring a large pot of lightly salted water to a boil. Add green beans and cook for 3 minutes. Turn off heat and remove to a bowl with a slotted spoon. Save water for Honeyed Sweet Potatoes, if desired (recipe at far right).

• Melt butter in a large nonstick skillet over medium-high heat. Add mushrooms and sauté for 3 to 5 minutes. Stir in green beans, thyme, oregano, salt and a few grinds of black pepper. Cook for 1 minute. Transfer to a platter or bowl and top with shaved Parmesan.

PER SERVING 84 CAL; 4 g FAT (3 g SAT); 4 g PRO; 7 g CARB; 3 g FIBER; 232 mg SODIUM; 12 mg CHOL

Smoky Southern Cornbread Dressing

MAKES 8 servings PREP 10 minutes
COOK 12 minutes BAKE at 375° for 52 minutes

1½	pounds purchased cornbread, cut into 1-inch cubes
6	ounces bacon (about 7 slices), chopped
1	medium onion, chopped
2	ribs celery, chopped

HONEYED SWEET POTATOES

CREAMY CORN AND BACON CASSEROLE

Creamy Corn and Bacon Casserole

MAKES 8 servings **PREP** 15 minutes **COOK** 13 minutes **BAKE** at 375° for 35 minutes

6	ounces (about 7 slices) center-cut bacon, chopped
1	medium red onion, chopped
1	medium red sweet pepper, cored and chopped
1	bag (16 ounces) frozen corn kernels, thawed
¼	cup fresh parsley, chopped
2	large eggs plus 1 egg white
½	cup heavy cream
¼	teaspoon salt
¼	teaspoon black pepper
¼	teaspoon ground cumin
1¼	cups shredded sharp cheddar cheese
1	teaspoon cornstarch

• Heat oven to 375°. Coat a 1½-quart baking dish with nonstick cooking spray. Heat a large skillet over medium-high heat. Add bacon and cook, stirring, 5 to 6 minutes; remove to a plate with a slotted spoon.

• Reduce heat to medium, and add onion and sweet pepper to skillet. Cook for 7 minutes, until softened. Remove from heat, and stir in corn and parsley.

• In a large bowl, whisk together eggs, egg white, heavy cream, salt, black pepper and cumin. Stir in vegetables and bacon. In a small bowl, toss together 1 cup of the cheddar and the cornstarch. Fold into corn mixture and transfer to prepared baking dish. Bake at 375° for 25 minutes. Top with remaining ¼ cup cheddar and bake 10 minutes more.

PER SERVING 250 **CAL**; 17 g **FAT** (9 g **SAT**); 11 g **PRO**; 15 g **CARB**; 2 g **FIBER**; 297 mg **SODIUM**; 99 mg **CHOL**

SPICED
OLIVE OIL
CAKE

Infused with traditional fall spices—including cardamom, cinnamon and ginger—this elegantly rustic cake has a moist, tender texture from the olive oil. If you have extra-virgin olive oil, it's fine to use that—but regular olive oil will give the cake a milder, more neutral flavor.

Spiced Olive Oil Cake

MAKES 12 servings **PREP** 25 minutes **BAKE** at 350° for 55 minutes **COOL** 10 minutes plus 2 hours

CAKE

2	cups cake flour (not self-rising)
1	teaspoon ground cardamom
1	teaspoon ground cinnamon
1	teaspoon ground ginger
½	teaspoon salt
½	teaspoon baking powder
½	teaspoon baking soda
3	large eggs, separated
1¼	cups sugar
½	vanilla bean
1¼	cups milk
¾	cup plus 2 tablespoons olive oil

FROSTING AND TOPPING

½	package Neufchâtel (reduced-fat cream cheese), softened
¼	cup (½ stick) unsalted butter, softened
¼	cup confectioners' sugar
	Pinch of salt
¼	cup heavy cream
	Dried orange slices or fresh lemon peel (optional)
	Pepitas (optional)

• Heat oven to 350°. Coat a 9-inch square baking pan with nonstick cooking spray. Line bottom with wax paper; coat paper with nonstick cooking spray.

• **Cake.** In a large bowl, whisk together cake flour, cardamom, cinnamon, ginger, salt, baking powder and baking soda. In a second large bowl, beat egg whites with an electric mixer until frothy. Add ¼ cup of the sugar and beat until stiff, shiny peaks form. Set aside. In a medium bowl, beat egg yolks. Split vanilla bean in half lengthwise and scrape seeds from pod. Add to egg yolks along with ½ cup of the sugar. Beat until pale yellow and fluffy, about 2 minutes. On low speed, beat in milk, oil and remaining ½ cup sugar. Whisk egg yolk mixture into flour mixture.

• Fold whipped egg whites into batter and pour into prepared pan. Bake at 350° for 55 minutes, until cake springs back when gently pressed.

• **Frosting.** Beat together Neufchâtel and butter until smooth and no lumps remain. On low speed, beat in confectioners' sugar and salt. Add heavy cream and beat on medium until fluffy and smooth.

• Cool cake in pan on a wire rack for 10 minutes. Invert cake onto a rack; remove wax paper and turn right-side-up onto rack. Cool completely (about 2 hours) and spread top with frosting. If desired, garnish with dried fruit or lemon peel and pepitas.

PER SERVING 384 **CAL**; 22 g **FAT** (7 g **SAT**); 5 g **PRO**; 43 g **CARB**; 1 g **FIBER**; 236 mg **SODIUM**; 72 mg **CHOL**

2-Hour Menu:

Whip up your feast while you watch the Macy's Thanksgiving Day Parade.

Cranberry-Glazed Turkey Breast • Roasted Fingerlings, Parsnips and Baby Carrots • Fig and Toasted Pine Nut Dressing • Mixed Lettuces with Pear and Blue Cheese • Eggnog Ice Cream Parfaits

Time Line

2 HOURS BEFORE: Simmer cranberry glaze; prep potatoes and vegetables

1½ HOURS BEFORE: Roast turkey breast, potatoes and vegetables

DURING LAST HOUR: Make fig and pine nut dressing; prep salad; whip cream and refrigerate

CRANBERRY-GLAZED TURKEY BREAST WITH ROASTED FINGERLINGS, PARSNIPS AND BABY CARROTS

If you prefer white meat—and have only a couple of hours to whip up the entire feast—this menu featuring a roasted turkey breast is for you.

MIXED LETTUCES WITH PEAR AND BLUE CHEESE

Cranberry-Glazed Turkey Breast

MAKES 6 servings **PREP** 15 minutes **ROAST** at 375° for 1 hour **COOK** 5 minutes
BROIL 5 minutes **LET REST** 10 minutes

- 1   large boneless turkey breast half (3–3½ pounds)
- 2   tablespoons olive oil
- ½   teaspoon salt
- ¼   teaspoon black pepper
- 1   can (14 ounces) whole cranberry sauce
- 1   can (14 ounces) jellied cranberry sauce
- 2   tablespoons brown sugar
- 1   tablespoon lemon zest
- ½   teaspoon ground cinnamon

• Heat oven to 375°. Fit a rack into a roasting pan.

• Place turkey in prepared roasting pan. Brush oil over turkey and season with salt and pepper. Roast at 375° for 1 hour or until temperature reaches 160°. (Potatoes and vegetables, at right, will be roasting at the same time.)

• Meanwhile, combine cranberry sauces, brown sugar, lemon zest and cinnamon in a medium saucepan and simmer 5 minutes over medium-high heat. Stir occasionally.

• After 30 minutes of roasting, brush ½ cup of the glaze over turkey; repeat with an additional ½ cup after 45 minutes. After turkey is done, broil 6 inches from heat source for 5 minutes.

• Allow turkey to rest 10 minutes before slicing. Serve remaining cranberry glaze with turkey.

PER SERVING 489 **CAL**; 6 g **FAT** (1 g **SAT**); 54 g **PRO**; 54 g **CARB**; 2 g **FIBER**; 317 mg **SODIUM**; 149 mg **CHOL**

Roasted Fingerlings, Parsnips and Baby Carrots

MAKES 6 servings **PREP** 15 minutes
ROAST at 375° for 55 minutes **BROIL** 3 minutes

- 1¾   pounds fingerling potatoes or small red-skin potatoes (1 inch in diameter)
- 1   pound parsnips, peeled and cut into 1-inch pieces
- ¾   pound baby carrots
- 2   tablespoons olive oil
- 1   tablespoon dark brown sugar
- ½   teaspoon salt
- ½   teaspoon dried Italian seasoning
- ¼   teaspoon black pepper

• In a large bowl, toss potatoes, parsnips and carrots with olive oil. Season with brown sugar, salt, Italian seasoning and black pepper. Place on a large rimmed baking sheet.

• Roast at 375° for 55 minutes at the same time as turkey breast. Rotate pan after 30 minutes. Just before serving, broil 6 inches from heat source for 3 minutes.

PER SERVING 233 **CAL**; 5 g **FAT** (1 g **SAT**); 3 g **PRO**; 46 g **CARB**; 8 g **FIBER**; 253 mg **SODIUM**; 0 mg **CHOL**

Mixed Lettuces with Pear and Blue Cheese

MAKES 6 servings **PREP** 10 minutes

- 6   cups mixed baby lettuces
- 2   tablespoons grapeseed oil
- 1   tablespoon pomegranate balsamic vinegar
- ⅛   teaspoon salt
- ⅛   teaspoon black pepper
- 1   Bosc pear, thinly sliced
- ½   cup crumbled blue cheese

• Place baby lettuces in a large salad bowl. Toss with oil and vinegar. Season with salt and pepper. Gently fold in pear slices and blue cheese. Serve immediately.

PER SERVING 105 **CAL**; 8 g **FAT** (3 g **SAT**); 3 g **PRO**; 6 g **CARB**; 1 g **FIBER**; 209 mg **SODIUM**; 8 mg **CHOL**

FIG AND TOASTED PINE NUT DRESSING

Finish the Thanksgiving feast with a forward-thinking dessert—eggnog parfaits that hint at the holiday to come.

Eggnog Ice Cream Parfaits

MAKES 6 servings **PREP** 10 minutes

½	**cup heavy cream**
1	**teaspoon sugar**
¼	**teaspoon vanilla extract**
24	**gingersnap cookies, crushed**
3	**cups eggnog-flavor ice cream**
3	**cups rum raisin ice cream** **Cinnamon, mint and cherries for garnish**

• In a large bowl, beat heavy cream on medium speed until foamy. Add sugar and vanilla; beat on medium-high until soft peaks form. Refrigerate until serving.

• In each of six 12-ounce dessert glasses, layer 2 tablespoons cookie crumbs, one ½-cup scoop eggnog ice cream, 2 tablespoons cookie crumbs and one ½-cup scoop rum raisin ice cream. Garnish with whipped cream, cinnamon, mint and cherries.

PER SERVING 467 **CAL**; 12 g **FAT** (6 g **SAT**); 5 g **PRO**; 55 g **CARB**; 0 g **FIBER**; 102 mg **SODIUM**; 27 mg **CHOL**

Fig and Toasted Pine Nut Dressing

MAKES 6 servings **PREP** 10 minutes **COOK** 3 minutes

1	**tablespoon vegetable oil**
1	**cup pre-chopped onion, carrot and celery**
2	**cups turkey or chicken broth**
6	**tablespoons unsalted butter**
4	**cups herb-seasoned bread stuffing cubes**
4	**dried Turkish figs, chopped (about ½ cup)**
¼	**cup toasted pine nuts**

• Heat oil in a medium saucepan over medium-high heat; add chopped vegetables and cook 3 minutes. Add broth, 1 cup water and 4 tablespoons of the butter. Bring to a simmer. Stir in stuffing cubes and figs; cover and let stand 5 minutes.

• To serve, fluff with a fork and dot with remaining butter. Sprinkle pine nuts over top.

PER SERVING 353 **CAL**; 19 g **FAT** (8 g **SAT**); 6 g **PRO**; 40 g **CARB**; 5 g **FIBER**; 856 mg **SODIUM**; 30 mg **CHOL**

EGGNOG ICE CREAM
PARFAITS

FALL FOR SWEETS

For the holidays or just because—here are some new ways to enjoy autumnal treats.

PUMPKIN CAKES

CANDY-COATED PRETZELS

ACORNS

OWL CUPCAKES

...15 minutes
...
...atch

...ice, vanilla

...ng

• H
two
Prep
direc
wate
cupc

• Bake
center
Transfe
5 minute
Using a sr
tops to ma

• Tint frosti
Spread a little frosting on cut side of 12 of
the cakes. Sandwich with remaining
12 cakes. Microwave remaining frosting
5 to 10 seconds, until smooth but not too
thin. Spoon some frosting on top of a
stacked cake, allowing it to drip down the
sides. Top with nonpareils or sprinkles.
Cut a Tootsie Roll in half diagonally and
reshape slightly with your hands. Add to
top of cake as stem.

• Repeat with other flavors of cake mix,
if desired.

Candy-Coated Pretzels

MAKES 16 servings (about 10 pretzels each)
PREP 25 minutes
MICROWAVE 1½ minutes per batch

1	cup each white, yellow and orange candy melts (such as Wilton brand)
1½	teaspoons vegetable oil
6½	cups mini pretzels
	Assorted nonpareils and sparkling sugars

• Place white candy melts in a
microwave-safe bowl. Microwave for
30 seconds, then stir. Continue to
microwave in 30-second increments
until smooth. Stir in ½ teaspoon of
the oil.

• Using two forks, dip a pretzel into
melted candy. Tap against side of bowl
to allow excess candy to drip off. Slide
off fork onto a wire rack set over a
rimmed baking sheet. Repeat with five
more pretzels, then decorate as desired
with nonpareils, sparkling sugars or
drizzled candy melts. Repeat with
remaining colors of candy melts,
pretzels and assorted decorations.

Acorns

MAKES 24 servings
PREP 30 minutes
MICROWAVE at 70% power for 1 minute

¾	cup peanut butter chips
½	teaspoon vegetable oil (if needed)
24	Nutter Butter Bites cookies (from an 8-ounce bag)
48	unwrapped Hershey's Kisses
48	semisweet chocolate chips

• Place peanut butter chips in a small
microwave-safe bowl. Microwave at
70% power per package directions to
melt. Stir in vegetable oil if stiff.

• Split Nutter Butter Bites. Dip the
bottom of one Kiss into melted chips.
Secure a Nutter Butter half onto Kiss.
Dip flat bottom of a semisweet chip into
melted chips and press onto top of
Nutter Butter. Place on wax paper to
dry. Repeat with remaining ingredients.

Owl Cupcakes

MAKES 6 servings **PREP** 15 minutes
BAKE per package directions

6	baked chocolate cupcakes
12	baked mini chocolate cupcakes
1	can (16 ounces) chocolate frosting
12	Double Stuf Oreo cookies
24	mini Oreo cookies
12	brown and 6 orange M&M's
24	brown and 12 orange mini M&M's

• Spread all cupcakes with frosting.
Separate Double Stuf Oreo cookies by
carefully slicing down, leaving filling on
one side of each sandwich. Scrape any
cookie crumbs off filling. Place two
cookie halves, filling side up, on each
frosted standard-size cupcake. Gently
press brown M&M's into Oreos to finish
eyes and an orange M&M's into frosting
as beak. Cut pointed ears out of leftover
cookie halves and tuck into top of each
cupcake behind eyes.

• Repeat process with mini cupcakes,
mini cookies and mini M&M's.

These whimsical and tasty
treats will please the palate
and tickle the fancy of
anyone—of any age—who
has a sweet tooth and a
sense of humor.

FLAVOR MAKEOVERS

Five cooking techniques that are big on taste but light on fat and calories.

BEER-BRAISED
BEEF WITH
POTATOES AND
CABBAGE

MOROCCAN SHRIMP AND COUSCOUS

1. BRAISING

Beer-Braised Beef with Potatoes and Cabbage

MAKES 4 servings **PREP** 15 minutes
COOK 1 hour, 10 minutes

- 1½ **pounds beef chuck, cut into 1-inch pieces**
- 1 **cup thinly sliced onion**
- 2 **cloves garlic, sliced**
- 2 **teaspoons chopped fresh thyme**
- 2 **tablespoons all-purpose flour**
- 1 **teaspoon salt**
- ½ **teaspoon black pepper**
- 1 **tablespoon tomato paste**
- 1 **cup unsalted beef broth**
- 1 **cup Guinness beer**
- 1½ **pounds red-skin potatoes, cut into 2-inch pieces (do not peel)**
- 3 **cups chopped green cabbage**
- ½ **cup plain nonfat yogurt**
- ½ **cup buttermilk**
  Fresh parsley (for garnish)

• In a Dutch oven or heavy-bottomed pot, toss beef cubes with onion, garlic, thyme, flour, ½ teaspoon of the salt and ¼ teaspoon of the pepper. Add tomato paste, broth and beer. Cover and bring to a boil. Reduce to a low simmer and cook 1 hour, until beef is tender. With a slotted spoon, remove beef to a bowl. Increase heat to high and bring sauce to a boil. Simmer 10 minutes, until thickened. Stir beef back into sauce, cover and remove from heat.

• Meanwhile, add potatoes to a medium pot and fill with cold water. Bring to a boil and cook 9 minutes. Stir in cabbage; cook 3 minutes more. Drain and return to pot. Add yogurt and buttermilk. Mash and stir in remaining ½ teaspoon salt and ¼ teaspoon pepper. Serve beef over potato-cabbage mash. Garnish with parsley.

PER SERVING 432 **CAL**; 8 g **FAT** (3 g **SAT**); 43 g **PRO**; 43 g **CARB**; 5 g **FIBER**; 769 mg **SODIUM**; 73 mg **CHOL**

2. COOKING IN PARCHMENT

Moroccan Shrimp and Couscous

MAKES 4 servings **PREP** 20 minutes **COOK** 12 minutes **BAKE** at 400° for 12 minutes

- 1 **teaspoon ground cumin**
- ½ **teaspoon salt**
- ½ **teaspoon ground cinnamon**
- ½ **teaspoon ground turmeric**
- ¼ **teaspoon ground ginger**
- ⅛ **teaspoon ground cayenne**
- 1 **tablespoon olive oil**
- ¼ **cup minced shallots**
- 2 **cloves garlic, minced**
- 1 **cup whole wheat Israeli couscous**
- 1¼ **pounds peeled and deveined shrimp (tails left on)**
- 1 **cup dried apricots**
- 1 **cup pitted dates**
- 8 **large Italian- or Spanish-style green olives with pits**
- 2 **tablespoons lemon juice, plus 1 teaspoon zest**
- 2 **tablespoons white wine, chicken broth or water**
- ½ **cup fresh parsley, chopped**
- ½ **cup fresh cilantro, chopped**
- ¼ **cup chopped almonds**

• Heat oven to 400°. In a small bowl, combine cumin, salt, cinnamon, turmeric, ginger and cayenne.

• Heat olive oil in a medium pot over medium heat. Add half each of the shallots, garlic and spice mixture. Cook 2 minutes, until soft. Stir in couscous and 1¼ cups water; cover and bring to a boil. Reduce to a simmer and cook for 8 to 10 minutes. Set aside, covered.

• In a large bowl, toss shrimp with apricots, dates, olives, lemon juice and zest, wine and remaining shallots, garlic and spice mixture. Transfer to two large parchment cooking bags (such as PaperChef brand) and seal per package directions. Place bags on a rimmed baking sheet. Bake at 400° for 10 to 12 minutes. Carefully open to release steam; toss in a bowl with parsley, cilantro and almonds. Serve shrimp over couscous.

PER SERVING 550 **CAL**; 10 g **FAT** (1 g **SAT**); 30 g **PRO**; 88 g **CARB**; 10 g **FIBER**; 882 mg **SODIUM**; 211 mg **CHOL**

3. GRILLING

Wheat Berries with Grilled Mushrooms and Kale

MAKES 4 servings **PREP** 20 minutes **COOK** 15 minutes **GRILL** 16 minutes

1¼	**cups quick-cook wheat berries**
5	**tablespoons balsamic vinegar**
3	**tablespoons extra-virgin olive oil**
½	**teaspoon Dijon mustard**
1	**teaspoon salt**
¼	**teaspoon plus ⅛ teaspoon black pepper**
12	**ounces kale, trimmed**
10	**ounces cremini mushrooms**
7	**ounces shiitake mushrooms, stems removed and discarded**
⅓	**cup walnuts, toasted and chopped**
4	**poached eggs (optional)**

• Add wheat berries to a medium pot and fill with water. Cover and bring to a boil. Reduce to a simmer and cook for 15 minutes, until tender. Drain.

• Meanwhile, heat a grill or grill pan to medium-high. In a bowl, whisk 3 tablespoons of the vinegar, 2 tablespoons of the oil, the mustard, ¼ teaspoon of the salt and ⅛ teaspoon of the pepper. Pour half the vinaigrette over kale leaves and toss well. Brush remaining vinaigrette over mushrooms (skewer cremini, if desired). Grill cremini 4 minutes per side and shiitakes 2 minutes per side, turning each once. Grill kale 2 minutes per side, in two batches. Quarter cremini, slice shiitakes and chop kale, discarding stems on the latter. Stir into cooked wheat berries with walnuts and remaining 2 tablespoons vinegar, 1 tablespoon oil, ¾ teaspoon salt and ¼ teaspoon pepper. Top each serving with a poached egg, if desired.

PER SERVING 434 **CAL**; 18 g **FAT** (2 g **SAT**); 15 g **PRO**; 55 g **CARB**; 9 g **FIBER**; 630 mg **SODIUM**; 0 mg **CHOL**

WHEAT BERRIES WITH GRILLED MUSHROOMS AND KALE

4. POACHING

Orecchiette with Chicken and Creamy Rosemary Sauce

MAKES 6 servings **PREP** 15 minutes
COOK 21 minutes

1	medium onion, diced
4	cloves garlic, sliced
2	whole sprigs fresh rosemary plus 1 tablespoon chopped
2	whole sprigs fresh thyme plus 1 tablespoon chopped
1	pound boneless, skinless chicken breasts
1	pound orecchiette pasta
2	tablespoons olive oil
2	tablespoons all-purpose flour
2½	cups skim milk
4	ounces plain goat cheese
¾	teaspoon salt
¼	teaspoon black pepper
	Chopped pistachios (optional)

• Add half the onion, 2 cloves of the garlic, the rosemary and thyme sprigs to a pot of lightly salted water. Bring to a boil. Reduce heat to a simmer and add chicken. Simmer 10 to 12 minutes, until cooked through. Using tongs, remove chicken to a cutting board and keep warm.

• Return water to a boil. Add orecchiette. Cook 9 minutes. Drain, removing rosemary and thyme stems.

• Meanwhile, heat oil in a large skillet over medium heat. Add remaining onion; cook 3 minutes. Add remaining 2 cloves garlic and 1 tablespoon each chopped rosemary and thyme; cook 2 minutes. Stir in flour; cook 1 minute more. Slowly whisk in milk; bring to a simmer and cook 5 minutes, until thickened. Stir in goat cheese, salt and pepper.

• Thinly slice chicken. Add to sauce with cooked orecchiette; stir well. Serve with chopped pistachios, if desired.

PER SERVING 505 **CAL**; 11 g **FAT** (4 g **SAT**); 35 g **PRO**; 66 g **CARB**; 3 g **FIBER**; 457 mg **SODIUM**; 55 mg **CHOL**

GINGER AND SCALLION
STEAMED SEA BASS

5. STEAMING

Ginger and Scallion Steamed Sea Bass

MAKES 4 servings **PREP** 20 minutes **MARINATE** 15 minutes **COOK** 15 minutes **STEAM** 8 minutes

¼	cup low-sodium soy sauce
3	tablespoons rice vinegar
2	tablespoons light brown sugar
1	teaspoon sesame oil
½	teaspoon five-spice powder
1	cup thinly sliced scallions
4	tablespoons julienned ginger
1¼	pounds sea bass or cod (4 fillets)
1	pound baby bok choy
1¼	cups jasmine rice
⅓	cup unsalted chicken stock
1	teaspoon cornstarch

• Mix soy sauce, vinegar, brown sugar, sesame oil and five-spice powder in a bowl. Pour ¼ cup of the soy mixture into a small saucepan and set aside. Stir ½ cup of the scallions and 3 tablespoons of the ginger into remaining ¼ cup soy mixture. Pour half over fillets in a resealable plastic bag. Marinate 15 minutes. Toss bok choy with remaining marinade.

• Meanwhile, bring 2½ cups water to a boil in a small lidded pot. Add rice, cover and return to a boil. Reduce heat and cook 15 minutes, until water is absorbed. Keep covered but remove from heat.

• Fill a large skillet with ½ inch water. Stack two bamboo steamer baskets on top with lid. Bring water to a boil. Place fish fillets in bottom basket and bok choy in top basket. Cover with lid; steam for 6 to 8 minutes, just until fish flakes easily with a fork.

• While fish and bok choy are cooking, add stock and cornstarch to contents in saucepan; bring to a boil. Cook 2 minutes, until thickened. Fluff rice. Serve fish and bok choy over rice, spoon sauce on top and garnish with remaining ½ cup scallions.

PER SERVING 313 **CAL**; 4 g **FAT** (1 g **SAT**); 33 g **PRO**; 34 g **CARB**; 2 g **FIBER**; 788 mg **SODIUM**; 62 mg **CHOL**

AMERICA'S BEST
CHOCOLATE CHIP
COOKIES, PAGE 315

CHOCOLATE CHIP
QUINOA COOKIES,
PAGE 315

DECEMBER

320

323

328

CLASSIC COOKIES WITH A TWIST

Best-loved cookies from our archives, plus a modern take on each.

PEANUT BLOSSOMS

SUNBUTTER BLOSSOMS

The classic version of these thumbprint cookies combines peanut butter and chocolate, while the twist swaps sunflower seed spread for the peanut butter. For either version, be sure to press the chocolate Kisses into the cookies as soon as they come out of the oven.

Peanut Blossoms

MAKES 5 dozen cookies **PREP** 15 minutes
BAKE at 375° for 12 minutes per batch

- 1¾ **cups all-purpose flour**
- ½ **cup granulated sugar, plus more for rolling**
- ½ **cup packed brown sugar**
- 1 **teaspoon baking soda**
- ¼ **teaspoon salt**
- ½ **cup solid vegetable shortening**
- ½ **cup peanut butter**
- 2 **tablespoons milk**
- 1 **teaspoon vanilla extract**
- 1 **large egg**
- 60 **milk chocolate Hershey's Kisses, unwrapped**

• Heat oven to 375°. In a large bowl, combine flour, ½ cup granulated sugar, brown sugar, baking soda, salt, shortening, peanut butter, milk, vanilla and egg. Beat on low speed until dough is stiff.

• Shape dough into 1-inch balls; roll in sugar. Place 2 inches apart on ungreased baking sheets.

• Bake at 375° for 10 to 12 minutes or until golden brown. Immediately top each cookie with a Kiss, pressing down firmly so that cookie cracks around edges. Transfer cookies to wire racks to cool.

PER COOKIE 80 **CAL**; 4 g **FAT** (2 g **SAT**); 1 g **PRO**; 9 g **CARB**; 0 g **FIBER**; 47 mg **SODIUM**; 5 mg **CHOL**

SunButter Blossoms

MAKES 3½ dozen cookies **PREP** 15 minutes
BAKE at 375° for 10 minutes per batch

- 1¾ **cups all-purpose flour**
- 1 **teaspoon baking soda**
- ¼ **teaspoon salt**
- ¾ **cup granulated sugar**
- ½ **cup packed dark brown sugar**
- ½ **cup (1 stick) unsalted butter, softened**
- ½ **cup SunButter (sunflower seed spread)**
- 1 **large egg**
- 1 **teaspoon vanilla extract**
- 42 **dark chocolate Hershey's Kisses, unwrapped**

• Heat oven to 375°. In a medium bowl, whisk flour, baking soda and salt. Set aside.

• In a large bowl, combine ½ cup of the granulated sugar, the dark brown sugar, butter and SunButter. Beat on medium speed until light and fluffy. Add egg and beat well. On low speed, beat in vanilla, followed by flour mixture, scraping down sides of bowl.

• Place remaining ¼ cup granulated sugar in a small bowl. Shape dough into 1-inch balls, roll in sugar and place 2 inches apart on baking sheets. Bake at 375° for 8 to 10 minutes. Immediately press a Kiss into each cookie. Transfer cookies to a wire rack and cool completely.

PER COOKIE 96 **CAL**; 5 g **FAT** (2 g **SAT**); 1 g **PRO**; 12 g **CARB**; 1 g **FIBER**; 59 mg **SODIUM**; 10 mg **CHOL**

BASIC SUGAR
COOKIES

PEPPERMINT
MITTENS

A must-have for the holidays, the rolled sugar cookie is infinitely versatile and open to all kinds of decoration interpretations. Crushed starlight mint candies add crunch and a cool touch to the twist.

Basic Sugar Cookies

MAKES 3 dozen cookies **PREP** 15 minutes **REFRIGERATE** at least 4 hours **BAKE** at 350° for 12 minutes per batch

- 1½ **cups all-purpose flour**
- ½ **teaspoon baking powder**
- ⅛ **teaspoon salt**
- ½ **cup (1 stick) unsalted butter, softened**
- ¾ **cup sugar**
- 1 **large egg**
- ¾ **teaspoon vanilla extract**
- **Frosting and nonpareils, for decorating (optional)**

• In a medium bowl, whisk together flour, baking powder and salt. Set aside.

• In a large bowl, beat butter and sugar until smooth, about 2 minutes. Beat in egg and vanilla. On low speed, beat in flour mixture until just combined. Divide dough in half and form each half into a disk. Wrap in plastic wrap and refrigerate for 4 hours or overnight.

• Heat oven to 350°. On a lightly floured surface, roll out one disk to ¼-inch thickness. Using a 2-inch tree-shape cookie cutter, cut out shapes. Place on an ungreased baking sheet. Bake at 350° for 10 to 12 minutes, until lightly golden around edges. Transfer cookies to wire racks to cool completely.

• Repeat with remaining half of dough. Gather scraps and refrigerate. Re-roll and cut into additional trees. Bake and cool as above. If desired, decorate with frosting (see Peppermint Mittens, at right) and nonpareils. When dry, cookies may be stored in an airtight container up to 2 weeks.

PER COOKIE 60 **CAL**; 3 g **FAT** (2 g **SAT**); 1 g **PRO**; 8 g **CARB**; 0 g **FIBER**; 16 mg **SODIUM**; 13 mg **CHOL**

Peppermint Mittens

MAKES 2 dozen cookies **PREP** 15 minutes **REFRIGERATE** overnight **BAKE** at 350° for 11 minutes per batch

COOKIES

- 1¾ **cups all-purpose flour**
- ½ **teaspoon baking powder**
- ¼ **teaspoon salt**
- ½ **cup (1 stick) unsalted butter, softened**
- ½ **cup finely crushed starlight mint candies (about 22)**
- ⅓ **cup granulated sugar**
- 1 **large egg**

FROSTING

- 1 **box (16 ounces) confectioners' sugar**
- 5 **tablespoons warm water**
- **Food coloring, sparkling sugar or nonpareils, for decorating**

• **Cookies.** In a medium bowl, whisk flour, baking powder and salt. In a large bowl, beat butter, crushed candies and sugar until blended. Beat in egg. On low speed, beat in flour mixture. Gather dough with your hands and divide in half. Flatten each half into a disk and wrap in plastic. Refrigerate overnight.

• Heat oven to 350°. Let dough stand for 10 minutes at room temperature. Line two baking sheets with parchment paper. On a floured surface, roll out one disk to ⅛- to ¼-inch thickness. Cut out mittens with cookie cutter. Transfer to prepared sheets. Re-roll scraps, cutting as many mittens as possible. Bake at 350° for 11 minutes. Transfer to a wire rack to cool; repeat with all dough.

• **Frosting.** In a bowl, combine confectioners' sugar and the warm water. Beat until smooth. If desired, transfer ¼ cup of the frosting into each of two bowls. Tint to desired colors.

• Spread a scant 2 teaspoons frosting onto each cookie. Top with sparkling sugar or nonpareils, or decorate with colored frosting. Let dry completely before stacking cookies.

PER COOKIE 172 **CAL**; 4 g **FAT** (2 g **SAT**); 1 g **PRO**; 33 g **CARB**; 0 g **FIBER**; 38 mg **SODIUM**; 19 mg **CHOL**

There's a reason salted caramel gained such popularity a few years ago. A sprinkle of sea salt both contrasts and enhances the sweetness of the caramel in any dessert form—such as this twist on classic buttery spritz.

Festive Wreaths

MAKES 6½ dozen cookies **PREP** 10 minutes
BAKE at 350° for 10 minutes per batch

1	cup (2 sticks) unsalted butter, softened
⅔	cup sugar
1	large egg
¼	teaspoon salt
2¼	cups all-purpose flour
	Green liquid food coloring
	Red candy "berries" or edible confetti, for decorating

• Heat oven to 350°. In a large bowl, beat butter, sugar, egg and salt until fluffy, about 3 minutes. On low speed, beat in flour until smooth. Tint pale green with food coloring.

• Spoon dough into a cookie press fitted with a standard wreath disc, following manufacturer's directions. Press out wreaths, about 1 inch apart, onto large baking sheets. If using, press in candy "berries" before baking.

• Bake at 350° for 8 to 10 minutes, until slightly puffed and set. Transfer cookies directly to wire racks to cool.

PER COOKIE 44 **CAL**; 2 g **FAT** (1 g **SAT**); 0 g **PRO**; 5 g **CARB**; 0 g **FIBER**; 9 mg **SODIUM**; 9 mg **CHOL**

Salted Caramel Spritz

MAKES 7 dozen cookies **PREP** 15 minutes
BAKE at 350° for 10 minutes per batch

COOKIES

¾	cup Kraft soft caramels, unwrapped (18 caramels)
¼	cup half-and-half
1	cup (2 sticks) unsalted butter, softened
⅓	cup packed dark brown sugar
1	large egg
¾	teaspoon sea salt
3	cups all-purpose flour
1	cookie press, fitted with a snowflake disc

GLAZE

¾	cup packed dark brown sugar
3	tablespoons half-and-half
	Sea salt, for sprinkling

• **Cookies.** Heat oven to 350°. Combine caramels and half-and-half in a small saucepan. Cook over medium-low heat, stirring occasionally, until caramels are melted, about 8 minutes. Cool slightly.

• In a large bowl, beat butter and sugar until fluffy, about 3 minutes. Beat in egg and salt, then cooled but still fluid caramel mixture. On low speed, mix in flour. Add some dough to cookie press. Press cookies out onto ungreased baking sheets. Bake at 350° for 10 minutes, until set and just beginning to brown around bottom. Transfer to wire racks to cool. Repeat with remaining dough.

• **Glaze.** In a small saucepan, combine sugar and half-and-half. Heat over medium-low heat until sugar is dissolved. Place wire rack with cookies over a baking sheet. Drizzle with glaze and sprinkle with salt. Let cookies dry until glaze is set before stacking or storing.

PER COOKIE 57 **CAL**; 3 g **FAT** (2 g **SAT**); 1 g **PRO**; 8 g **CARB**; 0 g **FIBER**; 31 mg **SODIUM**; 9 mg **CHOL**

SALTED CARAMEL
SPRITZ

FESTIVE
WREATHS

GINGERBREAD
COOKIES

MAPLE
GINGERBREAD
COOKIES

What would Christmas be without gingerbread? The warmly spiced classic is infused with real maple syrup in place of molasses in the modern adaptation of these cheery little cookie people.

Gingerbread Cookies

MAKES 2½ dozen cookies **PREP** 20 minutes
REFRIGERATE 2 hours **BAKE** at 350° for 13 minutes per batch

- 2¾ **cups all-purpose flour**
- ¾ **teaspoon baking soda**
- 1 **tablespoon ground ginger**
- 1 **teaspoon ground cinnamon**
- ½ **teaspoon ground cloves**
- ¼ **teaspoon salt**
- ½ **cup (1 stick) unsalted butter, softened**
- ½ **cup packed dark brown sugar**
- 1 **large egg**
- ½ **cup molasses**
  Royal Icing (optional; recipe below right)

- In a medium bowl, whisk flour, baking soda, ginger, cinnamon, cloves and salt.

- In a large bowl, beat butter and sugar until smooth. Beat in egg, then molasses. Stir flour mixture into butter mixture. Divide dough in half and wrap. Refrigerate for 2 hours.

- Heat oven to 350°. On a well-floured surface, roll half of dough to ⅛-inch thickness. Cut into shapes with assorted gingerbread cookie cutters; transfer to ungreased baking sheets. Re-roll scraps and cut. Repeat with rest of dough.

- Bake at 350° for 13 minutes. Transfer cookies to wire racks to cool. Decorate with Royal Icing, if using.

PER COOKIE 134 **CAL**; 3 g **FAT** (2 g **SAT**); 2 g **PRO**; 25 g **CARB**; 0 g **FIBER**; 62 mg **SODIUM**; 15 mg **CHOL**

Maple Gingerbread Cookies

MAKES 4½ dozen 3-inch cookies **PREP** 15 minutes
REFRIGERATE at least 3 hours **BAKE** at 375° for 10 minutes per batch

COOKIES
- ½ **cup solid vegetable shortening**
- ½ **cup packed dark brown sugar**
- ½ **cup maple syrup**
- 1 **large egg**
- 1 **tablespoon white vinegar**
- 2⅔ **cups all-purpose flour**
- 1 **teaspoon baking powder**
- ½ **teaspoon baking soda**
- 1 **teaspoon ground ginger**
- ½ **teaspoon ground cinnamon**
- ½ **teaspoon salt**
- ½ **teaspoon maple flavoring**

ROYAL ICING
- 2 **cups confectioners' sugar**
- 2 **tablespoons powdered egg whites**
  Red M&M's minis

- **Cookies.** In a large bowl, beat shortening, brown sugar and maple syrup on medium-high until well combined. On low, beat in egg and vinegar until blended.

- In a medium bowl, whisk flour, baking powder, baking soda, ginger, cinnamon and salt. Add flour mixture to shortening mixture, 1 cup at a time, stirring until incorporated. Stir in maple flavoring. If mixture is very soft, mix in a few extra tablespoons flour. Transfer to a sheet of plastic wrap and flatten. Wrap and refrigerate at least 3 hours or overnight.

- Heat oven to 375°. Line two baking sheets with parchment. Remove ¼ of the dough from refrigerator; rewrap the rest. On a well-floured surface, roll out dough (it will be soft) to ¼-inch thickness. Cut out gingerbread shapes and transfer to prepared baking sheets with a metal spatula, re-rolling scraps. Continue with remaining dough, lining each baking sheet with new parchment. Bake cookies at 375° for 8 to 10 minutes. Cool on baking sheets for 3 minutes, then transfer to wire racks to cool completely.

- **Royal Icing.** In a bowl, beat confectioners' sugar, powdered egg whites and 3 tablespoons water until thick and shiny, about 5 minutes. Transfer to a pastry bag with a writing tip. Outline cookies with frosting; add M&M's minis as buttons. Let dry.

PER SERVING 75 **CAL**; 2 g **FAT** (0 g **SAT**); 1 g **PRO**; 13 g **CARB**; 0 g **FIBER**; 43 mg **SODIUM**; 4 mg **CHOL**

These rich and buttery sugar-dusted cookies are shaped differently and flavored just a bit differently, too. Ground pepitas—pumpkin seeds—step in for pecans in the modern version, which is also flavored with a pinch of cardamom.

Meltaways

MAKES 4½ dozen cookies **PREP** 15 minutes **REFRIGERATE** 1 to 2 hours
BAKE at 325° for 20 minutes per batch

1	cup (2 sticks) unsalted butter, softened
1	cup confectioners' sugar
2	teaspoons vanilla extract
2	cups all-purpose flour
1	cup finely ground pecans
1	cup confectioners' sugar, for dusting

• In a bowl, beat butter and confectioners' sugar until smooth and creamy. Add vanilla.

• On low speed, beat in flour and pecans. Wrap dough in plastic wrap and refrigerate 1 to 2 hours, until firm.

• Heat oven to 325°. Pinch off pieces of dough in rounded teaspoonfuls. Roll into logs, taper ends and bend into crescents. Place on ungreased baking sheets.

• Bake at 325° for 19 to 20 minutes, until lightly browned.

• Transfer cookies to a wire rack. Sprinkle with a heavy coat of confectioners' sugar. Cool completely. Sprinkle again with confectioners' sugar.

PER COOKIE 77 **CAL**; 5 g **FAT** (2 g **SAT**); 1 g **PRO**; 8 g **CARB**; 0 g **FIBER**; 1 mg **SODIUM**; 9 mg **CHOL**

Pepita Snowballs

MAKES 2½ dozen cookies **PREP** 20 minutes
BAKE at 350° for 10 minutes, then 15 minutes per batch

1	cup pepitas (shelled pumpkin seeds)
2	cups all-purpose flour
¾	teaspoon salt
¼	teaspoon ground cardamom (optional)
1	cup (2 sticks) unsalted butter, softened
1¾	cups confectioners' sugar
1½	teaspoons vanilla extract

• Heat oven to 350°. Spread pepitas on a baking sheet. Bake at 350° for 10 minutes, until toasted.

• Combine 1 cup of the flour and the toasted pepitas in a food processor; pulse until pepitas are finely ground. Transfer to a bowl and whisk in remaining 1 cup flour, the salt and cardamom, if using.

• In a large bowl, beat butter, ¾ cup of the confectioners' sugar and the vanilla on high speed until light and fluffy, 2 minutes. Reduce speed to low; slowly add flour-nut mixture, beating just until combined.

• Shape dough into 1-inch balls between your palms and place 1 inch apart on baking sheets. Bake at 350° for 15 minutes or until bottoms just begin to brown. Transfer cookies to wire racks and let cool slightly, about 4 minutes.

• Place remaining 1 cup confectioners' sugar in a bowl. Working with four cookies at a time, roll in sugar, coating well. Transfer to a rack and let cool completely. Roll in sugar again.

PER COOKIE 105 **CAL**; 7 g **FAT** (3 g **SAT**); 2 g **PRO**; 10 g **CARB**; 0 g **FIBER**; 43 mg **SODIUM**; 11 mg **CHOL**

MELTAWAYS

PEPITA
SNOWBALLS

AMERICA'S BEST
CHOCOLATE CHIP
COOKIES

CHOCOLATE CHIP
QUINOA COOKIES

While some chocolate chip cookie fans wouldn't mess with perfection, we think this updated version is wildly interesting. Popped quinoa adds a toasty, nutty flavor and texture—and who could argue with the addition of more chocolate in the form of white baking chips?

While some chocolate chip cookie fans wouldn't mess with perfection, we think this updated version is wildly interesting. Popped quinoa adds a toasty, nutty flavor and texture—and who could argue with the addition of more chocolate in the form of white baking chips?

America's Best Chocolate Chip Cookies

MAKES 4 dozen cookies **PREP** 25 minutes
BAKE at 375° for 12 minutes per batch

- 2⅓ **cups all-purpose flour**
- ¾ **teaspoon baking soda**
- ¾ **teaspoon salt**
- 1 **cup (2 sticks) unsalted butter, softened**
- 1 **cup packed light brown sugar**
- ½ **cup granulated sugar**
- 1 **large egg**
- 1 **teaspoon vanilla extract**
- 1 **package (12 ounces) semisweet chocolate pieces**
- 1½ **cups chopped walnuts**

● Heat oven to 375°. Lightly coat baking sheets with nonstick cooking spray.

● In a large bowl, stir together flour, baking soda and salt.

● In a medium bowl, beat butter, brown sugar and granulated sugar until light and creamy, 3 minutes. Beat in egg and vanilla until blended.

● Stir in flour mixture until blended. Stir in chocolate pieces and walnuts. Drop batter by tablespoonfuls onto prepared baking sheets.

● Bake at 375° for 12 minutes or until golden. Cool baking sheets on wire racks for 5 minutes. Transfer cookies to wire racks to cool completely.

PER COOKIE 135 **CAL**; 9 g **FAT** (4 g **SAT**); 2 g **PRO**; 15 g **CARB**; 0 g **FIBER**; 50 mg **SODIUM**; 15 mg **CHOL**

Chocolate Chip Quinoa Cookies

MAKES 3½ dozen cookies **PREP** 20 minutes **COOK** 3 minutes
BAKE at 375° for 15 minutes per batch

- ½ **cup dry quinoa**
- 2¼ **cups all-purpose flour**
- ¾ **cup old-fashioned oats**
- 1 **teaspoon baking powder**
- ¾ **teaspoon salt**
- ¼ **teaspoon ground nutmeg**
- 1 **cup (2 sticks) unsalted butter, softened**
- ¾ **cup packed light brown sugar**
- ¾ **cup granulated sugar**
- 2 **large eggs**
- 2 **teaspoons vanilla extract**
- 1 **bag (10 or 11.5 ounces) bittersweet chocolate chips**
- 1 **bag (10 or 11.5 ounces) white baking chips**
- 1 **cup chopped walnuts**

● Heat oven to 375°. Heat a 2- to 3-quart sauté pan over medium heat. Add quinoa. Cook, stirring constantly, until quinoa pops, 2 to 3 minutes. Transfer to a bowl.

● In a medium bowl, whisk together flour, oats, baking powder, salt, nutmeg and popped quinoa. Set aside.

● In a large bowl, beat butter and both sugars until smooth and fluffy. Beat in eggs, one at a time, beating well after each addition. On low, beat in vanilla. Spoon flour mixture into bowl and beat on low just until combined. With a wooden spoon, stir in both kinds of chips and the walnuts. Drop dough onto baking sheets by large spoonfuls (about 3 tablespoons) 2 inches apart. Bake at 375° for 12 to 15 minutes per batch. Cool cookies for 2 minutes on baking sheet; transfer to a wire rack to cool completely.

PER COOKIE 196 **CAL**; 11 g **FAT** (6 g **SAT**); 3 g **PRO**; 24 g **CARB**; 1 g **FIBER**; 64 mg **SODIUM**; 22 mg **CHOL**

PERFECT PAIRINGS

Mix and match our nine party recipes for 27 winning combinations. Pick a main, a side and a vegetable that suit you and your guests perfectly.

SIDES

SPAGHETTI WITH BRUSSELS SPROUTS AND HAZELNUTS

CREAMY POLENTA

HOLIDAY SPELT SALAD

MAINS

ROASTED CHICKEN WITH TRUFFLED MUSHROOM SAUCE

MAPLE-MUSTARD GLAZED SALMON

PEPPERCORN-CRUSTED BEEF TENDERLOIN

VEGGIES

ROASTED KALE WITH POPPY SEED DRESSING

HONEYED BEETS WITH SPICED WALNUTS

CARROT-FENNEL SALAD

Spaghetti with Brussels Sprouts and Hazelnuts

MAKES 8 servings   **PREP** 15 minutes
COOK 8 minutes

1½	pounds Brussels sprouts (about 7 cups), trimmed
1	pound spaghetti
6	tablespoons extra-virgin olive oil
¼	cup sliced shallots
4	cloves garlic, sliced
½	cup hazelnuts, chopped
½	teaspoon salt
	Freshly cracked black pepper
1	cup grated Pecorino Romano cheese

• Shred Brussels sprouts in a food processor fitted with a slicing blade. Set aside.

• Bring a pot of salted water to a boil. Add spaghetti; cook 8 minutes. Drain, reserving ½ cup of the pasta water.

• Meanwhile, in a large skillet, heat oil over medium heat. Stir in shallots and garlic; cook 2 minutes. Mix in shredded Brussels sprouts; cook 4 minutes. Using tongs, add spaghetti to skillet. Stir in pasta water, hazelnuts, salt, freshly cracked pepper and ¾ cup of the Pecorino Romano. Toss well. Place in a serving bowl and sprinkle with remaining ¼ cup cheese.

PER SERVING 460 **CAL**; 21 g **FAT** (5 g **SAT**); 18 g **PRO**; 52 g **CARB**; 6 g **FIBER**; 422 mg **SODIUM**; 15 mg **CHOL**

The benefit of this array of recipes is that each entrée goes beautifully with each one of the sides and of the vegetable dishes to create a complementary menu for any occasion.

Creamy Polenta

MAKES 8 servings   **PREP** 5 minutes
COOK 30 minutes

2	teaspoons salt
2	cups polenta or corn grits (not instant)
4	ounces soft goat cheese
6	tablespoons unsalted butter
2	tablespoons chopped chives
¼	teaspoon black pepper

• In a large pot, bring 6 cups water and 1 teaspoon of the salt to a boil. Slowly whisk in polenta. Reduce to a very low simmer, cover and cook 30 minutes.

• Stir in goat cheese and butter until melted. Mix in chives, remaining 1 teaspoon salt and the pepper. Serve immediately.

PER SERVING 244 **CAL**; 12 g **FAT** (7 g **SAT**); 6 g **PRO**; 27 g **CARB**; 2 g **FIBER**; 635 mg **SODIUM**; 29 mg **CHOL**

Holiday Spelt Salad

MAKES 8 servings   **PREP** 10 minutes
COOK 75 minutes

2	cups spelt (see Note)
4	tablespoons pomegranate vinegar or balsamic vinegar
3	tablespoons extra-virgin olive oil
1¼	teaspoons salt
¼	teaspoon black pepper
2	cups packed arugula
1	cup pomegranate seeds
4	ounces feta cheese, crumbled

• In a large pot, combine spelt and 6 cups water. Bring to a boil. Cover and reduce heat to a low simmer. Cook 65 to 75 minutes, until tender. Drain and rinse under cool water.

• In a large bowl, whisk vinegar, oil, salt and pepper. Stir in cooked spelt, arugula, pomegranate seeds and feta.

PER SERVING 258 **CAL**; 10 g **FAT** (3 g **SAT**); 8 g **PRO**; 38 g **CARB**; 5 g **FIBER**; 525 mg **SODIUM**; 13 mg **CHOL**

Note: Swap Kamut or farro for spelt, if desired. Cook according to package directions.

SPAGHETTI WITH BRUSSELS SPROUTS AND HAZELNUTS

CREAMY POLENTA

HOLIDAY SPELT SALAD

ROASTED GARLIC CREAM SAUCE

PEPPERCORN-CRUSTED BEEF TENDERLOIN

RED WINE-SHALLOT SAUCE

MAPLE-MUSTARD GLAZED SALMON

Peppercorn-Crusted Beef Tenderloin

MAKES 8 servings **PREP** 10 minutes
ROAST at 400° for 45 minutes **REST** 10 minutes

1	beef tenderloin (about 3 pounds)
1	tablespoon olive oil
3	tablespoons rainbow peppercorns
4	teaspoons kosher salt
	Roasted Garlic Cream Sauce or Red Wine-Shallot Sauce

• Bring tenderloin to room temperature 30 minutes before cooking. Heat oven to 400°. Pat tenderloin dry and rub with oil.

• Crush peppercorns in a spice grinder (or coffee grinder reserved for spices). Mix in a bowl with salt and press onto entire surface of tenderloin. Roast at 400° for 45 minutes or until internal temperature reaches 137°. Let rest 5 to 10 minutes, until temperature reaches 145°, before

slicing. Serve with Roasted Garlic Cream Sauce or Red Wine–Shallot Sauce.

PER SERVING 347 **CAL**; 23 g **FAT** (9 g **SAT**); 33 g **PRO**; 1 g **CARB**; 0 g **FIBER**; 1,027 mg **SODIUM**; 111 mg **CHOL**

Roasted Garlic Cream Sauce

MAKES 8 servings **PREP** 5 minutes
ROAST at 400° for 1 hour **COOK** 11 minutes

1	head garlic
2	teaspoons olive oil
½	teaspoon salt
	Freshly cracked black pepper
1	tablespoon unsalted butter
1	tablespoon all-purpose flour
1	cup unsalted chicken stock
½	cup heavy cream

• Heat oven to 400°. Slice off top ¼ of garlic head, exposing tops of cloves. Place on a piece of aluminum foil and drizzle

with oil, ¼ teaspoon of the salt and freshly cracked pepper. Wrap in foil and roast at 400° for 1 hour, until softened.

• In a skillet, melt butter over medium heat. Stir in flour; cook for 1 minute. Whisk in stock and heavy cream, and squeeze in cooked garlic cloves (discarding skin). Bring to a boil. Simmer for 8 to 10 minutes, until thickened. Stir in remaining ¼ teaspoon salt and more freshly cracked pepper.

PER SERVING 86 **CAL**; 8 g **FAT** (4 g **SAT**); 1 g **PRO**; 3 g **CARB**; 0 g **FIBER**; 168 mg **SODIUM**; 24 mg **CHOL**

Red Wine-Shallot Sauce

MAKES 8 servings **PREP** 5 minutes
COOK 14 minutes

3	tablespoons unsalted butter
¼	cup finely diced shallots

ROASTED CHICKEN WITH TRUFFLED MUSHROOM SAUCE

until desired doneness. Garnish with parsley, if using.

PER SERVING 270 CAL; 12 g FAT (2 g SAT); 32 g PRO; 7 g CARB; 0 g FIBER; 408 mg SODIUM; 93 mg CHOL

Roasted Chicken with Truffled Mushroom Sauce

MAKES 8 servings   PREP 30 minutes
ROAST at 400° for 45 minutes   COOK 6 minutes

2	whole chickens (about 3 pounds each), cut into 8 pieces each (breasts halved; about 4 pounds after discarding wings and back)
3	tablespoons olive oil
1½	teaspoons salt
¼	teaspoon black pepper
1	pound wild mushrooms, halved or quartered
1	tablespoon unsalted butter
2	tablespoons finely diced shallots
1	tablespoon all-purpose flour
1	cup unsalted chicken stock
½	cup heavy cream
1	teaspoon chopped fresh thyme
1	teaspoon truffle oil, plus more (if desired) for drizzling
	Freshly cracked black pepper (optional)

• Heat oven to 400°. Place chicken pieces on a rimmed baking sheet and drizzle with 1 tablespoon of the olive oil, then season with 1 teaspoon of the salt and ⅛ teaspoon of the pepper. On a separate rimmed baking sheet, toss mushrooms in remaining 2 tablespoons oil, ¼ teaspoon of the salt and remaining ⅛ teaspoon pepper. Roast chicken and mushrooms at 400° for 35 minutes, until golden. Remove mushrooms. Roast chicken 10 minutes more, until cooked.

• In a large skillet, melt butter over medium heat. Stir in shallots and cook 2 minutes. Stir in flour and cook 1 minute. Whisk in stock, cream and mushrooms. Bring to a boil and cook 3 minutes, until thickened. Stir in thyme, truffle oil, remaining ¼ teaspoon salt and, if using, freshly cracked pepper.

• Place chicken on a platter and pour truffled mushroom sauce over top. If desired, drizzle with additional truffle oil.

PER SERVING 299 CAL; 14 g FAT (6 g SAT); 37 g PRO; 4 g CARB; 0 g FIBER; 558 mg SODIUM; 110 mg CHOL

1	tablespoon all-purpose flour
1	cup unsalted beef stock
¾	cup dry red wine
1	tablespoon chopped fresh thyme
¼	teaspoon plus ⅛ teaspoon salt
	Freshly cracked black pepper

• In a medium skillet, melt 2 tablespoons of the butter over medium heat. Stir in shallots and cook 2 to 3 minutes, until softened. Stir in flour; cook 1 minute. Whisk in stock, wine and thyme. Bring to a boil. Reduce by half and simmer 10 minutes, until thickened. Remove from heat and stir in remaining 1 tablespoon butter, the salt and freshly cracked pepper.

PER SERVING 65 CAL; 4 g FAT (3 g SAT); 1 g PRO; 2 g CARB; 0 g FIBER; 126 mg SODIUM; 11 mg CHOL

Maple-Mustard Glazed Salmon

MAKES 8 servings   PREP 10 minutes
ROAST at 400° for 15 minutes

1	whole skin-on salmon fillet (about 2½ pounds)
2	tablespoons light brown sugar
1	teaspoon salt
⅛	teaspoon black pepper
2	tablespoons maple syrup
1	tablespoon unsalted butter, melted
1	tablespoon grainy mustard
	Parsley, for garnish

• Heat oven to 400°. Dry salmon with paper towels and place in an oven-safe baking dish. In a small bowl, combine brown sugar, salt and pepper; pat onto salmon. In a bowl, stir maple syrup, butter and mustard. Pour evenly over salmon. Roast at 400° for 15 minutes or

ROASTED KALE WITH
POPPY SEED DRESSING

HONEYED BEETS WITH
SPICED WALNUTS

Roasted Kale with Poppy Seed Dressing

MAKES 8 servings PREP 15 minutes
ROAST at 400° for 15 minutes

1½	pounds bagged chopped kale, large stems removed
5	tablespoons extra-virgin olive oil
¾	teaspoon plus ⅛ teaspoon salt
¼	teaspoon plus ⅛ teaspoon black pepper
2	tablespoons cider vinegar
1	tablespoon light mayonnaise
1	tablespoon poppy seeds
1	teaspoon sugar
1	cup golden raisins
½	cup thinly sliced red onion

• Heat oven to 400°. In a very large bowl, toss kale with 3 tablespoons of the olive oil, ½ teaspoon of the salt and ¼ teaspoon of the pepper. Distribute between two rimmed baking sheets. Roast at 400° for 10 minutes. Stir with tongs and alternate location of baking sheets. Roast another 5 minutes, until some pieces are crispy.

• Meanwhile, make dressing: Whisk together remaining 2 tablespoons olive oil, the vinegar, mayonnaise, poppy seeds, sugar and ¼ teaspoon of the salt.

• Toss cooked kale with raisins, onion, dressing, remaining ⅛ teaspoon salt and remaining ⅛ teaspoon pepper.

PER SERVING 196 CAL; 10 g FAT (1 g SAT); 4 g PRO; 26 g CARB; 3 g FIBER; 310 mg SODIUM; 1 mg CHOL

Honeyed Beets with Spiced Walnuts

MAKES 8 servings PREP 25 minutes
ROAST at 400° for 45 minutes

2	pounds red and golden beets (about 3 bunches)
¼	cup honey
2	tablespoons olive oil
½	teaspoon salt
¼	teaspoon black pepper
2	sprigs fresh thyme plus 1 teaspoon chopped
¼	teaspoon ground coriander
¼	teaspoon ground cumin
⅛	teaspoon ground ginger
⅔	cup roughly chopped walnuts
2	ounces Roquefort cheese, crumbled

• Heat oven to 400°. Place a large piece of aluminum foil on a rimmed baking sheet. Trim beets and cut into 2-inch chunks. Place on foil and toss with 2 tablespoons of the honey, 1 tablespoon of the oil, ¼ teaspoon of the salt and ⅛ teaspoon of pepper. Place thyme sprigs on top and seal foil around beets. Roast at 400° for 45 minutes. Allow beets to cool slightly before peeling (use gloves to keep hands from staining). Toss with juices from foil.

• Make spiced nuts: In a small skillet, heat remaining 2 tablespoons honey, 1 tablespoon oil, ¼ teaspoon salt and ⅛ teaspoon pepper, the chopped thyme, coriander, cumin, ginger and 1 teaspoon water over medium heat. Stir in walnuts until coated. Remove skillet from heat.

• Top beets with spiced nuts and cheese.

PER SERVING 184 CAL; 12 g FAT (2 g SAT); 4 g PRO; 18 g CARB; 3 g FIBER; 332 mg SODIUM; 6 mg CHOL

Carrot-Fennel Salad

MAKES 8 servings   PREP 20 minutes

3	tablespoons olive oil
3	tablespoons white wine vinegar
2	teaspoons Dijon mustard
½	teaspoon salt
⅛	teaspoon black pepper
1	large fennel bulb or 2 small bulbs, very thinly sliced
1	pound carrots, shaved with vegetable peeler
½	cup shelled, unsalted pistachios
⅓	cup fresh parsley, chopped

• In a large bowl, whisk oil, vinegar, mustard, ¼ teaspoon of the salt and the pepper. Toss in fennel, carrots, pistachios and parsley. Season with remaining ¼ teaspoon salt.

PER SERVING 132 CAL; 9 g FAT (1 g SAT); 3 g PRO; 12 g CARB; 4 g FIBER; 251 mg SODIUM; 0 mg CHOL

CARROT-FENNEL SALAD

HEALTHY FAMILY DINNERS

Simmer down! Slow cooker suppers leave more time to make merry.

PORK CARNITAS TACOS

Pork Carnitas Tacos

MAKES 6 servings (12 tacos) **PREP** 15 minutes
SLOW COOK on HIGH for 3 hours or LOW for
5 hours

2	pounds thick-cut boneless loin pork chops
1	teaspoon dried oregano
1	teaspoon ground cumin
½	teaspoon salt
¼	teaspoon black pepper
2	cups tomatillo salsa
1	red sweet pepper, cored, seeded and diced
½	cup fresh cilantro leaves
3	scallions, trimmed and sliced
4	cloves garlic, chopped
12	hard taco shells
	Chopped tomato, shredded lettuce, chopped onion, lime wedges, sour cream and sliced radishes (optional)

• Coat a 3½- or 4-quart slow cooker bowl with nonstick cooking spray.

• Place pork chops in slow cooker; season both sides with oregano, cumin, salt and black pepper. Add 1½ cups of the salsa, the red pepper, cilantro, scallions and garlic.

• Cover and cook on HIGH for 3 hours or LOW for 5 hours.

• Remove pork and shred with two forks. Return meat to slow cooker. Stir in remaining ½ cup salsa.

• Serve pork in taco shells topped with garnishes, if using.

PER SERVING 361 **CAL**; 15 g **FAT** (5 g **SAT**); 32 g **PRO**; 21 g **CARB**; 1 g **FIBER**; 608 mg **SODIUM**; 83 mg **CHOL**

Hearty Tuscan Linguine

MAKES 6 servings **PREP** 15 minutes
SLOW COOK on HIGH for 4 hours or LOW for
6 hours

1	large onion, sliced
½	cup packed-in-oil sun-dried tomatoes, drained and sliced
4	cloves garlic, sliced

HEARTY TUSCAN LINGUINE

1½	cups reduced-sodium vegetable broth
¼	cup tomato paste
1	teaspoon fresh rosemary, chopped
½	teaspoon dried oregano
½	teaspoon salt
¼	teaspoon black pepper
2	cans (15 ounces each) cannellini beans, drained and rinsed
1	small bunch kale, rinsed and torn into bite-size pieces (about 6 cups)
1	pound linguine, cooked per package directions
2	tablespoons olive oil
½	cup grated Parmesan cheese
½	cup toasted pine nuts

• Coat a 3½- or 4-quart slow cooker bowl with nonstick cooking spray.

• Place onion, sun-dried tomatoes, garlic, broth, tomato paste, rosemary, oregano, ¼ teaspoon of the salt and the pepper in slow cooker. Stir to blend. Stir in beans; place kale on top.

• Cover and cook on HIGH for 4 hours or LOW for 6 hours.

• Add remaining ¼ teaspoon salt. In a large bowl, toss sauce with cooked linguine and olive oil. Stir in Parmesan and sprinkle with pine nuts.

PER SERVING 487 **CAL**; 17 g **FAT** (3 g **SAT**); 23 g **PRO**; 72 g **CARB**; 12 g **FIBER**; 762 mg **SODIUM**; 45 mg **CHOL**

INDIAN TOMATO AND LENTIL SOUP

Indian Tomato and Lentil Soup

MAKES 6 servings **PREP** 15 minutes
SLOW COOK on HIGH for 5 hours

3	cups low-sodium vegetable broth
4	plum tomatoes, seeded and chopped (about 2 cups)
1	cup brown lentils
1	large onion, chopped
2	ribs celery, diced
1	large carrot, peeled and diced
3	cloves garlic, chopped
4	teaspoons garam masala
1¼	teaspoons salt
1	can (15 ounces) chickpeas, drained and rinsed
1	bag (5 ounces) baby spinach
½	cup plain Greek yogurt
	Lemon wedges, for squeezing

• Coat a 4- to 6-quart slow cooker bowl with nonstick cooking spray.

• Add broth, 1 cup water, the tomatoes, lentils, onion, celery, carrot, garlic, garam marsala and 1 teaspoon of the salt to the slow cooker.

• Cover and cook on HIGH for 5 hours. During last 30 minutes, stir in remaining ¼ teaspoon salt, the chickpeas and spinach.

• Just before serving, stir in yogurt. Serve with yogurt and lemon wedges.

PER SERVING 230 **CAL**; 2 g **FAT** (0 g **SAT**); 15 g **PRO**; 41 g **CARB**; 14 g **FIBER**; 755 mg **SODIUM**; 1 mg **CHOL**

BUFFALO CHICKEN CHILI

Buffalo Chicken Chili

MAKES 6 servings   PREP 15 minutes
COOK 5 minutes   SLOW COOK on HIGH for
4 hours or LOW for 6 hours

1½	**pounds ground chicken or turkey**
1	**large onion, chopped**
2	**large carrots, peeled and chopped**
2	**ribs celery, chopped**
4	**cloves garlic, chopped**
1	**can (28 ounces) fire-roasted diced tomatoes**
2	**tablespoons chili powder**
1	**teaspoon ground cumin**
1	**teaspoon dried oregano**
¼	**teaspoon cayenne pepper**
1	**can (15 ounces) black beans, drained and rinsed**
½	**cup crumbled blue cheese**
3	**tablespoons white vinegar**
¼	**teaspoon salt**
	Celery and carrot sticks (optional)

• Coat a 3½- or 4-quart slow cooker bowl with nonstick cooking spray.

• Heat a large nonstick skillet over medium-high heat; add chicken and cook 5 minutes, stirring occasionally, until browned. Drain excess fat and spoon chicken into slow cooker. Stir in onion, carrots, celery, garlic, tomatoes, chili powder, cumin, oregano and cayenne pepper.

• Cover and cook on HIGH for 4 hours or LOW for 6 hours. Add beans during last 30 minutes.

• Stir in blue cheese, vinegar and salt. Serve chili with celery and carrot sticks, if using.

PER SERVING 343 **CAL**; 17 g **FAT** (6 g **SAT**); 28 g **PRO**; 23 g **CARB**; 7 g **FIBER**; 717 mg **SODIUM**; 145 mg **CHOL**

ASIAN CHICKEN
NOODLE BOWL

Asian Chicken Noodle Bowl

MAKES 6 servings   PREP 15 minutes   SLOW COOK on HIGH for 4 hours or LOW for 6 hours

1	**large onion, sliced**
2	**large carrots, peeled and cut into ¼-inch coins**
3	**cloves garlic, sliced**
2½	**pounds boneless, skinless chicken thighs, cut into 1-inch pieces**
1	**can (20 ounces) pineapple chunks in juice**
3	**tablespoons cornstarch**
¼	**cup sugar**
¼	**cup cider vinegar**
¼	**cup ketchup**
3	**tablespoons reduced-sodium soy sauce**
1	**large red sweet pepper, seeded and sliced**
¼	**pound snow peas, trimmed and thinly sliced lengthwise**
½	**teaspoon salt**
4	**cups cooked rice noodles**
⅓	**cup toasted almonds**

• Coat a 3½- or 4-quart slow cooker bowl with nonstick cooking spray.

• Place onion, carrots and garlic in slow cooker. Add chicken evenly over top. Drain pineapple and set aside, reserving ¼ cup of the juice in a bowl. Whisk together juice, cornstarch, sugar, vinegar, ketchup and soy sauce; pour over chicken.

• Cover and cook on HIGH for 4 hours or LOW for 6 hours.

• Stir in red pepper, snow peas, salt and pineapple during last 30 minutes.

• Serve with rice noodles and almonds.

PER SERVING 484 **CAL**; 11 g **FAT** (2 g **SAT**); 37 g **PRO**; 61 g **CARB**; 7 g **FIBER**; 758 mg **SODIUM**; 147 mg **CHOL**

HOLIDAY WHIMSY

Santa pops, character doughnuts and a red velvet cake on a peppermint plate.

PEPPERMINT RED
VELVET CAKE,
PAGE 328

MARSHMALLOW
SANTA POPS

PEPPERMINT PLATE,
PAGE 328

PEANUT BUTTER
CUP TREES

REINDEER AND SNOWMAN
DOUGHNUTS, PAGES 328 AND 329

These sweet treats will bring a smile to your lips in more ways than one. They're as much fun to look at as they are to eat—and readily available convenience products make them a snap to create.

Marshmallow Santa Pops

MAKES 12 pops **PREP** 20 minutes
MICROWAVE 1 minute **REFRIGERATE** 5 minutes
ASSEMBLY 45 minutes

- **18 white marshmallows**
- **12 white lollipop sticks, 8 to 10 inches long**
- **12 pink marshmallows**
- **6 mini white marshmallows**
- **1 cup red candy melts**
- **1 cup vanilla frosting**
- **1 cup white pearlized sprinkles**
- **12 red M&M's minis**
- **1 tube (4.25 ounces) brown or black decorating icing**
- **1 piece Styrofoam, for holding finished sticks**
   Candies, to fill a container (optional)

• Line a cookie sheet with wax paper. Cut six of the large white marshmallows in half crosswise with clean scissors. Insert a lollipop stick into center of uncut side of a marshmallow half and push it about 1½ inches onto stick. Thread a pink and then a whole white marshmallow onto lollipop stick, pressing them to marshmallow half. Make sure end of stick remains covered with whole white marshmallow. Cut a corner from opposite sides of whole white marshmallow to create a triangle for Santa's hat. Transfer stick to prepared cookie sheet. Repeat to make 11 more sticks. Cut mini marshmallows in half crosswise; set aside.

• Place red candy melts in a small microwavable bowl. Microwave, stirring every 10 seconds, until smooth, about

1 minute. Dip top of a marshmallow assembly in red candy to cover just the white triangular marshmallow, allowing excess candy to drip back into bowl. Return stick to cookie sheet. Place a mini marshmallow half, cut side down, at top of coated marshmallow. Repeat with remaining marshmallows and red candy. Transfer cookie sheet to refrigerator until set, about 5 minutes.

• Spoon vanilla frosting into a ziplock bag; press out excess air and seal bag. Place white sprinkles in a shallow bowl.

• Snip a small (⅛-inch) corner from bag with vanilla frosting. Working on one stick at a time, pipe a thin wavy line around edge of red candy and press sprinkles into frosting. Pipe Santa's beard, hair and mustache onto marshmallows, and gently press sprinkles into frosting. Adjust any stray sprinkles with a toothpick, if necessary. Add a red M&M for the nose and pipe eyes with decorating icing. Press stick end into Styrofoam. Repeat with remaining sticks.

• Arrange finished sticks in a cup filled with candy. Cover Styrofoam with candies, if using.

Peanut Butter Cup Trees

MAKES 12 trees **PREP** 10 minutes
REFRIGERATE 15 minutes

- **24 Reese's peanut butter cup miniatures (from a 12-ounce bag)**
- **12 standard-size Reese's peanut butter cups (0.75 ounce each)**
- **12 snack-size Reese's peanut butter cups (0.55 ounce each)**

- **12 Reese's peanut butter cup minis (from an 8-ounce bag)**
- **1 cup Royal Icing (recipe below)**
- **12 small red or white candy stars**
- **1 tablespoon assorted red or white sprinkles**

• Refrigerate all peanut butter cups for 15 minutes to chill (this makes for easier handling and unwrapping).

• Spoon Royal Icing into a ziplock bag. Press out excess air and seal bag. Line a cookie sheet with wax paper. Unwrap peanut butter cups and place on prepared cookie sheet.

• Snip a small (⅛-inch) corner from bag with icing. Place a miniature peanut butter cup, bottom side up, on work surface. Pipe a dot of frosting on top and attach one standard-size peanut butter cup bottom side up. Pipe a wavy line of vanilla frosting around top edge, allowing it to hang over edge. Add a snack-size peanut butter cup and repeat with icing, stacking with a second miniature cup and finishing with a mini cup, to make a four-layer (five with the base) Christmas tree shape.

• Add a star candy to top and scatter some sprinkles over tree. Repeat to create 11 more peanut butter cup trees.

Royal Icing

MAKES about 2½ cups **PREP** 5 minutes

- **1 box (16 ounces) confectioners' sugar**
- **6 tablespoons warm water**
- **3 tablespoons powdered egg whites (such as Just Whites)**

• Combine confectioners' sugar, the warm water and powdered egg whites in a large bowl. Beat with an electric mixer on medium speed until smooth and fluffy, about 5 minutes.

• Keep covered with plastic wrap until ready to use.

Peppermint Red Velvet Cake

MAKES 12 servings PREP 20 minutes
BAKE at 350° for 20 minutes
MICROWAVE 2 minutes CHILL 20 minutes
FREEZE 15 minutes

CAKE

1	box (16.5 ounces) red velvet cake mix
1	cup buttermilk
3	large eggs
⅓	cup vegetable oil

CHOCOLATE CURLS

8	ounces white chocolate
2	teaspoons vegetable shortening

FROSTING

1	package (8 ounces) cream cheese, softened
1	cup (2 sticks) unsalted butter, softened
4	cups confectioners' sugar
½	teaspoon vanilla extract
¼	teaspoon peppermint extract
½	cup heavy cream
	Peppermint Plate (at right)
	Peppermint balls

• Heat oven to 350°. Line bottoms of three 8-inch round cake pans with wax paper. Coat with nonstick cooking spray.

• **Cake.** Prepare cake mix according to package directions, substituting buttermilk for water. Divide batter evenly among prepared pans and smooth tops. Bake at 350° until firm and a toothpick inserted in center comes out clean, 17 to 20 minutes. Transfer pans to a wire rack and let cool 10 minutes. Invert and cool completely.

• **Curls.** Chop 4 ounces of the white chocolate. Place in a small microwavable bowl with shortening. Microwave, stirring often, until smooth, about 1 minute. Pour mixture into a small plastic-wrap-lined loaf pan. Tap on counter to smooth. Refrigerate until set, about 20 minutes. (You will have more chocolate than needed for curls, but to get good curls you need a block.)

• **Frosting.** Chop remaining 4 ounces white chocolate. Microwave 1 minute, stirring often until smooth; set aside to cool slightly.

• Beat cream cheese and butter in a large bowl until fluffy. Gradually add cooled chocolate, beating until smooth, making sure to scrape down sides of bowl. Add confectioners' sugar, vanilla and peppermint extract. Beat until smooth. Increase speed to high and beat frosting until light and fluffy, about 3 minutes.

• With a serrated knife, trim tops of cake layers to make even. Place one cake layer on a serving platter, trimmed side up. Spread a generous cup of frosting over top. Place another cake layer on top of frosting, trimmed side down, gently pressing into frosting to make level. Spread a generous cup of frosting over top. Place remaining cake layer on top of frosting, trimmed side down, pressing into frosting to make level. Spread a thin crumb coating of frosting all over cake. Place cake in freezer for 15 minutes to set.

• Meanwhile, whip heavy cream until fluffy and smooth. Fold into remaining frosting. Place Peppermint Plate on a flat serving platter. Transfer chilled cake to Peppermint Plate. Spread frosting over cake, making soft swirls with the tip of an offset spatula or a small spoon.

• Line a cookie sheet with wax paper. Remove chocolate block from loaf pan; peel away plastic. Holding chocolate with a piece of paper towel to prevent melting, make curls using a vegetable peeler. Place curls on prepared pan. If chocolate or curls become too soft, return to refrigerator.

• Decorate top of cake with curls and peppermint balls.

Peppermint Plate

MAKES one 10-inch plate PREP 5 minutes
BAKE at 350° for 13 minutes

2	bags (8 ounces each) starlight mints (about 78 mints)
	Heavy-duty aluminum foil

• Heat oven to 350°. Line a 10-inch spring-form pan or any 10-inch round pan with a sheet of foil and make smooth.

• Unwrap mints. Arrange a row of mints close together around outside edge of foil-lined pan. Add rows of mints until foil is covered.

• Bake at 350° until mints spread together and melt, 10 to 13 minutes. Transfer pan to a wire rack to cool completely. Remove candy plate from pan using foil and gently peel candy from foil.

• Store in an airtight container on the countertop up to 2 weeks. (Place plate on a flat platter or you risk breaking the candy.)

Reindeer Doughnuts

MAKES 12 reindeer PREP 10 minutes

12	mini (2-inch) chocolate glazed doughnuts
12	unsalted mini pretzels
¼	cup vanilla frosting
12	red M&M's megas
24	brown M&M's minis
1	tablespoon white nonpareils

PEPPERMINT PLATE

- Line a cookie sheet with wax paper. Lay doughnuts, smooth side up, on prepared cookie sheet. To make antlers, use a small serrated knife to cut ¾ inch from each rounded side of a pretzel, removing center piece.

- Spoon vanilla frosting into a ziplock bag. Press out excess air and seal bag. Snip a small (⅛-inch) corner from bag. Pipe a dot of vanilla frosting into center of doughnut and attach a red candy, flat side down, into frosting as the nose. Pipe two dots of frosting on doughnut above nose and attach brown candies as the eyes.

- Insert two pretzel pieces into top side of doughnut, cut sides facing each other and about ¾ inch apart, as the antlers. Pipe a few dots of frosting on pretzels and sprinkle with nonpareils. Repeat with remaining doughnuts.

Snowman Doughnuts

MAKES 12 snowmen PREP 5 minutes

12	mini (2-inch) powdered sugar doughnuts
4	orange candy slices
¼	cup vanilla frosting
24	brown M&M's minis
1	tube (4.25 ounces) brown or black decorating icing

- Line a cookie sheet with wax paper. Arrange doughnuts on prepared cookie sheet. Cut three triangles, about ¼ x ¾ inch, from each orange slice.

- Spoon frosting into a ziplock bag. Press out excess air and seal bag. Snip a small (⅛-inch) corner from bag. Pipe a dot of frosting into center of each doughnut and insert a piece of orange candy, wide end into frosting, as the nose. Pipe two dots of frosting on each doughnut above nose, brushing away powdered sugar as necessary, and attach brown M&M's as eyes. Pipe five or six dots of decorating icing below each nose as the mouth, brushing away powdered sugar as necessary.

Starlight Mint Wreath

MAKES 1 wreath PREP 20 minutes ASSEMBLY 30 minutes STAND overnight

	Hot-glue gun
2	9 x ¾-inch round Styrofoam wreath forms
	Aluminum foil
3	bags (8 ounces each) starlight mints (about 140 mints)
1	recipe Royal Icing (page 327)
	Ribbon, for hanging

- Hot-glue Styrofoam rings together to get a double thickness. Cool.

- Bevel from one outer and one inner edge of wreath. Discard trimmings.

- Cut foil into 12 x 3-inch strips. Wrap strips around Styrofoam wreath, making foil as smooth as possible.

- Line a cookie sheet with wax paper. Place foil-covered wreath on wax paper, flat side down. Unwrap mints.

- Spread some Royal Icing around outside edge of wreath and make smooth. Press starlight mints into frosting, flat side against wreath and very close together, all around base of wreath. Spread some icing around inside edge of wreath and repeat method with starlight mints.

- Spread more icing on top of the wreath, making sure to cover the foil, and add two more rows of mints, very close together.

- Spoon the remaining icing into a ziplock bag. Press out excess air and seal bag. Snip a small (⅛-inch) corner from bag. Pipe a dot of icing on a flat side of a mint and place as a top row of mints, covering any large gaps. Repeat with remaining mints and icing. Let wreath dry in a cool, dry spot until frosting is firm, at least overnight.

- Thread ribbon through wreath to hang.

INDEX

IN-A-PINCH SUBSTITUTIONS

It can happen to the best of us: Halfway through a recipe,
you find you're completely out of a key ingredient. Here's what to do:

When the Recipe Calls For:	You May Substitute:
1 square unsweetened chocolate	3 tbsp. unsweetened cocoa powder + 1 tbsp. butter/margarine
1 cup cake flour	1 cup less 2 tbsp. all-purpose flour
2 tbsp. flour (for thickening)	1 tbsp. cornstarch
1 tsp. baking powder	¼ tsp. baking soda + ½ tsp. cream of tartar + ¼ tsp. cornstarch
1 cup corn syrup	1 cup sugar + ¼ cup additional liquid used in recipe
1 cup milk	½ cup evaporated milk + ½ cup water
1 cup buttermilk or sour milk	1 tbsp. vinegar or lemon juice + enough milk to make 1 cup
1 cup sour cream (for baking)	1 cup plain yogurt
1 cup firmly packed brown sugar	1 cup sugar + 2 tbsp. molasses
1 tsp. lemon juice	¼ tsp. vinegar (not balsamic)
¼ cup chopped onion	1 tbsp. dried minced onion
1 clove garlic	¼ tsp. garlic powder
2 cups tomato sauce	¾ cup tomato paste + 1 cup water
1 tbsp. prepared mustard	1 tsp. dry mustard + 1 tbsp. water

HOW TO KNOW WHAT YOU NEED

Making a shopping list based on a recipe can be tricky if you don't know
how many tomatoes yields 3 cups chopped. Our handy translations:

When the Recipe Calls For:	You Need:
4 cups shredded cabbage	1 small head cabbage
1 cup grated raw carrot	1 large carrot
2½ cups sliced carrots	1 pound raw carrots
4 cups cooked cut fresh green beans	1 pound green beans
1 cup chopped onion	1 large onion
4 cups sliced raw potatoes	4 medium-size potatoes
1 cup chopped sweet pepper	1 large pepper
1 cup chopped tomato	1 large tomato
2 cups canned tomatoes	16-oz. can
4 cups sliced apples	4 medium-size apples
1 cup mashed banana	3 medium-size bananas
1 tsp. grated lemon rind	1 medium-size lemon
2 tbsp. lemon juice	1 medium-size lemon
4 tsp. grated orange rind	1 medium-size orange
1 cup orange juice	3 medium-size oranges
4 cups sliced peaches	8 medium-size peaches
2 cups sliced strawberries	1 pint
1 cup soft bread crumbs	2 slices fresh bread
1 cup bread cubes	2 slices fresh bread
2 cups shredded cheese	8 oz. cheese
1 cup egg whites	6 or 7 large eggs
1 egg white	2 tsp. egg white powder + 2 tbsp. water
4 cups chopped walnuts or pecans	1 pound shelled